Issues
AND
Innovations
IN
Literacy Education

Readings From *The Reading Teacher*

Richard D. Robinson

EDITOR

University of Missouri–Columbia
Columbia, Missouri, USA

INTERNATIONAL
Reading Association
800 BARKSDALE ROAD, PO BOX 8139
NEWARK, DE 19714-8139, USA
www.reading.org

The International Reading Association attempts, through its publications, to provide a forum for a wide spectrum of opinions on reading. This policy permits divergent viewpoints without implying the endorsement of the Association.

Director of Publications   Dan Mangan
Editorial Director, Books and Special Projects   Teresa Curto
Managing Editor, Books   Shannon T. Fortner
Acquisitions and Developmental Editor   Corinne M. Mooney
Associate Editor   Charlene M. Nichols
Associate Editor   Elizabeth C. Hunt
Production Editor   Amy Messick
Books and Inventory Assistant   Rebecca A. Zell
Permissions Editor   Janet S. Parrack
Assistant Permissions Editor   Tyanna L. Collins
Production Department Manager   Iona Muscella
Supervisor, Electronic Publishing   Anette Schütz
Senior Electronic Publishing Specialist   R. Lynn Harrison
Electronic Publishing Specialist   Lisa M. Kochel
Proofreader   Stacey Lynn Sharp

Project Editor   Shannon T. Fortner

Cover   Design, Linda Steere; Photo, Clipart.com

Library of Congress Cataloging-in-Publication Data
Issues and innovations in literacy education : readings from The Reading Teacher / Richard D. Robinson, editor.
     p. cm.
Includes bibliographical references and index.
ISBN 0-87207-599-0
1. Reading. I. Robinson, Richard David, 1940-
LB1050.I79 2006
428.4'071--dc22

2005035294

This book is dedicated to the memory
and legacy of William S. Gray,
a true pioneer in literacy
teaching and research.
1885–1960

Contents

SECTION THREE

Reading Comprehension   77

SECTION FOUR

Literacy Assessment   121

Foreword

This edited collection deserves much praise. First, because Richard Robinson has selected a set of incredibly useful articles for inclusion in this book. Each article adds, layer upon layer, ideas for improving reading instruction. Second, because the selected articles provide a historical perspective for the six broad themes that are addressed. As I read through the collection I found myself thinking, "Why wasn't that recommendation wholly accepted and in common practice today?" Third, because the historical articles remind us that we have too often neglected the advice of those giants of the field that went before us. Hopefully, this collection will prompt all of us to remember the contributions of so many early literacy leaders.

The very first article in this collection, "Challenges Facing the Teacher of Reading in 1957" by Gerald A. Yoakam, well sets the tone by reminding us, 50 years later, that far too many challenges of that era remain challenges today. The section on the "slow learner" in that article may shock some younger readers for its forthright assertion that, "The dull child has always been a problem to teachers..." (p. 6). In our modern era wherein the U.S. Congress has mandated that every child will achieve grade-level reading proficiencies, the conventional wisdom of the last century—that we should set our sights quite a bit lower for those "slow" children—seems dangerously biased. However, Yoakam's call for more differentiated instruction for slow learners could be understood as a call for instruction that provided more expert and more intensive reading lessons for those students who struggle with reading, or with schooling for that matter. Such recommendations would well address the current challenge of developing reading proficiencies in every student.

No one will be able to read this book and think, Everything new is old. The organization of the articles chronologically in each section provides clear evidence of the progress we've made in the past half century on each of the six broad topics considered here. But progress does not mean that we have arrived at the solution to the historically vexing problems that surround attempts at teaching every child to read. Still, progress is what is needed, continual progress, if we are ever to achieve the goal of universal literacy.

—*Richard L. Allington*
University of Tennessee
Knoxville, Tennessee, USA

Preface

> *This year each issue of* The Reading Teacher *includes several articles presenting different points of view concerning controversial issues in the teaching of reading. [The conclusion of this work] is that there is no magic formula for the teaching of reading. Teaching is far too complex to admit a pat formula. And of all the phases of teaching, perhaps the teaching of reading is the most complex.*
>
> —NANCY LARRICK (1951b)

In the first issue of *The Reading Teacher* in 1951, editor Nancy Larrick set the purpose and editorial direction of the publication when she stated that it was to be "focused on the needs and interests of the classroom teacher of reading at all grade levels" (1951a, p. 18). This basic belief in the inherent value of the classroom teacher as the foundation of effective literacy instruction has been the guiding light of *The Reading Teacher* for more than 50 years.

This journal, which began as a relatively obscure typewritten bulletin of approximately 25 pages per issue, has become a major educational publication of international reputation and influence. First published as the *ICIRI Bulletin* (International Council for the Improvement of Reading Instruction) in 1948, the name was officially changed to the *Bulletin* in 1950. In 1951, the publication subsequently became *The Reading Teacher*.

Noted educators such as William S. Gray, Arthur Gates, Edward Dolch, Albert Harris, and Helen Robinson were prominent early contributors in addition to a wide variety of classroom teachers and educators. This inclusion of literacy authorities from differing viewpoints and educational backgrounds has been a hallmark of *The Reading Teacher* throughout its publishing history.

Purpose of This Book

This book was written with a single purpose in mind and that is to allow literacy teachers of the past to speak to today's teachers about issues, problems, and innovative educational solutions of common interest. Richard de Bury, one of the first authors to write about the lasting values of reading, noted over 600 years ago,

Issues and Innovations in Literacy Education: Readings From The Reading Teacher, edited by Richard D. Robinson. © 2006 by the International Reading Association.

For the meaning of voice perishes with the sound, truth lying in the mind is wisdom that is hid and treasure that is not seen; but truth which shines forth in books desires to manifest itself when it is read.... (as cited in Thomas, 1966, pp. 10–11)

Although time separates us from the important literacy educators of the past, their thoughts and words live on in the pages of *The Reading Teacher* as if they were present today. This valuable legacy of thought and practice often has gone relatively unnoticed, if for no other reason than it is considered to be dated and, thus, of no current use to modern literacy practices. Careful consideration of the many educational writings of the past clearly reveals the fallacy of this belief. It is unfortunate that what often is considered today to be "innovative or new" is in reality little more than teaching philosophies and techniques that have been tried and found lacking in the past.

Unfortunately, there is a seemingly endless circle of change in literacy education that continually repeats itself. The topics that educators argue about today—such as phonics, assessment, use of materials, and the role of the teacher—have been issues of debate for many years. Knowledge of what literacy teachers of the past thought and did about these concerns should provide current teachers the basis for making intelligent and useful decisions about their present teaching practices.

Selection Process

The selection process of the articles included in this book began with a careful review of past issues of *The Reading Teacher* in order to choose those that clearly met the selection criteria discussed below. Of primary importance throughout this procedure was careful consideration of the information that this editor believed would be most beneficial to today's practicing classroom literacy teachers. From what began as a large pool of possible articles, many were eliminated gradually for a variety of reasons, most often because they were dated and no longer relevant for today's literacy teacher. Once articles were selected on a particular subject, then a final de-

cision was made as to whether to include them as a complete reference or as an annotated reference.

Selection Criteria

The final selection of articles was made based on the following criteria:

- The relevance of the article for today's literacy teacher

Because an individual article may have been written 20, 30, or even 50 years ago does not necessarily mean that the information or the author's viewpoint is not important or relevant for the teaching of reading today.

- The importance of the material from a historical standpoint

The Reading Teacher has a notable history of publishing articles that, because of their originality of content, have been identified as fundamental contributions in many aspects of reading education. Many of these contributions were written by some of the most notable reading educators of the past and are recognized today as important in the historical development of literacy instruction.

- The effect of the specific article on related research and teacher practice

The Reading Teacher has always been in the forefront in describing the latest literacy developments. Often these noteworthy articles established a foundation on which future classroom literacy practices, as well as related research agendas, would continue long after initial publication.

- The position taken when related to a controversial issue in literacy education

The field of literacy education has often been marked by controversy and disagreement on many issues. Examples include reading philosophies, assessment procedures, and use of various types of materials.

The editor wishes to give special recognition to the publication *20 Year Annotated Index to* The Reading Teacher (Barrett et al., 1969), which proved to be of great value in the review and final selection of materials for this book. The contributors to this volume have provided immense help to literacy researchers of today who value the early history of *The Reading Teacher*.

Organization of This Book

Each section in this book is organized around a central literacy issue or topic such as comprehension, assessment, or word recognition. At the beginning of each section, quotations by educators are included about the central topic. Following a brief introduction of the topic, *The Reading Teacher* articles are included chronologically so that readers can see the historical and educational development of ideas and concepts related to the specific literacy topic. Each section additionally includes a list of annotated articles, also arranged in chronological order, for further reading on the topic.

A Personal Note From the Editor

Finally, I hope that readers of this book sense the enthusiasm and dedication of the literacy teachers rep-

resented here. These educators of the past experienced many of the same successes and problems we face today. Their excitement and pleasure in helping students to learn to read successfully is clearly evident in their writing. Their legacy of excellence is a worthy foundation on which modern literacy teachers can build for the future. Again, as Nancy Larrick stated in her first editorial in which she set the purpose for *The Reading Teacher*, "[W]e hope the articles [in this journal] will be so provocative that every reader will be so stimulated to do more reading and more experimenting in his own teaching" (1951a, p. 18).

REFERENCES

Barrett, T.C., Burnett, R., Dykstra, R., Harris, L.A., Kerfoot, J., & Simula, V. (1969). *20 Year annotated index to* The Reading Teacher: *1948–1949, 1966–1977*. Newark, DE: International Reading Association.

Larrick, N. (1951a). *The Reading Teacher* and the ICIRI [International Council for the Improvement of Reading Instruction]. *The Reading Teacher, 5*(1), 18.

Larrick, N. (1951b). There is no magic formula. *The Reading Teacher, 5*(2), 18.

Thomas, E.C. (1966). *The love of books: The Philobiblon of Richard de Bury*. New York: Cooper Square.

SECTION ONE

Effective Teachers of Reading

The improvement of the reading situation [training of reading teachers] can be and is being accelerated. This is the beginning of a new era.

—EMMETT BETTS (1962, p. 414)

In the current climate of learner-centered, experienced-based education, we [reading teachers] have been encouraged to become learners ourselves. I think it goes deeper than this, however. We must become childlike—children again—unencumbered by suspicions and conditioning.

—PATRICIA TELLIER (1990, p. 327)

Teachers must decide whether to focus on what is wrong in order to "fix" things, or they must use what is right as a springboard to delve into deeper learning [in reading].

—MARGARET TAYLOR STEWART (2003, p. 540)

Issues and Innovations in Literacy Education: Readings From The Reading Teacher, edited by Richard D. Robinson. © 2006 by the International Reading Association.

From the beginning of its publication, a primary goal of *The Reading Teacher* has been to address the important pedagogical issue of what constitutes the good teaching of reading. Any historical review of this journal quite clearly shows the depth and sophistication of the many articles that have been published in its pages on various aspects of the role of the teacher in effective literacy instruction. Whether it has been commentary on language theories, the results of relevant related research, or information on effective instructional techniques, *The Reading Teacher* has been consistently at the forefront in reporting the latest information on these subjects. This writing has been done by a wide spectrum of authors ranging from successful classroom teachers to noted college and university faculty. Although each has brought a unique and at times differing view of what constitutes the good teaching of reading, there have been common threads throughout much of this work. The following points summarize much of this writing found in the history of *The Reading Teacher*:

- Regardless of the approach, method, or materials used to teach reading, the overwhelming factor in successful literacy instruction has always been the knowledgeable classroom teacher.
- The teacher as a role model for reading is one of the most powerful incentives for students to want to read.
- The effective teacher of reading is one who has a clear understanding of the reading process and is able to convey this information to all students.
- The successful literacy teacher views each student as a unique individual with distinctive learning characteristics and traits that need to be addressed.

Section Readings

The first article in this section was written almost 50 years ago by Gerald A. Yoakam. Even though the title refers to the year 1957, note how current the issues are to literacy education today. Although teachers of reading still face criticism from a wide spectrum of media sources about issues such as dealing with the problem reader, phonics, and reading in the content areas, consider the progress that has been made in dealing with these seemingly persistent literacy issues.

Next is a one-page article by Russell G. Stauffer, editor of *The Reading Teacher* from 1958 to 1967. In his article, as an instructional leader in literacy and an understanding and insightful reader as well, Stauffer sets a standard for classroom teachers.

Do you feel that our good work as reading teachers often goes unnoticed? The third piece in this section, a short article by Paula J. Gaus, should do much to revive our spirits, noting that "good reading instruction is a marketable commodity." Specific suggestions are provided on how to better promote our invaluable work as teachers of reading.

The article by John C. Manning argues persuasively that to be a successful teacher of reading, there is more required than just basic knowledge of the reading process. Although this foundation information is important, there also needs to be "a love of language and books" shown by the teacher as both a scholar and romanticist as well.

Next, a position statement of the International Reading Association describes a research-based discussion of the important qualities often found in the effective teacher of reading.

These characteristics include knowledge of how children effectively learn to read and write, the role of various literacy methods and materials in the classroom reading program, and the development of a positive attitude in their interactions with students.

Section One concludes with a more recent article by Carla C. Dearman and Sheila R. Alber, who describe how classroom teachers and administrators can come together to cooperatively make positive changes in a school's curriculum. Emphasized here is the importance of collaboration and reflective study as basic components of this change process.

REFERENCES

Betts, E.A. (1962). Who shall teach reading? *The Reading Teacher, 15*(6), 409–414.

Stewart, M.T. (2003). Building effective practice: Using small discoveries to enhance literacy learning. *The Reading Teacher, 56*(6), 540–547.

Tellier, P. (1990). The walls are shaking: An appreciation of how we grow through change. *The Reading Teacher, 44*(4), 326–328.

For Further Reading on Effective Teachers of Reading

The following articles have been selected from *The Reading Teacher* because they represent a wide spectrum of viewpoints and positions on this important aspect of literacy instruction. They are listed chronologically so that the reader can better understand the historical development of the important issues related to the training as well as the roles of the effective reading teacher.

Dawson, M.A. (1951). Keeping abreast in reading. *The Reading Teacher, 4*(4), 3–5.
   Notes ways in which the classroom teacher can stay abreast of the latest developments in reading such as independent reading, in-service activities of various types, conferences, and the visiting of effective literacy classrooms.

Betts, E.A. (1962). Who shall teach reading? *The Reading Teacher, 15*(6), 409–414.
   Recommends fundamental changes in the professional training of prospective teachers of reading in terms of increased emphasis on both liberal arts courses as well as pedagogical experiences in the fundamentals of literacy.

Burnett, R.W. (1963). The diagnostic proficiency of teachers of reading. *The Reading Teacher, 16*(4), 229–234.
   Presents information on the development and use of a diagnostic procedure for measuring the proficiency of classroom teachers in the examination of reading problems of various types.

Artley, A.S. (1975). Good teachers of reading—Who are they? *The Reading Teacher, 29*(1), 26–31.
   Describes the results of a survey of what undergraduate students remembered most about their elementary school reading experiences.

Robinson, R.D., & Pettit, N.T. (1978). The role of the reading teacher: Where do you fit in? *The Reading Teacher, 31*(8), 923–927.
   Suggests various specific ways in which classroom teachers can expand their roles in the effective teaching of the reading curriculum.

Stern, P., & Shavelson, R.J. (1983). Reading teachers' judgments, plans, and decision making. *The Reading Teacher, 37*(3), 280–286.
> Describes the importance of the classroom reading teacher's role as a decision maker in terms of pedagogical judgments related to effective literacy instruction.

Neilsen, L. (1990). The reading professional: The challenge of change. *The Reading Teacher, 44*(1), 58–59.
> Comments on the rapid change of the knowledge base in effective literacy instruction and the importance of the classroom's preparation for these new developments.

Lefever-Davis, S. (2002). The preparation of tomorrow's reading teacher. *The Reading Teacher, 56*(2), 196–197.
> Reviews recent developments in the area of teacher certification and professional development as they relate to literacy education, noting the need for a multifaceted approach in these educational activities.

Dreher, M.J. (2002–2003). Motivating teachers to read. *The Reading Teacher, 56*(4), 338–340.
> Emphasizes the importance of the classroom teacher's personal life as a reader and as a literacy role model for his or her students.

Challenges Facing the Teacher of Reading in 1957

Gerald A. Yoakam

The modern teacher of reading is challenged by problems unknown to the teacher of a quarter of a century or more ago. This is because she knows more about the teaching of reading than her predecessor and also because publicity, both favorable and unfavorable, has made parents and interested laymen more critical of the teaching of reading than ever before. Practically every magazine that reaches into the American home has carried articles on the teaching of reading since Mr. Nameless published his book a couple of years ago.

As I see it, there are several challenging problems facing the reading teacher today that should receive her most careful thought. True, the teacher of reading is so busy teaching the children of America to read that she seldom has time to draw a breath much less to reply to the critics of public education, the most obnoxious of whom are those who indulge only in negative criticism and wish to go back to the good old days when "all children learned to read" without any failures whatever. What a race of men and children there were then, my hearers!

Critical Articles in Magazines Create Challenges

What should we do about the critical articles appearing in the magazines and the newspapers? This is a question that has been annoying teachers for two or three years now. Every now and then some prophet speaks out against the teaching of reading and some of the more intelligent, but ill-informed patrons, rush to the schoolhouse in wild-eyed indignation. They want to know "how come little Reginald is not reading as well as mama or papa did at his age." Generally they say mama, for it is well known that women are smarter than men and that mama always could beat papa talking and reading by two or three laps. Some teachers will say that when this happens the thing to do is to send them to the principal. Let him or her do it. Aren't they paid for it? That, however, will not solve the problem.

Criticism of reading instruction is a staff problem and should be taken up by the Reading Committee. Every school should have a reading or language arts committee which should be composed of all teachers. This committee should take up the public relations problem that is involved here and use the best possible strategy to cope with it. There are several possibilities: (1) the parent-teachers' organizations; (2) articles in the newspaper; (3) school bulletins to parents; (4) open letters to the parents; (5) parents' day reading demonstrations; (6) informal conferences with parents; and (7) carefully formulated reports to the parents on the reading situation. The latter two or three measures are probably the most effective, although they take time.

The problem is so crucial, however, that principals and teachers, as well as administrative officers higher up, must give it top-level professional consideration and treatment. If teachers and principals don't know the answer to the problem of

Reprinted from *The Reading Teacher*, 10(2), pp. 67–70, 96. © 1956 by the International Reading Association.

criticism, they must get the answer. Reading consultants may help temporarily, but the permanent remedy is for teachers and principals to become thoroughly informed. How has reading been doing in the local schools? What evidence is there that it is better, or worse, than it was ten years or five years ago? Are children reading and how much? What outstanding examples of good reading can be cited? Answers to these and other questions properly presented to patrons will allay their anxiety and secure their allegiance. Many times the schools are criticized because neither the administrative nor teaching staff has time to answer the critics. In spite of over-crowding and overloading, however, ways must be found to report intelligently to the public concerning their children. And in the meantime, intelligent and capable teachers should be writing for the magazines and newspapers, to keep the public informed.

Challenges Created by the Slow-Learner

Another crucial problem facing the reading teacher is and always has been, *What to do about the slow-learning child?* Mr. Nameless blithely passes these by on the other side when he discusses the teaching of reading. To him all children should learn to read, regardless of their ability. All you need is a magic formula. It is very simple: just use my method of teaching to read and all will be well. This is in spite of the fact that there have always been slow-learners in school and there have always been failures to learn to read. We used to drop such children as soon as possible. Now we keep them all up to the age of 16, or thereabouts, and try to teach the slow child as if he were bright. The result is that we do not do justice either to the fast learning or the slow-learning child.

The schools must definitely adjust the load to the child's ability and allow for different rates of progress. Children of different abilities perform at different levels now and will do so in the future. Adults are also highly different in the levels at which they read. It is definitely more wholesome to differentiate instruction for children of different ability levels than

to have them founder and fail. The dull child has always been a problem to teachers and always will be until the schools decide to teach each child to the limits of his ability and enrich laterally on different levels instead of accelerating children beyond their mental and educational ages.

Of course many teachers will say, "It's all right to talk about differentiation, but just try and do it. With all the children I have, all the things to teach, all the reports and meetings to attend, I am poohed out by the end of the day and devastated by the end of the week." There's a lot of truth in this statement, but it doesn't solve the problem. Perhaps the easiest way is the common-sense way. Give the slow-learning child things which he can read. Differentiate materials as much as possible. Go slower with the slow learner. Help the child informally as much as time and strength will permit. And don't give up, but keep on trying. If the modern teacher is to be respected by laymen, she must become as competent to handle individuals as the expert in other fields. Excuses won't help. The problem must be faced squarely and solved.

What to Do About Phonics

One of the most torrid problems which faces the reading teacher is, *What to do about phonics?* To some critics of the public schools, phonics seems not to be a professional problem but rather a religion. Without the slightest knowledge of the nature and constitution of the English language and with no knowledge of the psychology of teaching reading, they immediately rush to the conclusion that it is best to go back to the good old days. Having forgotten all about the way they learned to read, they reason logically and say that since words are made up of letters and represent sounds, all you need to do is to teach the child the sounds of the letters and he will be able to read and write anything. Would that it were as simple as that. The record shows, however, that one can't depend upon phonics alone to teach the child independence in word recognition.

Since the storm over phonics arose, many teachers have yielded to public criticism, and have gone back to teaching phonics after some fashion which they may have learned twenty or more years ago. Unfortunately, they will find that after a time they will still have reading problems on their hands. For English is far from a phonetic language and a considerable amount of reconstruction will have to take place if it is ever to become fully phonetic.

As it looks from here, the thing to do is to teach phonics sensibly and functionally. Whenever phonics will help to unlock a word, use it. Use phonics as soon as the mental age of the child will allow him to cope with it. Teach the phonics of speech—ear phonics—as well as the phonics which functions in reading and spelling. But don't neglect to emphasize word-form analysis, structural analysis, syllabication, and the use of the dictionary as an aid to word recognition and pronunciation. Teach phonics as long as it will help the child in his reading and writing and in any situation where it will improve his ability to identify words. Teach a combination of approaches to word recognition rather than depend upon a single one and you will in the long run develop reading power.

Television Has Its Problems

Another crucial problem which, in spite of much effort spent upon it, still challenges the reading teacher: *What to do about radio and television?* The present writer does, of course, not have a perfect answer to this problem any more than you have. We are living in an age of electronic marvels. This is the first generation of children who ever were weaned and reared on radio and television. Howdy Doody and Mr. Temple bid for the child's time and compete with good reading for his attention. For a time it may appear that the advertisers have it and that the schools should go along with the trend, install television studios, and prepare to instruct the children electronically.

The answer to the problem, as it seems to me, is to development more attractive and interesting reading programs. If Paul Witty is correct, all is not yet lost to television. There is some evidence that children at first become almost unmanageable in their

television conduct and then gradually become more sane and teleview somewhat less. At any rate, neither teacher nor school can stop the trend. The thing to do, therefore, is to evaluate the school's reading program (some schools don't have any) and to begin the development of a balanced program of reading which will satisfy the child's need for information and recreation. Here again the Reading Committee of the school should deliberate and plan a long-range program of enrichment in the reading program. Parents, local librarians, and interested laymen should be enlisted in a program to retard the influences which interfere with the personal development of the child. Properly used television is an educational asset. The teacher and the school must plan and develop a program that will utilize television as an educational force but not permit it to drive out other important educational agencies.

Problems of Reading in Curricular Areas

Another challenging problem which will occupy the attention of the reading teacher now and in the future still is, *How can I get the children to read effectively the materials of the school curriculum?* This problem has faced us ever since we discovered silent reading and became conscious that reading is a tool for learning. It is still unsolved. There are several things that prevent progress. Among them are textbooks in the curricular areas that are too difficult for the children to read, lack of supplementary material of an informational character for use in the curricular areas, and lack of know-how on the part of teachers. This problem must be met and solved. It is not a passing problem but will remain with us until reading is taught functionally. This year every teacher should attempt to do something about it.

One of the most practical ways to deal with the problem is the organization of materials on different levels of difficulty for use in the curricular fields. Another is to teach the common basal study-skills more effectively. All the study skills that are common to all curricular situations should definitely be initiated and taught in the basal reading program.

All teachers should be responsible for the development and use of these basic reading-study skills.

As a start this year, the teacher might well take one small area in which books are used as tools for learning and map out a beginning program. Experience will then be gained that will enable her to spread the program to other areas in the years to come.

And now this article will have to come to a close, not because there are no other challenging problems that will face the reading teacher in 1957, but because there are other articles which demand a place in this magazine. May *The Reading Teacher* continue to deal as effectively with the challenging problems that face the reading teacher in the future as it has done in the past. The teachers of America are winning the race against ignorance by teaching the child to read better decade by decade and year by year.

More Than Words

Russell G. Stauffer

To stimulate personal and social growth through reading, the most experienced person in the classroom (the teacher) must also be the most experienced person about books for children. Books and authors, fact and fiction, old stories and new provide the starting point. However, love for reading is not taught, it is created; not required, but inspired; not demanded, but exemplified; not exacted, but quickened; not solicited, but activated.

A human mind can be directed. This is why promoting desirable social and personal growth is of tremendous importance. This is why Thomas Jefferson advocated so strongly the law for educating the common people, and swore eternal hostility against every form of tyranny over the mind of man. Unless our educational program is devised so as to accomplish this compact with our people our civilization can disintegrate.

To better understand themselves and others, children must learn to be responsible and responsive. To do this they need opportunities for critical inquiry, for cultivation of open-mindedness, and for freedom of inquiry. But they also need opportunity for realistic practice in living with other people and achieving better human relations.

If, as John Dewey says, the beginning of instruction is made with experiences learners already have, then teachers must realize at the outset that they must see equally to a number of things. To provide boys and girls with realistic practice in living as well as with books about living is the best way to teach them to behave properly when alone and with others.

Even more important than practices in living and books about living, in a sound educational program, is understanding about living. Both practice and reading might not result in much insight and understanding. The good teacher does more. She helps her pupils to generalize from their experiences. As pupils abstract and generalize, more understanding results because such procedures more fully utilize the values of learning through personal experience. The important thing is to enable the children more adequately to appreciate and more intensely to live the lives they know.

Reprinted from *The Reading Teacher*, *12*(1), p. 29. © 1958 by the International Reading Association.

The Indispensable Reading Teacher

Paula J. Gaus

School mailboxes can tell a lot about their owners. Here are some sample notes from the indispensable reading teacher's mailbox.

The *Citizen's Gazette* called to arrange the interview. They'd like to get some photos of the kids working on computers in the lab.

The principal would like to see you as soon as possible. She wants to discuss the proposal for a reading program in the L.D. class.

Call Mrs. Parelli regarding the possibility of alternative low level social studies materials for her son Joey.

Call Mrs. Peabody. Should she worry because Amanda's vocabulary test scores have slipped from 9th to 8th stanine?

The Curriculum Director would like you to make an appointment to discuss the improved reading test scores in our school. He would like to discuss expansion of the content area consulting program to the junior high school.

The secretary of the Parent Advisory Council called. The meeting is scheduled for 8 p.m. Wednesday. Your presentation is third on the agenda.

Marketing Our Services

If your mailbox is not spilling over with notes like these, it is probably not because you are dispensable. But it may be because you are not telling people how indispensable you are. In the private sector, letting people know how much they need you is known as marketing. Good public relations strategies are a significant part of marketing. With educational budgets shrinking, it is our duty to explore anything that protects our budgets and personnel. Our services must be considered indispensable.

Reading teachers have never had a problem getting and keeping "customers." In fact, we must often make painful decisions about which students most need our help. As for keeping customers, our goal is obviously to send them on their way as soon as they are successful readers and students.

We offer more than just reading instruction; our customers are more than just the students we teach. We offer a great service to the school, the parents, and the community. Actually, we offer the *promise* of a service (Levitt, 1981). Reading instruction is an intangible it can't be tasted, touched, or seen. It is even questionable whether reading instruction can be tested; if it can, the testing and resulting evaluation occurs after the service has already been provided—when the student goes out into the world. So we promise to provide a service and we ask our customers to trust us.

Frequently, people willingly invest in something that can't be evaluated until after they've committed time, energy or money to it. "Travel,...insurance, repair,...investment banking, brokerage, health care, accounting can seldom be tried out, inspected, or tested in advance" (Levitt, 1981, p. 96). We can only ask satisfied customers about surgeons, hair stylists, maintenance firms, or caterers, but none of these service providers wait modestly for people to find them and ask about them.

Marketing Ourselves

If you are basically fading into your assignment-laden blackboard, you shouldn't be. The average reading teacher I meet is really quite extraordinary. He or she

Reprinted from *The Reading Teacher*, 37(3), pp. 269–272. © 1983 by the International Reading Association.

holds goals and objectives for ten, tens, or hundreds of students; has a plan of action to match the goals; coordinates formal and informal testing; schedules instructional sessions with teachers and students; selects instructional materials; offers suggestions and makes reports to parents; organizes the school reading programs; participates in district decisions related to reading; promotes reading throughout the school and community; and participates in professional organizations (Professional Standards and Ethics Committee, 1978). The person who can carry all that responsibility is a person who is fulfilling the promise of service. And the community has a right to be informed of that fulfillment.

If your mailbox is filled with complaints like these, you are probably not marketing your accomplishments.

> Ms. Deter wants to know why Jerry got a D. Please call her at work.
>
> Please call Mary Mart's mom. She has a complaint about too much homework.
>
> Sam Soldett's dad wants to know why Sam never has any homework. Please call.

Unfortunately, people seldom realize when things are going well. They notice when things are going wrong. If you keep "what's going well" out front, many of the questions which sound like complaints will be answered before they are asked. Further, genuine complaints can be viewed by parents, teachers, and administrators in terms of the larger perspective of your good works.

The P.R. Campaign

Here are some suggestions for letting the world know just how indispensable you are.

- Contribute to the school or district newsletter. If your school doesn't have this public relations vehicle, suggest that one be instituted. Offer to edit it, if necessary. Parents want to see the baseball scores, one more time, in print. They want to know why they can't find a period marked "lunch" on their daughter's schedule (it is part of the new 90 minute fourth period). More importantly for us, parents want to know the criteria for acceptance into the remedial reading program, an interpretation of the standardized test scores, the rationale for the reading in the content area program.

- Report special programs to local newspapers. Local papers, particularly in small towns, are looking for *good* news to print. There is no better news than that the schools care about teaching and students. Report on the new all-school vocabulary development program or the skills reinforcement exercises offered by computer.

- Consider writing a monthly educational column for the local newspaper. The column could promote all educational ventures supported by the district. If you put out the word that you are interested in writing about any special event in grades K–12, you should be inundated with leads. The Renaissance Festival held in the junior high school, the slide and tape show "Journey to Paris with Dr. Hertz" scheduled for the fourth grade, and the ski club trip are all newsworthy.

- Make regular reports on the progress of the reading program(s) to the Parent Advisory Council.

- Request time to address the school board on a yearly basis; outline your successes and make clear your continued and future needs.

- Send monthly update reports on conspicuously bright-colored paper to the teachers and administrators in your school, the reading teachers throughout the district, and the personnel in central office. Update reports may contain any information about reading: changes in the reading programs offered in your school, descriptions of an existing program, mini-case studies of anonymous students or teachers that you have helped, "book talks" suggesting a book for professional development, changes in laws related to certification or promotion/graduation requirements, an all-school best sellers list.

- Offer to provide inservice programs for the entire school staff and for the teachers in individual content areas. We all have our own inservice favorites; one of mine is a variation on a suggestion by Osburn (1974). Early in the year, tape record several of the less able students reading short selections from their content texts. Tape record the same students reading the same or similar selections at the end of the year. Edit the tapes so that a cogent before-and-after presentation can be made the following year. This inservice offers evidence that your intangible services have tangible results (Berry, 1980). It provides a starting point for dialogue about essential services you offer and what your peers can do to help.

- Join professional organizations. Get involved with your local and regional affiliates as well as the national organizations. Offer to serve on committees. The *IRA Directory* (International Reading Association, 1982) offers a starting point for finding contacts in all these organizations. Attend conferences; conferences offer the possibility of professional development as well as professional contacts. (Hint: Remember to tell people what you are doing.)

- Present papers at local, regional, or national conferences. Write articles for professional journals. These activities are undertaken by professionals. You lend credence to your own professionalism when you indulge in writing for and speaking to your colleagues.

- Invite influential community members, as well as Board of Education members and dis-trict administrators, to observe your work. Offer to explain complex testing concepts or your projected budget. Offer to provide a cup of coffee and a sympathetic ear (Landsmann, 1983).

These suggestions are only a sampling of what a public relations campaign might include. We are limited only by our imaginations. Our goal is simple: Make sure everyone realizes that we make good on the promise to provide service. We want to remind our fellow teachers, school and district administrators, and the community that there is value in the reading instruction which is constantly and competently delivered. We need to remind ourselves that competence and professionalism are not synonymous with silence. We need to reassert our presence in the school continually.

REFERENCES

Berry, Leonard L. "Service Marketing Is Different." *Business*, vol. 30 (May–June 1980), pp. 22–25.

International Reading Association. *1982–1983 Directory*. Newark, Del.: International Reading Association, 1982.

Landsmann, Leanna. "Researching Out to Save the Schools." *The Journal of Reading Education*, vol. 9 (February 1983), pp. 95–102.

Levitt, Theodore. "Marketing Intangible Products and Product Intangibles." *Harvard Business Review*, vol. 59 (May–June 1981), pp. 95–102.

Osburn, Bess. "Shock Treatment Inservice Program Adds New Life to Reading." *Journal of Reading*, vol. 18 (November 1974), pp. 122–126.

Professional Standards and Ethics Committee. "Specific Attitudes, Concepts, and Skills." In *Guidelines for the Professional Preparation of Reading Teachers*. Newark, Del.: International Reading Association, 1978.

What's Needed Now in Reading Instruction: The Teacher as Scholar and Romanticist

John C. Manning

Then said a teacher, speak to us of teaching
and he said
No man can reveal to you aught but that
which already lies half asleep in the
dawning of your knowledge.
The teacher who walks in the shadow of
the temple, among his followers
gives not of his wisdom but rather of
his faith and his lovingness.

Khalil Gibran, *The Prophet*

Kahlil Gibran, like John Donne, William Blake and T.S. Eliot, perceived teaching as the universal expression and explanation of the eternal communion which binds us together as individual people in a sometimes unfeeling, chaotic and tragic world. That metaphysical history is certainly part of our legacy as teachers, and we must communicate that human common inheritance to all who come to the school to learn to read.

But we also live in a secular world, the world of the school, the world of our work and of our professional calling. What knowledges are essential for the effective teaching of reading in our schools? What wisdoms will ensure that children and adults will use reading as a means of personal and societal fulfillment? I believe there are two—those knowledges characteristic of the teacher of reading as scholar, and those wisdoms characteristic of the teacher of reading as romanticist.

The Reading Teacher as Scholar

Knowledge of the professional literature. All who serve the schools in various capacities as teachers of reading must be aware of and understand that body of information found in our professional reading literature. We must be cognizant of the conclusions and the instructional implications of appropriate and well designed reading and language research studies. We need to seek means of applying those significant research results to improve school reading practice. It is imperative that we read the research journals of our own professional organization, the International Reading Association, and the various monographs and texts that augment and enlarge this theoretical and foundational research base. We must have teachers of reading who are aware of and conversant with both historical and contemporary reading research studies and findings.

As teachers of reading we must also be alert to the journals and monographs which report the experiences and intuitions of successful practitioners in the schools—those learned and gifted teachers who by their instructional skills, practical reflections, and creative methods most effectively teach students to read in the schools. There is much to be learned from conversation with and observation of the highly skilled and accomplished practitioner. Unfortunately, there is a puzzling and distressing notion that

Reprinted from *The Reading Teacher*, 39(2), pp. 132–138. © 1985 by the International Reading Association.

there are some higher and some lower level cognitions that separate college and university research efforts from classroom reading practice. Colleges of teacher education and the various departments within them exist solely for one purpose—to improve the quality of learning in the schools. It is incumbent on these same colleges of education and university faculties to demonstrate the relevance and appropriateness of reading and language research findings to such school improvements.

We paid much notice to but followed little the wise counsel of James Bryant Conant in *The Education of American Teachers* (1962). Conant proposed "the most realistic alternative that has come to my attention is the clinical professor of education prepared by training to understand what other professionals have to say and inclined to listen to them and prepared by continuing experience in the elementary or secondary school to demonstrate in concrete teaching situations the implications of expert judgment."

We have in no manner achieved the goal which Conant described. Indeed, I continue to perceive a drift away from research confrontation with the practical day to day problems of reading instruction in the schools.

For their part, the elementary and secondary schools need to open their classroom doors to allow greater applied research efforts conducted by college and university faculty and graduate students. There need to be school adjustments of classroom schedules and teaching personnel to allow this much needed applied reading research to move forward in schools.

When such reciprocal efforts, through research findings and enlightened school reading practice, find their way separately into some professional journals and jointly into others and when such journals are read by researchers and practitioners, the teaching of reading will be improved in the schools and our discipline will be more honored and esteemed.

Knowledge of the subject matter. The subject matter of our reading profession is language and the ability to teach the uses of language and an understanding of language in oral and written forms. It is clearly not enough that teachers of reading are knowledgeable about teacher's manuals and reading curriculum guides. It is patently insufficient when teachers know only the procedures specified and outlined in the various developmental reading programs; it is calamitous when teachers of reading are unaware of the content, structure, and function of the language they teach.

That we can speak and listen, read and write our language is inadequate for the teacher scholar of reading in the schools. We must return to the colleges and universities for courses in language development and learning, for courses in linguistics, cognition, and the psychology of language.

We need to turn to the bibliographies, monographs, and texts of language, turn on the lamps beside our chairs and read and read and read. Our profession demands all of that and more. Our schools and our children and our children's children cannot survive with less than that.

Knowledge of the reading curriculum. It is appropriate at this point to acknowledge with gratitude the support we receive as a professional association and as reading teachers from the book publishing industry. Historically they have enthusiastically endorsed our professional efforts and, in the vast majority of instances, with benevolent grace and financial resource. Our local councils, state organizations, regional conferences, and annual convention appreciate the support of our friends and colleagues in the publishing industry.

Knowledge of reading curriculum. The vast majority of students in our schools are taught to read through developmental reading programs. These programs have various gestalt, linguistic, orthographic stress or phonic emphases. Most children in the elementary schools, however, are taught through gestalt or whole word programs. The sequence of the lessons of those programs has not changed substantively in over 60 years.

There are three sequential parts or components to the contemporary reading lesson—a written vocabulary to be learned, a story or selection to be read either orally or silently, and reading skills to be acquired and practiced. Though the sequence of these lessons has not changed significantly over the years, the content of two of the three component parts has changed dramatically. In one instance the change has been inestimably for the better. In the other, the change is open to serious critical inquiry.

It is entirely proper that basal reader stories which stereotyped individuals and races, demeaned ethnic groups and national origins, and did not illustrate equality among men and women and boys and girls are no longer found in our reading textbooks. That content has changed and all for the better.

The other change in content, the shift of emphasis which needs to be gravely questioned, is in the reading skill component of the lessons at all grade levels and all book levels. It is a startling change which becomes increasingly disquieting and professionally unsettling. The amount of reading skill instruction taking place in today's schools is, in my view, entirely disproportionate to that necessary in learning to read. Upwards of 60% of the total time devoted to a reading lesson in the elementary school is focused on reading skill instruction.

For many children this is clearly inappropriate, unnecessary and perhaps even impedimentary in learning to read and in developing text fluency. Much of the skill instruction is unnecessary and inappropriate for bright children who have already internalized these reading skills through daily practice in pleasurable personal reading. And much of this skill instruction may very well be unintelligible for many lower ability children who do not understand the language used to explain it. All too many explanations regarding reading skills provided to pupils in the schools are more appropriate to a college class in applied linguistics than to a class of little children trying to learn to read.

As teachers of reading we must have thorough knowledge of the reading curriculum programs we teach. Through careful analysis and reflection we must exercise our professional judgments and discard those purported reading skills that are confusing and baffling to children. We must reduce the number of skill practices that are meaningless, overly repetitive and dulling, and we must eliminate much of the mindless skill practice exercises that we require students to complete in our classrooms.

The higher mental process reading skills of the developing and mature readers are best attained in school in the same way they are attained in our homes and in our libraries—through poetry and drama, through short story and novel. The reading curriculum in our schools must be the active reading and thoughtful reflection of all these literary forms or it is no reading program at all. Children learn to read fluently by reading.

This skills problem which I and many others perceive is not exclusively the fault of extant basal reading programs. The publishers respond as they have always responded to the expressed needs and demands of teachers and schools. Though the exact cause of this skill overkill is elusive, one cannot ignore the fact that all too many teachers of reading are becoming managers of material, shifters of paper, and collectors and filers of the inconsequential.

In addition, entirely too many classroom instructional procedures are being dictated by management schemes and testing programs of very dubious worth, and by administrative decisions far removed from the dynamics of classroom reading practice. As teachers of reading we have been led to believe that accountability is to be found in numbers, percentile ranks and grade equivalent scores. Distressingly, as a reading profession we are being measured and judged by a yardstick of relative numbers without a shred of literary calibration. There is an unfortunate and misguided zeal on the part of many educators who bear allegiance to the cause of basic education. In a quantum leap of intellectual misdirection, they have equated basic education with basic skill instruction in reading. With encouragement from legislators and from parents who are justifiably concerned about the quality of education, various skill accountability schemes have been implemented in the schools. While the intent and demands of legislators at all levels of government and parents at all levels of involvement are noble, the means which the schools are using to attain these goals are, in my judgment, clearly wrong.

There are two major thrusts needed to redirect school reading curricula away from the restrictive and confining testing programs which currently define and closet them and toward more intelligent, humane, and purposeful educational objectives.

First, reading researchers need to discover and validate more enlightened measures of pupil reading achievement. We need tests and measures of applied skills in reading performance rather than in disjointed skill subtests whose only validity appears to be that they are standardized.

Second, schools need to increase the time available for children to read, to read to themselves and to others, and for teachers to read to children and to share books with them. We need to insist that the reading of the story is the ultimate goal of the reading lesson, not the skill instruction which follows it...and follows it...and follows it.

With considerable thought I offer the suggestion that school may very well be the last refuge for children to engage in purposeful leisure and recreational reading. And I, for one, encourage that tranquil and holy sanctuary.

As teachers of reading we *are* indeed accountable. We are accountable for our professional decisions regarding the uses of reading materials and appropriate classroom methods in the schools, we are accountable to the parents and communities who invest their faith in our judgments and decisions, and we are certainly and ultimately accountable to all who come to the school to learn to read.

Knowledge of reading methodology and instructional practice. There is no problem more vexing or so critical to our development as a universally accepted profession than the problem of improving classroom reading instruction. Classroom reading methodology is the least understood area of current reading research. It is the least understood area of applied school practice.

Many teachers of reading erroneously believe that "methods" are those written procedures prescribed in the teacher manuals which accompany basal reader programs. Method, properly understood, is that unique, highly subjective, affectively charged condition which occurs when this teacher interacts with those students using these guidebook or manual procedures. These encouraged manual or guidebook procedures do not teach, they do not instruct. They do not in any manner take into account the two most critical variables of instructional process, the dynamics of the teacher and of the learner.

The major problems I perceive in our present instructional practices are two. First, they are basically socratic in procedure. The "instruction" begins with a question, proceeds with a question and concludes with a question—to which I have two additional questions: If the students know the answer to the question...why ask? And two, and more culpably, if the students do not know the answer to the question...why ask?

The second problem is equally evident. The procedures we employ in teaching children to read in our schools are essentially bimodal—they assume the attentive eye and ear of the learner. But many children who come to our schools have not learned to attend to print with the eye nor to language with the ear. Many come to school from very restricted home language environments. Many come who have not been read with consistently at home. For such pupils these bimodal instructional procedures found in most developmental reading programs are clearly inappropriate and ineffective. The major research efforts still to be completed are in the areas of teacher instruction and learner-teacher-text interaction.

In my view, there are two reasonable and common sense temporary solutions that can be implemented by sensitive teachers of reading *now*.

First we must translate the existing socratic questioning procedures into more direct teacher instructional processes. We must ask far fewer questions during the reading lesson and provide more appropriate modeling behaviors in our teaching. We must do much more reading of directions and of text during the reading lesson itself. We should read from the skill charts and the vocabulary charts. We should read from the practice sheets and from the skill sheets that are relevant to learning to read and we should read the stories from the basal readers so that pupils will learn to attend to print. Where teachers of reading see a question mark at the end of a sentence of directions in the teachers manual, that sentence should be addressed to the pupils as a declarative one.

Children learn to read in school in exactly the same manner that they would have learned to read at home on a mother's lap or father's knee. Children learn to read by learning to follow along visually with print as the fluent reader reads. And that is the only way a child who is sighted and can hear will learn to read in the schools.

Second, we must implement methods which will actively involve the learner during reading instruction. In active pupil involvement, the learner cannot *not* pay attention. If the learner is not attending, that condition is immediately apparent to the teacher. We must search for more ways to engage the student through printing, writing and other overt responses so that the learner is more directly and responsibly involved during the reading lesson. When we read our teacher manuals and the directions on how to teach the lesson, we should ask ourselves a fundamental question: "What will the pupils be doing during the time that I am doing what the manual suggests?"

For many children in beginning reading programs and for all children experiencing difficulty in learning to read, the teacher should never assume the pupils are attentive to the directions nor to the text. We have by no means either through research or through classroom experience resolved these major problems of instruction which prevent so many children from learning to read in our schools and prevent them from experiencing pleasurable and successful academic and personal lives.

The Reading Teacher as Romanticist

Yet, schools are more than basal readers and pencils, chalk and board. Schools are places of people, of great hopes, high expectation and achieved promise, places of human emotions, psychological needs and spiritual values, place where intellects are aroused, ideas thought and shared, sensitivities explored,

character developed. In the words of one metaphysical poet, John Donne, from *Songs and Sonnets*:

> Go and catch a falling star,
> Get with child a mandrake root
> Tell me where all past years are
> Or who cleft the Devil's foot.
> Teach me to hear mermaids singing
> Or to keep off envy's stinging.
> And find
> What wind
> Serves to advance an honest mind.

And William Blake's "Nurse's Song" from *Songs of Innocence*:

> When the voices of children are heard
>   on the green
> And laughing is heard on the hill
> My heart is at rest within my breast
> And everything else is still
> The little ones leaped and shouted
>   and laughed
> And all the hills echoed

And Kahlil Gibran from *The Prophet* "On Children":

> And a woman who held a babe against her
>   bosom said, Speak to me of children
> And he said
>   You may give them your love but not your thoughts
>   For they have their own thoughts
>   You may house their bodies but not their souls
>   For their souls dwell in the house of tomorrow,
>   which you cannot visit, not even in your dreams.
>   You may strive to be like them, but seek not to
>   make them like you.
>   For life goes not backward nor tarries with yesterday.

And T.S. Eliot from *Gerontion*:

> Here I am an old man in a dry month
> Being read to by a boy, waiting for rain

Therein lies the artistry and the eternity of the reading teacher as romanticist.

Those of us who serve the schools as teachers of reading need to immerse ourselves in the world of books, stories, poetry and drama. We need to know the literature appropriate and appealing to the children, adolescents and adults who come to the schools to learn to read. We need to know that historical and contemporary literature graces our profession and adds literary substance to our reputation as teachers of reading. We need to seek within literature those lines that speak to eternal truths, those stories that have taught through the ages, that poetry which has opened our intellects and consciences to an understanding of goodness, truth and beauty. We must ourselves be at all times well read, so that we may use the literature and history of our birthright as teachers to inform, to entertain and to inspire.

Above all else, teachers of reading must be literate exemplars, demonstrating by their knowledge and by their language familiarity with literature that has guaranteed personal liberty and intellectual freedom for all who have known it. We need to be ever alert to the uses of language in our school and public lives and in our personal lives as well. We need to appreciate the various language patterns which children and young adults bring with them to school. There is again with language as there is with research in colleges and practice in the schools an unfortunate confusion which places exalted values on certain language patterns and stigmata and intolerance on others. There is an inherent beauty and propriety, rhythm and cadence, charm, grace and, indeed, eloquence to all language forms both standard and nonstandard.

As teachers of reading we must understand and accept why students communicate as they do. Equally important, and again by our example of language manners and styles and forms, we need to teach our students other appropriate forms of language for social, economic and personal needs. That we are teachers of reading demands that we are teachers of language in the fullest sense of the term.

Through the teaching and use of language we need to enlighten our students to recognize and appreciate the inherent dignity of all human labor through words of gratitude and thanks, to relieve physical and emotional pain through words of understanding and compassion, to seek justice and equality through words of good moral sense and common decency. And for all of us to seek through language and reading a universe of peace in our families, neighborhoods, cities, states and nations in the only world that we together share.

The greatest gift we can give to the children and students who come to our schools is the unbridled romantic love affair with language and books in historical context and literary form. It is that gift which shall remain long after the sweet gentle memories of school have dimmed and faded forever more.

Excellent Reading Teachers

A Position Statement of the International Reading Association

Every child deserves excellent reading teachers because teachers make a difference in children's reading achievement and motivation to read.

This position statement provides a research-based description of the distinguishing qualities of excellent classroom reading teachers. Excellent reading teachers share several critical qualities of knowledge and practice:

1. They understand reading and writing development and believe all children can learn to read and write.

2. They continually assess children's individual progress and relate reading instruction to children's previous experiences.

3. They know a variety of ways to teach reading, when to use each method, and how to combine the methods into an effective instructional program.

4. They offer a variety of materials and texts for children to read.

5. They use flexible grouping strategies to tailor instruction to individual students.

6. They are good reading "coaches" (that is, they provide help strategically).

(See the Table for resources that address each of these characteristics.)

In addition, excellent reading teachers share many of the characteristics of good teachers in general. They have strong content and pedagogical knowledge, manage classrooms so that there is a high rate of engagement, use strong motivation strategies that encourage independent learning, have high expectations for children's achievement, and help children who are having difficulty.

What Evidence Is There That Good Reading Teachers Have a Positive Effect on Children's Reading Achievement and Motivation to Read?

Teachers make a difference. There is a growing body of evidence that documents teacher effects on children's reading achievement scores (Jordan, Mendro, Weerasinghe, & Dallas Public Schools, 1997; Sanders & Rivers, 1996; Wright, Horn, & Sanders,

Reprinted from *The Reading Teacher*, 54(2), pp. 235–240. © 2000 by the International Reading Association.

Characteristics of excellent reading teachers: Research support

Articles	1	2	3	4	5	6
Anders, P.L., Hoffman, J.V., & Duffy, G.G. (2000)	p. 7 p. 16					p. 6
Briggs, K.L., & Thomas, K. (1997)		p. 27 p. 28 p. 33		p. 8 p. 9	p. 14	p. 527
Brophy, J. (1982)		p. 259	p. 527		p. 529	p. 527
Duffy, G.G., Roehler, L.R., & Herrmann, B.A. (1988)	p. 762	p. 763	p. 766			p. 766
Haberman, M. (1995)		p. 19				p. 19 p. 20 p. 86
Hoffman, J., & Pearson, P.D. (1999)		p. 16	p. 17			
Knapp, M.S. (1995)		p. 127 p. 128	p. 126	pp. 127–128 pp. 130–133 pp. 136–137 p. 142		
Ladson-Billings, G. (1994)	p. 123	p. 124				p. 124
Metsala, J.L. (1997)	p. 520	p. 519	p. 519 p. 520	p. 519	p. 519	p. 520
Moll, L. (1988)	p. 466 p. 468	p. 469		p. 468		p. 468
Pederson, E., Faucher, T.A., & Eaton, W.W. (1978)	p. 22					
Pressley, M., Rankin, J., & Yokoi, L. (1996)	p. 371 p. 375 p. 377				p. 373	
Ruddell, R.B. (1995)	p. 456	p. 455	p. 455 p. 456		p. 455	
Sweet, A.P., Guthrie, J.T., & Ng, M.M. (1998)	p. 217 p. 220	p. 218 p. 220	p. 215 p. 217 p. 220			
Taylor, B.M., Pearson, P.D., Clark, K.F., & Walpole, S. (1999)	p. 3	p. 45 p. 46	p. 3	pp. 44–46	p. 11	
Teddlie, C., & Stringfield, S. (1993)	p. 192					
Tharp, R.G. (1997)		p. 6	p. 6			p. 5
Thomas, K.F., & Barksdale-Ladd, M.A. (1995)		p. 171 p. 172	p. 171 p. 172 pp. 176–177	p. 173		
Wharton-McDonald, R., Pressley, M., & Hampston, J.M. (1998)	p. 119		p. 111 p. 112	p. 112		p. 116

1997). Teacher effectiveness—which can be measured as scores on teacher proficiency tests (Ferguson, 1991), past records of students' improved scores, teachers' level of education, type of appointment (tenured, probationary, substitute), and years of experience (Armour, Clay, Bruno, & Allen, 1990)—is strongly correlated with children's reading achievement. Moreover, teachers have strong effects on children's motivation to read (Ruddell, 1995; Skinner & Belmont, 1993).

What Do Excellent Reading Teachers Know About Reading Development?

Excellent reading teachers know that reading development begins well before children enter school and continues throughout a child's school career. They understand the definition of reading as a complex system of deriving meaning from print that requires all of the following:

- the development and maintenance of a motivation to read

- the development of appropriate active strategies to construct meaning from print

- sufficient background information and vocabulary to foster reading comprehension

- the ability to read fluently

- the ability to decode unfamiliar words

- the skills and knowledge to understand how phonemes or speech sounds are connected to print

(International Reading Association, 1999; see also Snow, Burns, & Griffin, 1998).

Excellent teachers understand that all components of reading influence every stage of reading, but they also realize that the balance of instruction related to these components shifts across the developmental span and shifts for individual children. Excellent teachers understand how reading and writing development are related, and they effectively integrate instruction to take advantage of the child's development in both areas. They are familiar with the sequence of children's reading development. They believe that all children can learn to read and write.

How Do Excellent Reading Teachers Assess Student Progress?

Excellent reading teachers are familiar with a wide range of assessment techniques, ranging from standardized group achievement tests to informal assessment techniques that they use daily in the classroom. They use the information from standardized group measures as one source of information about children's reading progress, recognizing that standardized group achievement tests can be valid and reliable indicators of group performance but can provide misleading information about individual performance. They are well aware that critical judgments about children's progress must draw from information from a variety of sources, and they do not make critical instructional decisions based on any single measure.

Excellent reading teachers are constantly observing children as they go about their daily work. They understand that involving children in self-evaluation has both cognitive and motivational benefits. In the classroom, these teachers use a wide variety of assessment tools, including conferences with students, analyses of samples of children's reading and writing, running records and informal reading inventories, anecdotal records of children's performance, observation checklists, and other similar tools. They are familiar with each child's instructional history and home literacy background. From their observations and the child's own self-evaluations, they draw knowledge of the child's reading development, and they can relate that development to relevant standards. They use this knowledge for planning instruction that is responsive to children's needs.

What Do Excellent Reading Teachers Know About Instructional Methods and How to Combine Them to Meet the Needs of the Children They Teach?

Excellent reading teachers know a wide variety of instructional philosophies, methods, and strategies. They understand that excellent reading instruction addresses all the essential elements of reading. They are aware that instructional strategies vary along many dimensions, including the component of reading targeted by the instruction (for example, pronouncing words, understanding text, building motivation), the degree to which the instruction is teacher- or student-directed, and the degree to which the instruction is explicit or implicit. They understand that children vary in their responses to different types of instruction, and they select the most efficient combination of instructional strategies to serve the children in their classrooms. They know early intervention techniques and ensure that children get the help they need as soon as the need becomes apparent. For example, in a single middle-grade classroom, teachers have children who still recognize very few words and struggle with decoding, children who are fluent and avid readers who can and do read everything they get their hands on, and children who are fluent decoders but struggle with comprehension and motivation. In the case of a struggling reader, excellent reading teachers know enough about the child and the child's instructional history to provide access to very easy books on topics studied by the class. The teacher can work with similar children in a small group to build sight vocabulary and decoding fluency, and the teacher can provide appropriate accommodations so that these children can benefit from comprehension instruction and continue to learn critical content despite their reading difficulties.

What Kinds of Texts and Reading Materials Do Excellent Reading Teachers Use in Their Classrooms?

Excellent reading teachers include a variety of reading materials in their classrooms. Sometimes they rely on one or several reading series as the anchor of their reading program, but they also have supplemental materials and rich classroom libraries that contain at least seven books per child. They read to their students, and they provide time in class for children to read independently. They are aware of the reading abilities and interests of the children, and they constantly provide a selection of books that will be both interesting to the children and within the children's reading capabilities. Excellent reading teachers are familiar with children's literature. They include a wide variety of fiction and nonfiction genres (such as storybooks, novels, biographies, magazines, and poetry). Excellent reading teachers also use school and public libraries to ensure children's access to appropriate books.

How Do Excellent Reading Teachers Organize Their Classrooms for Instruction?

Excellent reading teachers organize their classrooms so that schedules are predictable and children know what is expected of them in a variety of activities throughout the instructional day. They use flexible grouping strategies. When there is new and difficult information to convey that most of the class needs to learn, excellent reading teachers use large-group, direct, explicit instruction. They model the focal strategy or skill, demonstrate how and when to use it, and explain why it is important. They guide the children in their use of the skill or strategy, gradually diminishing support and assistance and requiring students to assume greater responsibility as the children become more skilled. They provide opportunities for individual practice and observe children in their use of the skill or strategy. During practice activities, they observe children closely, intervening when necessary with a question or comment that moves children forward. They also know which children will benefit from all elements of a direct instruction lesson in a particular skill or strategy and which children will need only a brief period of guided instruction or review followed by independent practice. They use efficient grouping practices to accommodate these differences.

Excellent reading teachers also understand that large-group, direct instruction is time consuming and costly and that, often, many children in the class will not benefit from this instruction. They know when to organize children in large groups for direct, explicit instruction, when small-group or individual instruction is more appropriate, and when children will learn more efficiently on their own. They help children advance in reading by differentiating the type of instruction, the degree of support, and the amount of practice children receive. They do not allow children to spend time learning what they already know and can do.

How Do Excellent Reading Teachers Interact With Children?

Excellent reading teachers interact with individual children frequently in the course of their daily teaching activities. As they help children solve problems or practice new skills and strategies, they "coach" or "scaffold" children by providing help at strategic moments. They are skilled at observing children's performance and using informal interactions to call children's attention to important aspects of what they are learning and doing. They often help children with a difficult part of the task so that the children can move forward to complete the task successfully. It is important to note that such teaching is neither incidental or unsystematic. Excellent reading teachers know where their children are in reading development and they know the likely next steps. They help children take these steps by providing just the right amount of help at just the right time.

Recommendations for Developing Excellence in Reading Instruction

- Teachers must view themselves as lifelong learners and continually strive to improve their practice.

- Administrators must be instructional leaders who support teachers' efforts to improve reading instruction.

- Teacher educators must provide both a solid knowledge base and extensive supervised practice to prepare excellent beginning reading teachers.

- Legislators and policy makers must understand the complex role of the teacher in providing reading instruction and ensure that teachers have the resources and support they need to teach reading. Legislators and policy makers should not impose one-size-fits-all mandates.

- Parents, community members, and teachers must work in partnership to assure that children value reading and have many opportunities to read outside of school.

REFERENCES

Anders, P.L., Hoffman, J.V., & Duffy, G.G. (2000). Teaching teachers to teach reading: Paradigm shifts, persistent problems, and challenges. In M.L. Kamil, P.B. Mosenthal, P.D. Pearson, & R. Barr (Eds.), *Handbook of reading research: Volume III* (pp. 719–742). Mahwah, NJ: Erlbaum.

Armour, T.C., Clay, C., Bruno, K., & Allen, B.A. (1990). *An outlier study of elementary and middle schools in New York City: Final report.* New York: New York City Board of Education.

Briggs, K.L., & Thomas, K. (1997). *Patterns of success: Successful pathways to elementary literacy in Texas spotlight schools.* Austin, TX: Texas Center for Educational Research.

Brophy, J. (1982). Successful teaching strategies for the inner-city child. *Phi Delta Kappan, 63,* 527–530.

Duffy, G.G., Roehler, L.R., & Herrmann, B.A. (1988). Modeling mental processes helps poor readers become strategic readers. *The Reading Teacher, 41,* 762–767.

Ferguson, R. (1991). Paying for public education: New evidence on how and why money matters. *Harvard Journal on Legislation, 28,* 465–498.

Haberman, M. (1995). *Star teachers of children of poverty.* West Lafayette, IN: Kappa Delta Pi.

Hoffman, J., & Pearson, P.D. (1999). *What your grandmother's teacher didn't know that your granddaughter's teacher should.* Austin, TX: University of Texas at Austin.

International Reading Association. (1999). *Using multiple methods of beginning reading instruction: A position statement of the International Reading Association.* Newark, DE: Author.

Jordan, H.R., Mendro, R.L., Weeringhe, D., & Dallas Public Schools. (1997). *Teacher effects on longitudinal student achievement.* Presentation at the CREATE Annual Meeting, Indianapolis, IN.

Knapp, M.S. (1995). *Teaching for meaning in high poverty classrooms.* New York: Teachers College Press.

Ladson-Billings, G. (1994). *The dreamkeepers: Successful teachers of African American children.* San Francisco: Jossey-Bass.

Metsala, J.L. (1997). Effective primary-grades literacy instruction = Balanced literacy instruction. *The Reading Teacher, 50,* 518–521.

Moll, L. (1988). Some key issues in teaching Latino students. *Language Arts, 65,* 465–472.

Pederson, E., Faucher, T.A., & Eaton, W.W. (1978). A new perspective on the effects of first-grade teachers on children's subsequent adult status. *Harvard Educational Review, 48,* 1–31.

Pressley, M., Rankin, J., & Yokoi, L. (1996). A survey of instructional practice of primary teachers nominated as effective in promoting literacy. *The Elementary School Journal, 96,* 363–384.

Ruddell, R.B. (1995). Those influential literacy teachers: Meaning negotiators and motivation builders. *The Reading Teacher, 48,* 454–463.

Sanders, W.L., & Rivers, J.C. (1996). *Cumulative and residual effects of teachers on future student academic achievement: Research progress report.* Knoxville, TN: University of Tennessee Value-Added Research and Assessment Center.

Skinner, E.A., & Belmont, M.J. (1993). Motivation in the classroom: Reciprocal effects of teacher behavior and student engagement across the school year. *Journal of Educational Psychology, 85,* 571–581.

Snow, C.E., Burns, M.S., & Griffin, P. (Eds.). (1998). *Preventing reading difficulties in young children.* Washington, DC: National Academy Press.

Sweet, A.P., Guthrie, J.T., & Ng, M.M. (1998). Teacher perception and student reading motivation. *Journal of Educational Psychology, 90,* 210–223.

Taylor, B.M., Pearson, P.D., Clark, K.F., & Walpole, S. (1999). *Beating the odds in teaching all children to read.* Ann Arbor, MI: Center for the Improvement of Early Reading Achievement.

Teddlie, C., & Stringfield, S. (1993). *Schools make a difference: Lessons learned from a 10-year study of school effects.* New York: Teachers College Press.

Tharp, R.G. (1997). *The five generic principles: Current knowledge about effective education of at-risk students.* Santa Cruz, CA: Center for Research on Education Diversity and Excellence, University of California.

Thomas, K.F., & Barksdale-Ladd, M.A. (1995). Effective literacy classrooms: Teachers and students exploring literacy together. In K.A. Hinchman, D.J. Leu, & C.K. Kinzer, (Eds.), *Perspectives on literacy research and practice* (Forty-fourth yearbook of the National Reading Conference). Chicago: National Reading Conference.

Wharton-McDonald, R., Pressley, M., & Hampston, J.M. (1998). Literacy instruction in nine first-grade classrooms: Teacher characteristics and student achievement. *The Elementary School Journal, 99,* 101–128.

Wright, P.S., Horn, S.P., & Sanders, W.L. (1997). Teacher and classroom context effects on student achievement: Implications for teacher evaluation. *Journal of Personnel Evaluation in Education, 11,* 57–67.

The Changing Face of Education: Teachers Cope With Challenges Through Collaboration and Reflective Study

Carla C. Dearman and Sheila R. Alber

One size does *not* fit all. To accommodate diversity, we have to change the way we teach. We can do that if we actually have *time* to collaborate and plan effective interventions for each individual child.

Mississippi fifth-grade teacher

Our district provided us with two hours each week to collaboratively study the needs of our students and to plan the best way to meet those needs. We've come to really know each individual child and how to intervene effectively.

Mississippi second-grade teacher

We have been working collaboratively with our fellow teachers for the past three years. When reflective conferencing was added to collaboration, it was a lot easier to solve problems and make good instructional decisions.

Mississippi third-grade teacher

As illustrated by these quotes, Mississippi teachers recognize they must initiate and develop instructional changes that will improve individual student achievement. They also realize they need time to plan and implement effective changes. Mississippi teachers are not alone; their comments mirror the sentiment of teachers elsewhere in the United States. The shared experiences of these teachers may inspire educators to modify their current practice to have a positive impact on literacy instruction nationwide.

Only 31% of U.S. fourth graders scored at or above the proficient level in reading on the 2003 National Assessment of Educational Progress (NAEP). This statistic alone highlights the urgency of meeting diverse student needs, especially in these times of legislative mandates for increased teacher accountability. Consequently, educators (i.e., administrators and teachers) are joining together to study, plan, and meet the challenges of their diverse populations and the legislative mandates. Research has documented effective strategies for schools to address these challenges (Blythe, Allen, & Powell, 1999; Fullan, 2003; King & Newmann, 2000; National Institute of Child Health and Human Development [NICHD], 2000; Showers & Joyce, 1996; Snow, Burns, & Griffin, 1998). However, the literature stops short of uniting proven strategies into a step-by-step process. This article presents a three-pronged plan for coping with the changing face of education: (1) educators face the process of change, (2) educators find the time to study together, and (3) educators reflectively review student work in study teams and adjust research-based instructional practices to improve both teaching and learning.

Around the United States public outcries for accountability have challenged the nation's educational

---

Reprinted from *The Reading Teacher*, 58(7), pp. 634–640. © 2005 by the International Reading Association.

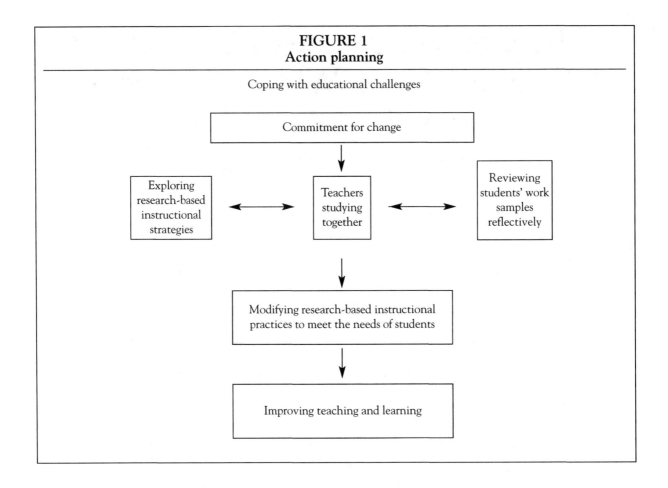

FIGURE 1
Action planning

Coping with educational challenges

Commitment for change

Exploring research-based instructional strategies

Teachers studying together

Reviewing students' work samples reflectively

Modifying research-based instructional practices to meet the needs of students

Improving teaching and learning

system. On January 8, 2002, the No Child Left Behind Act (NCLB) became law and outlined the principles of Reading First. Public Law 107-110 was enacted to close the achievement gap between high- and low-performing students. This law advocates that no child will be left behind if educators are accountable, flexible, and have choices. NCLB (2002) presents a multifaceted educational challenge for teachers and administrators across the nation. Not only are the school administrators and classroom teachers responsible for the measured growth of their students in reading, mathematics, and language, but also they are accountable for the diverse student needs in the following subgroups: economically disadvantaged students, students from various racial and ethnic groups, students with disabilities, and students with limited English proficiency.

Over time the laws may change, but the general consensus is that a system of accountability is here to stay (Fullan, 2003; King & Newmann, 2000). Therefore, debating the issues will neither change the mandates for accountability nor improve student achievement. Rather than suffer the consequences of fate, educators must now choose a plan of action that changes the way schools conduct business (NICHD, 2000; Snow et al., 1998). Figure 1 suggests such a process for administrators and teachers committed to coping with the challenges of education today. This process includes reflectively reviewing student work together to modify research-based instructional strategies and improve student achievement.

Regardless of mandates for accountability, any effective change takes planning, inquiry, and time to facilitate (Fullan, 2000, 2003). All schools must focus teachers and students on the processes of effective teaching and learning, but the legislative mandates of NCLB do not dictate precisely how schools should achieve their success. Neither does NCLB determine the reading curricula, methods, or the materials to be used for classroom instruction —only that reading instruction must encompass research-based programs and practices. The districts and schools are allowed to consider the school's culture and needs to make the programmatic decisions for improving reading performance (U.S. Department of Education, 2002). Therefore, state officials, school administrators, and teachers must assume control over choosing the processes they use to meet these legislative mandates.

Teachers and the Process of Change

There is abundant research concerning how change occurs in educational systems (Fullan, 2000, 2003; Swafford, 1998). Change rarely occurs merely as a reaction to a mandate. Research suggests that the change process is very complex, and, for change to actually occur, teachers must experience a paradigm shift in philosophy (Fullan, 2000). One aspect of change, addressing the learning capacity of both educators and students, is at the heart of school improvement and accountability (King & Newmann, 2000). Educator dialogue and problem solving have been demonstrated to be effective for building a school's capacity to improve student achievement (Fullan, 1998, 2000). Looking for "quick fixes" outside of school wastes time and resources. Furthermore, faculties that work together can set clear goals for teaching and learning, monitor student progress over time, and develop action plans to increase student achievement and establish a learning community.

If change is to occur in classrooms across the United States—and it must—the change forces will be the administrators and teachers in each local school. Educators committed to change will strive to make a difference in the lives of children and engage in the adjustment of classroom practices (Fullan, 2000). Furthermore, instead of randomly grasping for new reading programs or practices, educators should employ an action plan that includes the following (Blythe et al., 1999; Showers & Joyce, 1996): holding conversations to understand what works according to research (collaborative inquiry), studying each student's assessment and work samples, and reflecting upon the practices under which the student's work was constructed. Accordingly, these reflective conversations will guide the school faculty in the process of action planning for differentiating classroom reading instruction to reach all students.

Administrators and teachers who meet the challenges of education today will find the time to interpret the mandates, establish a unified, across-the-board commitment for change, and acquire the skills to implement and support those changes (Fullan, 2003). Therefore, rather than take the one-size-fits-all approach to mandated educational change, administrators and teachers must have time to work together, adjust classroom practices, perfect teaching skills to meet diverse needs, and thereby improve student achievement (Darling-Hammond, 1999). Educators must make the change a positive, powerful process. The change process at the local level can build a community of learners as well as maintain program fidelity through the unification of a school's purpose and vision (King & Newmann, 2000).

Educators Find the Time to Study Together

Educators are challenged with finding the time to translate research-based strategies into classroom practices and to modify these practices for their diverse student populations (NICHD, 2000; Snow et al., 1998). Research indicates that teachers who work in isolation rarely change instructional practices, thereby widening the research-to-practice gap (Greenwood & Maheady, 2001). In addition, effective application of instruction increases when administrators and teachers collaboratively study student data and plan the use of evidence-based practice (Baker & Smith, 2001; Fuchs & Fuchs, 2001; Greenwood & Maheady). Furthermore, according to Showers and Joyce (1996), classroom practice improves as a result of teachers implementing the following sequential process:

- Presenting the rationale or theory of a research-based innovative strategy
- Demonstrating the skills required for implementation
- Practicing the skills required to fine-tune the processes
- Collaborating with peers to develop a plan for the incorporation of the skills with classroom practices
- Supporting one another in the implementation process
- Collecting and using student data to adjust the proven practices to meet individual needs.

As teachers engage in a process of questioning and investigating teaching and learning with their peers, they gradually revise their beliefs to incorporate those new practices in their classrooms (Fullan, 2000). Therefore, district and school administrators must provide an environment that enables teachers to study together regularly, to build a strong commitment to meeting the needs of each student through effective instruction, and to support one another as the changes occur (Strickland, 2002). In other words, school faculties must create an atmosphere of one for all and all for one (Joyce & Showers, 1995).

With traditional staff development, classroom application of innovative strategies is minimal because teachers do not have adequate time to study together (Showers & Joyce, 1996). Study teams, however, can provide teachers with opportunities to improve their practice by sharing and discussing their reflections, knowledge, and solutions. For example, high school teachers who studied together reported that collaboration improves the development of new professional ideas and yields positive changes in their teaching (Slater & Simmons, 2001). Likewise, elementary faculties express that

the reflective process supports changes in beliefs and improves teacher quality (Swafford, 1998).

With the mandates of NCLB, meaningful professional development is more important than ever. Because professional development is very expensive, activities should be connected to improving both teaching and learning. Perhaps too often the school or district leadership assumes the responsibility for planning professional development opportunities for the teachers. However, effective educational leaders also elicit teacher input to construct professional development activities that review the research and evidence-based programs, model new skills, provide opportunities for teachers to practice the skills, and support study teams (Blase & Blase, 1998). Involving teachers in these decisions fosters the commitment necessary to achieve and sustain change in the classroom.

When the administrators designate time during the school day for faculty members to study together, teachers can make a positive change (Fullan, 2000; Murphy, 1997). Allowing time for change to occur is of the utmost importance (Fullan, 2003). For example, Mississippi has well-established study teams in many of its lowest performing schools. The schools' plans for improvement designate approximately two hours weekly for teachers to study teaching and learning together. These schools studied examples of how other schools find the time for teachers to work together (Murphy). The following provisions proved successful:

- Grouping teachers whose students attend art, music, physical education, and other special areas at the same time
- Grouping teachers by free periods
- Starting the school day 30 minutes later and having teachers arrive 30 minutes early one day a week to have 1 hour weekly for collaborative study (these teachers are provided release time as compensation for the extended day)
- Using trained assistant teachers and tutors in classrooms during study team times to implement whole-group strategies for fluency and comprehension

- Scheduling weekly reading camps by hiring and training a core of substitutes to conduct one-on-one reading tutorials until study teams begin meeting (during study teams the substitutes conduct whole-group strategies for fluency and comprehension)
- Amending school board policy to allow the early release of students one day a week
- Using federal, state, local, or grant funds to buy time for faculties to study together.

According to Kelleher (2003), "Research has shown unequivocally that professional development is most effective when it is embedded in teachers' work" (p. 3). In other words, teacher learning is most effective in the context of teaching. Teachers must collaboratively engage in study teams that devise curricula and assessments, look at student work to reflect upon their practice, and plan together to meet the needs of students (Kelleher).

Teachers Reflectively Review Student Work in Study Teams

Typically, faculty, grade-level, or subject area meetings are conducted to plan events, learn of new trends or mandates, and review assessment data. Rarely, however, do teachers use this time to collaboratively examine student work or analyze the instruction that produced that work. If schools elect to address their staff development needs through collaborative study teams, it is imperative that teachers be taught to structure productive conversations about improving instruction for individual students. Without establishing a structured process and a regularly scheduled meeting time, teachers may find this step nonproductive as well as intimidating. Because of the challenges of education today, teachers must have a step-by-step process that narrows the research-to-practice gap and accommodates the specific needs of individual students. Therefore, it is noteworthy to return to the experience of the Mississippi schools that regularly engaged in the practice of teachers studying together over the past

three years. The feedback from school administrators and teachers participating in collaborative study affirms the research of Showers and Joyce (1996). Some of the changes in these faculties' beliefs are as follows:

- Planning instruction collaboratively, rather than in isolation, reduces the workload
- Learning to engage in conversations that affect teaching and learning may be foreign to some and takes time
- Studying new research-based programs and strategies in the context of their own teaching promotes understanding
- Structuring conversations to examine student work and ongoing assessments in the context of teaching encourages instructional modifications to meet individual needs.

Many of these same schools report that study teams add more value to the reform effort than do other components of the model. On the other hand, some schools indicate that that time would be better spent in the classrooms. There is a need for empirical research, but it appears that when teachers actively engage in reflective conversations with team members, their students show promising gains in reading. Perhaps schools that find the study team nonproductive would benefit from the use of a structured protocol that guides the reflective process.

Several groups are leading the field concerning the use of protocols to structure reflective conversations:

- Coalition of Essential Schools in California
- Annenberg Institute for School Reform at Brown University in Massachusetts
- Project Zero at Harvard Graduate School in Massachusetts
- Teachers College at Columbia University in New York.

Each has contributed to the literature by stressing the need for a structured process or protocol to elicit teacher conversations about individual students'

FIGURE 2
Resources

Website resources for study teams and reflective conferences

1. Reading Success Network and study teams www.sedl.org/secac/rsn/peer.pdf

   The Southwest Educational Development Laboratory (SEDL) carries out an integrated program of education applied research and development. Reading Success Network is a professional development program sponsored by the U.S. Department of Education to improve reading instruction. This site includes a training manual on the rationale and use of study teams to increase professional and student learning.

2. Looking at student work www.lasw.org/methods.html

   This site provides an overview of different methods of looking at student work together. Schools may determine an appropriate method for reflective conferences by reviewing the work of others such as the Harvard Project Zero, National School Reform Faculty, Education Trust, and the Coalition of Essential Schools.

3. Free protocols www.teacherscollegepress.com

   Many different free protocols are available. This site provides the ordering information for the book The Power of Protocols: An Educator's Guide to Better Practice by Joseph P. McDonald, Nancy Mohr, Alan Dichter, and Elizabeth C. McDonald (2003, Teachers College Press).

4. Virtual collaborative assessment process www.lasw.org/protocols.html

   This site allows the reader to participate in an actual collaborative assessment conference. The virtual reflective conference takes the reader through the eight-step process of examining student work to reflect upon the practice that produced the work.

5. The Tuning Protocol: A process for reflection on teacher and student work www.essentialschools.org/cs/resources/view/ces_res/54

   This site outlines the seven-step process for looking at student work developed and used by the Coalition of Essential Schools.

---

work and the teaching that produced the work (Blythe et al., 1999). The structure of one such protocol, the Collaborative Assessment Conference (Seidel, 1991), requires teachers to use analytical questioning of the context in which student work is produced (Blythe et al.). Surprisingly, however, the literature lacks evidence of this protocol's use to enhance teachers' conversations in well-established study team schools.

Perhaps schools with regularly scheduled study team meetings should designate a portion of the time to look at student work reflectively. Reflective conversations involve two primary inquiries: (1) assessing the quality of the student's work and (2) assessing the context of work production. The dialogue should include elements of background information about the student, the teacher's instructional process, and the assignment itself. Both steps are critical, but the order in which they are conducted may vary from team to team (Blythe et al., 1999). For example, some may prefer to assess the quality of the student's work first. Assessing the quality of students' work has been labeled by Blythe et al. as "describing, interpreting and evaluating" (p. 12) work samples to determine the student's understanding and growth over time using several work samples. Others may choose to examine the context in which the work is produced prior to assessing its quality (Blythe et al.). The study teams should choose the conference protocol that meets the specific needs of the school culture and accommodate individual teachers' needs. According to Blythe et al., the following steps should be used to choose a protocol:

- Taking stock of current ways of looking at student work
- Establishing goals and framing questions
- Choosing, adapting, or developing a process for looking collaboratively at student work
- Implementing the process
- Reflecting on and revising the process.

The websites in Figure 2 provide a wealth of step-by-step processes using various protocols, including a virtual collaborative conference assessment. Teachers can actually participate in a reflective conference with an expert. Considering the repercussions of failure to meet the demand of the changing face of education today, school study teams should investigate different structures or protocols to begin reflective conversations about student work to improve teaching and learning.

Summary

High-stakes testing for accountability and recent legislative mandates have required that educators must make an important choice. The choice is whether to allow policymakers to determine the fate of children in the United States or to become a force for change by planning action steps to improve teaching and learning. The action steps must include (1) building a collective mission; (2) restructuring professional development to provide time for faculties to study and make classroom decisions based on the educational mandates, research-based programs and practices, and student data; (3) developing and implementing a plan of reflective conversations, all of which will lead to improved teaching and learning; and (4) seeking funding to support the change process from federal, state, local, and private sources. Fate or action planning— the right choice for children is evident.

REFERENCES

Baker, S., & Smith, S. (2001). Linking school assessments to research-based practices in beginning reading: Improving programs and outcomes for students with and without disabilities. *Teacher Education and Special Education, 24,* 315–332.

Blase, J., & Blase, J. (1998). Inquiry and collaboration: Supporting the lifelong study of learning and teaching. *International Electronic Journal for Leadership in Learning, 2*(7), 3–4.

Blythe, T., Allen, D., & Powell, B. (1999). *Looking together at student work: A companion guide to assessing student learning.* New York: Teachers College Press.

Darling-Hammond, L. (1999). Target time toward teachers. *Journal of Staff Development, 20*(2), 1–8.

Fuchs, D., & Fuchs, L. (2001). One blueprint for bridging the gap: Project promise. *Teacher Education and Special Education, 24,* 304–314.

Fullan, M.G. (1998). Breaking the bonds of dependency. *Educational Leadership, 55*(7), 6–10.

Fullan, M.G. (2000). *Change forces: Probing the depths of educational reform.* Levittown, PA: Falmer.

Fullan, M.G. (2003). *Change forces with a vengeance.* New York: Routledge Falmer.

Greenwood, C.R., & Maheady, L. (2001). Are future teachers aware of the gap between research and practice and what should they know? *Teacher Education and Special Education, 24,* 333–347.

Joyce, B., & Showers, B. (1995). *Student achievement through staff development: Fundamentals of school renewal.* New York: Longman.

Kelleher, J. (2003). A model for assessment-driven professional development. *Phi Delta Kappan, 84,* 751–757.

King, M.B., & Newmann, F.M. (2000). Will teacher learning advance school goals? *Phi Delta Kappan, 81,* 576–582.

Murphy, C. (1997). Finding time for faculties to study together. *Journal of Staff Development, 8*(3), 29–32.

National Institute of Child Health and Human Development. (2000). *The report of the National Reading Panel. Teaching children to read: An evidence-based assessment of the scientific research literature on reading and its implications for reading instruction* (NIH Publication No. 00-4769). Washington, DC: U.S. Government Printing Office.

No Child Left Behind Act of 2001, Pub. L. No. 107-110, 115 Stat. 1425 (2002).

Seidel, S. (1991). *Collaborative assessment conferences for the consideration of project work* [Data file]. Harvard Graduate School of Education: Project Zero. Available: http://www.pz.harvard.edu/ProdServ/Pubsmore.htm

Showers, B., & Joyce, B. (1996). The evolution of peer coaching. *Educational Leadership, 53*(6), 12–16.

Slater, C.L., & Simmons, D.L. (2001). The design and implementation of a peer coaching program. *American Secondary Education, 9*(3), 67–76.

Snow, C.E., Burns, S., & Griffin, P. (Eds.). (1998). *Preventing reading difficulties in young children.* Washington, DC: National Academy Press.

Strickland, D.S. (2002, November). *Improving reading achievement through professional development.* Paper presented at the meeting of the National Invitational Conference on Improving Reading Achievement Through Professional Development, Washington, DC.

Swafford, J. (1998). Teachers supporting teachers through peer coaching. *Support for Learning, 13*(2), 54–58.

U.S. Department of Education. (2002). *Reading First guidance.* Retrieved August 30, 2003, from http://www.aft.org/esea/downloads/ReadingFirstGuidanceFINAL.pdf

Word Recognition

Instruction in phonics should
never be apart from a need nor
separated from meaning.
—EDNA MORGENTHALER
(1952, p. 2)

It is doubtful that a topic [word
recognition] so basic to "breaking the
code" should become a subject for any
more than thoughtful, well-designed,
and impartial research as well as
careful and discerning analysis of the
process involved.
—CAROL K. WINKLEY (1970, p. 611)

The goal of early reading instruction is to
help students move as quickly as possible
toward independent comprehension of a
broad range of texts. Phonics instruction is
one gateway toward this goal by providing
students with the skills to decode
unfamiliar words encountered in new and
challenging passages.
—KIMBERLY A. NORMAN
& ROBERT C. CALFEE (2004, p. 42)

Issues and Innovations in Literacy Education: Readings From The Reading Teacher, edited by Richard D. Robinson. © 2006 by the International Reading Association.

The debate concerning word recognition has been a long, and at times contentious, one. Rather than a reasoned and coherent discussion of the basic issues involved, this dispute frequently has been characterized by heated attacks from those with little knowledge of or association with education instruction. For instance, adamant views about the role of word recognition often are expressed as part of many political agendas, commercial publishers' philosophies, and opinions from misinformed members of the general public. In contrast to this divisive situation, educators who are familiar with the contents of *The Reading Teacher* have found that, almost without exception, contributions to this journal have represented a fair and reasoned response to this continuing debate over the role of word recognition in an effective classroom literacy program.

In one of the earliest volumes of what was to become *The Reading Teacher*, Nila Banton Smith (1950), an early pioneer in literacy education, wrote about the role of word recognition. She provided a detailed discussion as to when and why phonics should be a part of all literacy instruction, ending her article by saying, "So in answer to the question 'When shall we teach phonics?' we might well answer: 'All through the elementary school, adjusting instruction continuously to maturity levels and individual needs'" (p. 15). This topic of word recognition has been and continues to be an important issue in *The Reading Teacher*. Very recently, Norman and Calfee (2004) addressed similar issues related to helping primary-grade students effectively apply various decoding skills to unfamiliar words. Each of these articles views word recognition through a different lense, and yet there are many similarities between them.

Although authors of articles published in *The Reading Teacher* have expressed a variety of opinions and positions on the role of word recognition in literacy instruction, the following points generally summarize these views:

- Word recognition is a fundamental aspect of most effective classroom literacy programs.

- The specific components of any word recognition program vary according to the literacy abilities and needs of individual students.

- There is no preferred method or approach to word recognition instruction for all students.

- The role of the classroom teacher must always take preference in any specific decisions related to the effective teaching of word recognition.

Section Readings

The first article in this section is by William S. Gray, one of the leading literacy researchers of the last century and the first president of the International Reading Association. In terms of both basic research and classroom application, Gray's work was profound and of great practical importance for literacy teachers. This article is included because of its clear and coherent overview of an effective, classroom word recognition program of instruction. In the introduction to this article, Gray comments on the history of the phonics controversy and his view of the importance of this aspect of language in the effective teaching of reading.

The second article is by A. Sterl Artley, who was a leading reading authority at the University of Missouri–Columbia with special teaching and research interests in the training of undergraduate teachers, as well as the diagnosis and remediation of reading difficulties. In the late 1940s, he founded one of the first reading clinics in the United States that was designed primarily to train reading specialists at all levels. His article is a well-reasoned discussion of the controversy that has often been associated with the phonics issue. As you read this brief discussion, consider how Artley's remarks, now 50 years old, apply to the current debate taking place on the role of word recognition in reading instruction.

The article by Theodore Clymer is considered by many to be one of the most important articles written on the very controversial topic of phonics instruction. Although it was written more than 40 years ago, it still speaks to the current debate about the role of the sound–symbol relationship in the effective teaching of reading. The author identifies 45 phonics generalizations, often taught in the typical classroom reading program, and then discusses how effective they are in the identification of vocabulary words. As you read this article, consider Clymer's conclusions about the usefulness of these phonics generalizations and the implications of his findings for today's effective teaching of reading.

Steven A. Stahl moves the discussion of word recognition ahead some 20 years and reflects the then-latest thinking on the phonics controversy. It is important to note that many of the relevant points made here are based on and reflective of some of the positions taken by previous authors in this section. An interesting aspect of this article is the discussion of the influence of politics on the role of phonics in literacy education. As we are all aware, politics, not only as they relate to word recognition but also in other areas of education, were destined to become a critical factor in most instructional decisions made today.

In the next article, Diane Lapp and James Flood review "the phonics wars" and the seemingly endless debates over the role of word recognition in an effective classroom literacy program. Through a number of examples, these authors illustrate extreme positions on the phonics question such as teaching "phonics systematically and explicitly, separate from rather than as an integrated segment of a text." They note that phonics as well as any other aspect of literacy instruction needs to be considered primarily in terms of how these various techniques enhance meaning for the reader. They conclude that a balanced view of literacy teaching "helps children integrate what they already know with new strategies, skills, and content that will best serve their new and developing reading interests."

The final article in this section, by Kathleen F. Clark, is an excellent summary of effective practices in the area of word recognition. Particular emphasis is given to the importance of the student's and teacher's role through a teaching technique called "coaching." The emphasis is placed on the student as an "active learner" in this process.

REFERENCES

Morgenthaler, E. (1952). Phonics: An essential tool. *The Reading Teacher, 5*(3), 1–2, 16.

Norman, K.A., & Calfee, R.C. (2004). Tile Test. A hands-on approach for assessing phonics in the early grades. *The Reading Teacher, 58*(1), 42–52.

Smith, N.B. (1950). When shall we teach phonics? *ICIRI Bulletin, II*(4), 13–15.

Winkley, C.K. (1970). Why not an intensive-gradual phonic approach. *The Reading Teacher, 23*(7), 611–617, 620.

For Further Reading on Word Recognition

The following articles on the role of word recognition have been selected from *The Reading Teacher* because they represent a wide spectrum of viewpoints and positions on this important aspect of literacy instruction. They are listed chronologically so that the reader can better understand the historical development of some of the important issues related to word recognition.

Morgenthaler, E. (1952). Phonics: An essential tool. *The Reading Teacher, 5*(3), 1–2, 16.
Discusses the role of phonic knowledge with emphasis on the importance of the reader comprehending effectively what is being read.

Gray, W.S. (1955). Phonic versus other methods of teaching reading. *The Reading Teacher, 9*(2), 102–106.
Summarizes the results of three surveys of word recognition that identify six phonics generalizations that are most applicable in a variety of reading situations.

Staiger, R.C. (1955). Your child learns phonics. *The Reading Teacher, 9*(2), 95–99.
Presents a discussion for parents on the role of phonics in an effective classroom literacy program with a particular emphasis on the role of parents in effective phonics instruction.

Winkley, C.K. (1970). Why not an intensive-gradual phonic approach. *The Reading Teacher, 23*(7), 611–617, 620.
Recommends a combination phonics approach based on both an analytic and synthetic view of this subject following a student pretest of related knowledge.

Durkin, D. (1974). Phonics: Instruction that needs to be improved. *The Reading Teacher, 28*(2), 152–156.
Reports the results of a series of classroom observations of phonics instruction that do not enhance effective literacy experiences for most readers.

Lamb, P. (1975). How important is instruction in phonics? *The Reading Teacher, 29*(1), 15–19.
Takes the position that as "little phonics instruction as possible" is the best approach to this aspect of literacy teaching.

Rosso, B.R., & Emans, R. (1981). Children's use of phonics generalizations. *The Reading Teacher, 34*(6), 653–658.
Concludes that there is a positive relationship between a student's ability to apply phonics generalizations and their overall reading ability.

Groff, P. (1986). The maturing of phonics instruction. *The Reading Teacher, 39*(9), 919–923.
Reports on the current teaching of phonics and the effectiveness of this approach to the teaching of reading.

Maclean, R. (1988). Two paradoxes of phonics. *The Reading Teacher, 41*(6), 514–517.
Suggests that the use of phonics as a primary method of reading instruction has little to do with helping students become better readers. Presents several solutions to this instructional problem.

Trachtenburg, P. (1990). Using children's literature to enhance phonics instruction. *The Reading Teacher, 43*(9), 648–654.

    Describes a literacy teaching strategy that encourages the extensive use of children's literature as a basis for the use of various types of phonics principles.

Morrow, L.M., & Tracey, D.H. (1997). Strategies used for phonics instruction in early childhood classrooms. *The Reading Teacher, 50*(8), 644–651.

    Presents information that shows that phonic relationships often taught in preschool classrooms are not consistent when students enter kindergarten and the primary grades.

Baumann, J.F., Hoffman, J.V., Moon, J., & Duffy-Hester, A.M. (1998). Where are teachers' voices in the phonics/whole language debate? Results from a survey of U.S. elementary classroom teachers. *The Reading Teacher, 51*(8), 636–650.

    Details the results of a nationwide survey that indicates that most literacy teachers are eclectic in their teaching of reading as opposed to being either a phonics or whole language instructor.

Yopp, H.K., & Yopp, R.H. (2000). Supporting phonemic awareness development in the classroom. *The Reading Teacher, 54*(2), 130–143.

    Encourages the development of phonemic awareness as an important aspect of early literacy instruction.

Jenkins, J.R., Vadasy, P.F., Peyton, J.A., & Sanders, E.A. (2003). Decodable text—Where to find it. *The Reading Teacher, 57*(2), 185–189.

    Discusses how classroom teachers can best match students' word recognition skills with appropriate text materials.

Smith, M., Walker, B.J., & Yellin, D. (2004). From phonological awareness to fluency in each lesson. *The Reading Teacher, 58*(3), 302–307.

    Reviews the latest research and practice on the role of phonological awareness as a significant aspect of word recognition.

Developing Word Recognition

William S. Gray

Since written or printed words are the keys that unlock meanings, the development of efficient habits of word recognition is of first importance in any sound reading program. It has received so much emphasis at times that methods of teaching reading have often been characterized by the specific techniques used in teaching accuracy and independence in word recognition. On the other hand, there have been vigorous opponents to the use of any form of word analysis in teaching reading. During the last half century emphasis has shifted repeatedly from one extreme position to another. However, as a result, of carefully conducted research, the fact has become clear that skill in independent word attack is essential. As an approach to an understanding of the teaching problems involved in developing needed skills, let us consider how words are recognized.

How Printed Words Are Identified

A good reader instantly identifies and associates meanings with the words of a passage. In reading familiar words he perceives them as wholes, often in units of two or three and as parts of a meaningful whole. But when he meets new and unfamiliar words, he centers attention on the details of each word. He tries to find a clue either within the word or in the accompanying context that helps him to identify the word and its meaning.

There are four such aids to word perception: (a) meaning clues from the context that surrounds the word; (b) its form or appearance; (c) structural clues; and (d) phonetic clues. If these are not adequate, he may secure help from the teacher or consult the glossary or dictionary. In most reading activities the first two aids suffice; when unfamiliar words are encountered even the good reader makes conscious use of all five aids or various combinations of them. When attacking a new word independently, he checks the results of his efforts by asking two questions: Is this a word I know? Does it make meaning in the sentence?

A Sight Vocabulary

At the outset in learning to read, the child acquires a basic vocabulary as words that he uses orally are presented to him as wholes in meaningful context. The necessity for developing such a sight vocabulary, however, is not limited to the early stages in learning to read.

In establishing a sight vocabulary, there are several important principles to be observed. The first is richness of association; the second is that the word must be in the center of undivided attention; the third is that there must be sufficient repetitions to insure adequate mastery. As the number of words increases, familiarity with general contour is not enough. For example, children must be led to notice that *bump* and *jump* look alike except at the beginning and that *the* and *this* look alike except at the end. At more advanced levels, pupils face a similar responsibility in differentiating *quiet* and *quite*, and *noise* and *nose*.

In the case of children who learn slowly, special techniques may be needed, such as tracing or writing words. These steps help direct attention to the general form of the word and to its left-to-right pattern, and increase the number of associations with it.

Reprinted from *Bulletin*, IV(4), pp. 1, 11–12. © 1951 by the International Council for the Improvement of Reading Instruction/International Reading Association.

Under the method of learning new words as wholes, most children make rapid progress in reading and their interest in content soon carries them into wider reading. It is at this point that the effectiveness of a sight vocabulary alone breaks down. Unless children are taught simple techniques of word attack, they are unable to advance.

Meaning Clues

Just as meaning clues aid in identifying sight words, so they aid in inferring the meaning and pronunciation of a word whose printed form is unfamiliar. Indeed, meaning clues are the most important aids available in attacking many words. Their use is clearly illustrated in the oft-used example, "The boy hit the *ball*." In some cases context clues make meanings unmistakable; in other cases they merely limit possibilities. Because of their great value, however, teachers should make every effort to teach children to use them effectively.

Word-Form Clues

As children acquire a sight vocabulary, they learn to scrutinize word forms, carefully noticing likenesses and differences. This habit carries over to their attack on new words and becomes a most useful aid. An illustration may help at this point. Suppose George knows the word *name*, but has never seen the printed word *same*. If as a result of his first scrutiny of the word he says, "It looks like *name* except at the beginning," he has effectively used word-form clues in attacking the word. If he sees *same* in the sentence, "The two balls are the same color," the content clues plus the word-form clues (and knowledge of the sound of "s") should enable him to identify the word accurately. In each such effort he must check the results with two questions: "Is this a word I know?" "Does it make sense here?"

Skill in making visual discriminations is also essential. Training often begins during the reading readiness period through the use of pictured forms. It is continued when discriminating between the forms of sight words. Special practice is often provided when pupils are asked to distinguish between the words *went* and *want*, *supper* and *suffer*, *trickle* and *tickle*. In developing skill in word attack, use should be made of exercises that lead from a known to an unknown word; for example, from *day* (known) to *say* (unknown).

Structural Analysis

In attacking new words, the child soon begins to make use of structural analysis as well as word form clues and meaning. For example, he encounters variant forms of known words such as the plural of *dog* or the past tense (*ed*) and the participial form (*ing*) of known words. The first step in identifying a new word is that of visual scrutiny of the whole word, which aids in identifying the familiar word and the variant element. As the child becomes familiar with these endings, structural analysis is of great aid in enlarging his recognition vocabulary. It aids also in recognizing compound words made up of two known words (*schoolhouse*), variant forms of adjectives (*shorter, shortest, shorten, shortly*). At a more advanced stage it aids also in attacking such derivatives as *discourage, courageous, courageously, encourage, encouraging, encouragement*. Similarly, it aids in identifying root words of more than one syllable.

As a pupil progresses in reading ability, an increasing proportion of the new words that he meets are words of two or more syllables. When he sees the word *potato*, his scrutiny of the word will not reveal a known prefix, suffix, or inflectional ending. He must attack the work in terms of syllables or sound units. To make this analysis, he needs the help which comes from training in phonetic analysis. For example, he must know that each syllable or pronounceable unit has one or more vowels. He must know also that if there are two consonant letters between two vowels in a word (*let-ter*), the first syllable usually ends with the first of the two consonants. If there is one consonant between two vowels (*ba-con*), the first syllable often ends with a vowel. Thus, the foundation is laid for identifying pronounceable units through a combination of word scrutiny and phonetic analysis.

Phonetic Analysis

Phonetic analysis is a natural accompaniment of the scrutiny of word forms and of the use of structural analysis. As a child notes the general form and details of words, he consciously or unconsciously associates sounds with certain parts—the *c* at the beginning of *cat*. Thus a start is made in the use of phonetic clues in recognizing words whose meanings and pronunciations are known.

Phonetic analysis in reading is based on a knowledge of the sounds of our language and the symbols that stand for them. There are 43 such sounds represented by 26 letters. Because there are more sounds than letters, some letters represent more than one sound (*at, age, car, all, care, ago*). Likewise, the same sound is sometimes represented by different letters (*cat* and *kite*). Just as the meaning of a word is determined by its use in a sentence, so the sound of a phonetic element is determined by its use in a word. It follows that we must teach the child to be aware of variant sounds in words and how to select from the variants the one that applies in a particular instance.

The phonetic elements may be classified under two headings: (1) consonants, of which there are three types—consonants with a single sound, consonant blends (*bl, cl, scr*) and speech consonants (*th, ch, ng*), and (2) vowels of which there are three types—single vowel letters, two-vowel letters (*ai* in *rain* or *oo* in *food*), or diphthongs (*ou* in *house*, or *oi* in *oil*). One of the essentials in identifying these sounds is good auditory perception. Needed training begins often during the reading readiness period. Ultimately, pupils should see and recognize these sounds as integral parts of word wholes.

A knowledge of phonetic elements is most frequently used in what is known as phonetic substitution. A child knows the word *bump*, for example. To recognize the word *lump*, he notes that it looks like *bump* except the first letter. He then substitutes the sound of *l* for *b* and pronounces the word. Special exercises promote ability to make such substitutions; for example, *jump—lump, slump; but—bug, bus; big—hag, heg*

Although our language is non-phonetic to a considerable extent, there are a few phonetic principles that may be safely applied. (1) In words or syllables containing only one vowel, the vowel is usually short unless it comes at the end of the word (*pan, shut, met, hit*). (2) In words having two vowels, one of which is final, the first is usually long (*gate, kite, hole*). (3) In words or syllables containing such vowel combinations as *ie, ea, oe, ai, ay*, the first is long and the second is silent. (4) In a word in which *r* follows the vowel, the sound of the vowel is governed by *r* (*curl, car, jar*). (5) The sound of *a* is modified by *l* or *w* if either follows that letter (*claw, halt*).

In attacking longer words, the pupil should become skillful in the use of various word attack skills. The first step is to scrutinize the word as a whole. In the word *notation*, for example, he spots a familiar ending, *tion*. He next identifies the number of syllables in the rest of the word by noting the vowels. He then applies the rule that if a consonant comes between two vowels, it belongs with the vowel that follows, thus deriving the visual units *no* and *ta*. His previous training has taught him that the sounds of these vowels are long—hence, he is able to pronounce each syllable successfully. As was pointed out earlier, any such effort must be checked with the questions, "Is this a word I know?" "Does it make sense here?"

Some children learn to use phonetic analysis with little or no help; others need much guidance. The amount of attention required, therefore, varies widely amount individuals.

The Dictionary

Because the pronunciations and meanings of odd words cannot be identified accurately for many reasons by the methods already discussed, the child is often forced to seek help from the teacher in the lower grades or from the dictionary in the later grades. Training in the skillful use of the dictionary is an essential step in developing accuracy and independence in word recognition, but one which has been grossly neglected during the last two decades. Background for such training is the development of efficient habits of word attack through the use of context, form clues, structural analysis, phonetic analysis.

Controversial Issues Relating to Word Perception

A. Sterl Artley

Of all the issues facing teachers of reading, it is safe to say that none is so controversial as that of word perception, and we might add, so surrounded with emotional overtones. In the last two decades there have been a number of articles written on the subject. Because in many cases the issues and the basic assumptions behind them have not been clear, much of the writing has resulted in confusion rather than clarification.

It is my intent this afternoon, in the limited time available, to look at three problems related to word perception and the word perception program. In each case I shall try to identify and briefly discuss the issues involved. In doing so I have discovered that it is impossible to conceal my own point of view.

Word Perception and Goals of Reading Instruction

The first issue has to do with the relation of the word perception program to the over-all goals of reading instruction. In question form we would state it as follows: What part of the total reading program shall be given over to the teaching of sight words and to the development of independent techniques of word perception?

A point of view implicit in a number of reading programs is that instruction in word perception is the most important part of the program. In fact the teaching of reading *is* the teaching of word recogni-

tion, with only a modicum of attention directed to other goals of instruction. Consequently, we find much of the program given over to word drill, word games, separate phonics periods, and word recognition activities divorced from functional reading. A great deal of the instructional material is unrelated to story content, being made up of lists of words and nonsense syllables used for the purpose of drill.

This type of program is characterized by a certain supplementary phonics drill book of some 125 pages where only a total of eight pages is given over to connected (?) discourse. Though presumably built for the primary grades the drill words that are supplied are those that are completely foreign to the vocabulary of a typical primary child. In fact, one word isn't even in the dictionary. Another program, almost exclusively phonics in nature, claims that a first grader can be taught to recognize words commonly found on fifth-grade word lists. By the amount of drill material provided, and the recommended amount of time the teacher is supposed to give these materials apart from reading, the validity of this claim would not be doubted. But what virtue is attached to an average first grader learning to pronounce fifth-grade words? What a terrific price we ask children to pay for their whistle.

The opposing point of view holds to the idea that the word perception program is merely a *part* of the total reading program—an important part, let there be no doubt about that, but a part that serves as a *means* to interpretation rather than as an

Reprinted from *The Reading Teacher*, 8(4), pp. 196–199. © 1955 by the International Reading Association.

end of reading instruction. This point of view is held by Gray and others who conceive of the total interpretative act as being made up of the identifiable components of word perception, comprehension, reaction, and integration. Word perception is then a part of the total act of reading.

This being true the word perception program must be closely integrated with the reading act, not set apart in separate instructional periods, nor handled through extraneous drill materials. The words from which recognition principles are inductively derived are those the child has met in his daily reading. As he acquires a new perception skill he applies it directly to new words which he meets in his daily reading. Emphasis throughout is on interpretation, with perception skills serving that end. Otherwise, the reader runs the risk of being able to "phonics his way through any word," but unable to derive or react to the author's meaning.

Content of Word Perception Program

The second issue I should like to discuss has to do with the content of the word perception program. In what areas shall we attempt to develop word perception skills and abilities? On this issue the lines are clearly drawn between those who would limit the program to a single area, namely phonics, and those who would advocate the development of abilities in several areas, such as context, structural analysis, and the use of the dictionary.

Within the last year, in several popular magazines, have appeared articles extolling the merits of the phonics approach to reading instruction. One of the writers contends that the teaching of reading is simple. Since reading means getting meaning from certain combinations of letters all the teacher needs to do is to teach the child what each letter stands for and he will be able to read. He adds that this is the "natural system" of learning to read, and that the "ancient Egyptians...the Romans...Germans...Estonians... and Abyssinians" learned to read that way.

Though we may smile at these broad and sweeping generalizations, there are those who believe that a return to the methods and content in vogue at the turn of the century would be the solution to all our reading problems. The number of so-called "phonetic systems" on display at the bookstands at professional meetings is mute testimony to the belief of many in the philosophy of the old oaken bucket.

The point of view most widely accepted by reputable reading people today—Gates, Gray, Witty, Durrell, Betts, and others is that phonics is merely one of several methods that the child may use to unlock words. This contention gets its strength from basic research done in the late 30's and early 40's by Tate, Tiffin and McKinnis, Russell, and others who conclude:

- Phonics is only one method of word recognition.
- Phonics instruction should be closely integrated with purposeful reading.
- Though intensive phonics instruction may improve ability to recognize words, it makes little contribution to silent reading comprehension.

There is not a series of basic materials on the market today that does not include instruction in phonics, but it is a functional phonics, not a superimposed system of reading. It is closely integrated with meaningful reading, and taught in close conjunction with other procedures such as context clues, structural clues, and word-form clues. The basis for this practice rests in the following assumptions:

- English is a language that follows no lawful pattern of pronunciation as German or Spanish. Consequently, no single method of word attack can be depended upon. This become increasingly obvious as the reader meets more involved polysyllabic words.
- Whereas one can sound out simple three- and four-letter words with only a minimum loss of time, one's rate of perception is slowed down materially as he attempts to use a highly synthetic approach on more involved words.

- Since meaning is the primary consideration, those devices which give the child clues to meaning as well as to form are of primary value—hence, the importance of context clues, structural analysis, (emphasizing root elements, prefixes, suffixes, inflectional endings, etc.), and the dictionary.

True independence in reading is attained when the child can with dispatch and confidence unlock any word he meets on his own terms, be it short or long, simple or complex.

The Teaching of Word Perception Skills

The last issue I propose to discuss is somewhat related to the preceding one. Assuming that we are committed to the development of a versatility of word attack by equipping the child with skills, abilities, and understandings in several methods of word perception, the question then arises as to how this program shall be carried out. Shall one begin by teaching the sounds of the elements, leading eventually into the synthesis of the word whole from known components, or shall one begin with sight words, withholding until later the teaching or analytical procedures?

A writer in one of the popular articles to which I have already alluded, would begin his program by teaching the sounds of the letters. He says, "As soon as you switch to the common sense method of teaching the sounds of the letters, you can give them a little primer, and then proceed immediately to anything from this magazine to Treasure Island." Let us examine this contention critically. Reading is the process of creating meaning from word symbols. It must be a meaningful experience, an interesting vital experience. But what meaningful experience can be associated with the sounds of *m*, or *b*, or *st*, or any other auditory or visual component? Possibly the most important thing the teacher can do with beginning children is to *help them develop a favorable attitude toward reading.* From the time she begins, reading must be an interesting, pleasurable, mean-

ingful experience. It is difficult to see how the teaching of meaningless, discrete sounds or elements, and "doing phonetic gymnastics" can go very far toward developing this essential attitude.

Those who understand that potency of motivation in the learning process insist that the initial contract with reading be through meaningful words, *perceived as wholes*, not as parts. Because the child's concern is with the meaningful unit he comes to see that reading is fun—a pleasurable experience. Some would take issue with me on this point and say that we need not be concerned with making reading fun. They contend that children might as well learn early that learning to read is a matter of blood, sweat, and tears. Yet, I will defend to the last the point that unless children see early that reading is an avenue to new and exciting experiences they are not going to turn to it in their free time nor use it as a source of information. They will become the avid readers of comic books and viewers of television. They will also be the ones who haunt the reading clinics because they see no point and purpose to an uninteresting activity.

Phonics Should Be Functional

As I have already pointed out, there is a place for phonics as well as other procedures of word perception, but they should not take precedence over the primary function of reading which is to create meaning. They should be introduced after a basic stock of sight words has been established. This basic stock of sight words serves two purposes: first, that of developing desirable attitudes toward reading; and second, that of providing the stock-in-trade for the inductive development of generalizations about sounds, endings, prefixes, similar and dissimilar elements, etc. After these principles have been developed from the basic stock of sight words they may then be applied to new words. The young reader is on his own in reading. It seems to me this is sound psychology.

Furthermore, research shows that a typical child should have a mental age of seven before phonics generalizations can be meaningfully learned and applied. As a result, much of this work is reserved for the second year and beyond. However, this does not preclude a rich and meaningful program in readiness for phonics and structural analysis. Of course, it is during this time that the basic stock of sight words is being developed.

I regret that time does not permit the discussion of other controversial issues related to word perception. However, I am quite sure that they will be live issues next year, or five years from now. There's something about word perception that makes it a perennial conversation topic.

The Utility of Phonic Generalizations in the Primary Grades

Theodore Clymer

The origins of this study go back to Kenneth, an extraordinary elementary pupil. Prior to my encounter with Kenneth I had completed a reading methods course in a small teachers college which provided a background in the principles of teaching reading as well as a good introduction to techniques. Among these techniques were procedures to develop phonic generalizations and also *the* list (not *a* list) of the most valuable generalizations to develop. (To those of you who might like copies of the list, I am sad to report that somehow through the years it has been lost.)

Difficulties with Kenneth began as the class reviewed phonic generalizations at the start of the school year. Our procedures were like those used in many classrooms: Groups of words were presented, and the class analyzed their likenesses and differences with a view toward deriving a generalization about relationships between certain letters and sounds or the position and pronunciation of vowels.

Throughout these exercises, following the dictum of my reading methods teacher, we were careful not to call the generalizations "rules," for all our statements had a number of exceptions. As the class finally formulated a generalization regarding the relationships of letters, letter position, and sounds, such defensive phrasing as "most of the time," "usually," and "often" appeared as protective measures. We also spent time listing some of the exceptions to our generalizations.

At this point Kenneth entered the discussion. While the class was busily engaged in developing the generalization, Kenneth had skimmed his dictionary, locating long lists of exceptions to the generalization. In fact, he often located more exceptions than I could list applications. When I protested—somewhat weakly—that the dictionary contained many unusual words, Kenneth continued his role as an educational scientist. He turned to the basic reader word list in the back of his text and produced nearly similar results. Today, of course, Kenneth's behavior would be rated as "gifted," "talented," or "creative"—although I remember discussing him in other terms as I sat in the teachers' lounge.

As Kenneth had provided a memorable and even a "rich" learning experience for me, he furnished the impetus for a series of studies which will attempt to answer three questions: (1) What phonic generalizations are being taught in basic reading programs for the primary grades? (2) To what extent are these generalizations useful in having a "reasonable" degree of application to words commonly met in primary grade material? (3) Which of the generalizations that stand the test of question 2 can be learned and successfully applied to unknown words by primary children?

What Generalizations Are Taught?

Four widely used sets of readers were selected to determine the phonic generalizations being taught in

Reprinted from *The Reading Teacher*, 16(4), pp. 252–258. © 1963 by the International Reading Association.

the primary grades. After a preliminary study of the manuals, workbooks, and readers, the manuals were selected as the source of the generalizations. The manuals presented the generalizations in three ways: (1) statements to be taught to the pupils, (2) statements to be derived by the pupils after inductive teaching, and (3) statements with no clear indication as to what was to be done. Generalizations presented by all three means were included in the analysis.

Five general types of generalizations emerged from the study of the teachers manuals. These types dealt with (1) vowels, (2) consonants, (3) endings, (4) syllabication, and (5) miscellaneous relationships. Arbitrary decisions were made in assigning some generalizations to one or another of the five types since certain statements might easily be classified under two or more headings.

If we eliminate from our consideration the miscellaneous type of generalization, a total of 121 different statements were located. There were 50 vowel generalizations, 15 consonant generalizations, and 28 generalizations in each of the ending and syllabication groups. In evaluating these figures it should be kept in mind that any statement was considered a separate generalization when its phrasing excluded or included different sets of words than another statement. For example, the generalization, "When there are two vowels side by side, the long sound of the first is heard and the second one is usually silent" and "When *ea* come together in a word, the first letter is long and the second is silent" were counted as two separate generalizations, although the second statement is a special application of the first.

While not directly related to our discussion here, note should be made of the wide variation of grade level of introduction, emphasis, and phrasing of the generalizations. Of the 50 different vowel generalizations, only 11 were common to all four series. None of these 11 was presented initially at the same half-year grade level in all four series. Some series gave a much greater emphasis to the generalizations than did other series. One publisher introduced only 33 of the 121 generalizations, while another presented 68. These comments are not meant to detract from the usefulness of basic materials, but simply to point out some of their differences. These differences do call for careful adjustments in the classroom when pupils are moved from one set of materials to another. The teacher who changes from series X to series Y may need to make some important revisions in his word recognition program. These findings may indicate also the need for further experimentation on emphasis and the developmental aspects of our word recognition program.

Which Generalizations Are Useful?

Forty-five of the generalizations given in the manuals were selected for further study. The selection of these was somewhat arbitrary. The main criterion was to ask, "Is the generalization stated specifically enough so that it can be said to aid or hinder in the pronunciation of a particular word?" An example or two will make our criterion clear. The generalization, "Long *o* makes a sound like its name," is undoubtedly a valuable generalization, but it was not specific enough to meet our criterion. On the other hand, the statement, "When a vowel is in the middle of a one syllable word, the vowel is short," was included because we could judge by reference to a word list how often one syllable words with a vowel in the middle do in fact have a short vowel sound.

Our next problem was to develop a word list on which we could test the generalizations. A reasonable approach seemed to be that of making up a composite list of all the words introduced in the four basic series from which the generalizations were drawn, plus the words from the Gates Reading Vocabulary for the Primary Grades. Once this list of some twenty-six hundred words was prepared, the following steps were taken:

1. The phonetic respelling and the syllabic division of all words were recorded. Webster's *New Collegiate Dictionary* was used as the authority for this information.

2. Each phonic generalization was checked against the words in the composite list to de-

termine (a) the words which were pronounced as the generalization claimed and (b) the words which were exceptions to the generalization.

3. A "per cent of utility" was computed for each generalization by dividing the number of words pronounced as the generalization claimed by the total number of words to which the generalization could be expected to apply. For example, if the generalization claimed that "When the letters *oa* are together in a word, *o* always gives its long sound and the *a* is silent," all words containing *oa* were located in the list. The number of these words was the total number of which the generalization should apply. Then the phonetic spellings of these words were examined to see how many words containing *oa* actually did have the long *o* followed by the silent *a*. In this case thirty words were located which contained *oa*. Twenty-nine of these were pronounced as the generalization claimed; one was not. The per cent of utility became 29/30 or 97. This procedure was followed for all generalizations.

When the per cent of utility was computed for each generalization, we set two criteria as to what constituted a "reasonable" degree of application. We have no scientific evidence to demonstrate that these criteria are valid; it can only be said that they seem reasonable to us.

The first criterion was that the composite word list must contain a minimum of twenty words to which the generalization might apply. Generalizations with lower frequencies of application do not seem to merit instructional time.

The second criterion was a per cent of utility of at least 75. To state the matter another way, if the pupil applied the generalization to twenty words, it should aid him in getting the correct pronunciation in fifteen of the twenty words.

The table gives the results of our analysis of the forty-five phonic generalizations. An inspection of the data leaves me somewhat confused as to the value of generalizations. Some time-honored customs in the teaching of reading may be in need of revision.

Certain generalization apply to large numbers of words and are rather constant in providing the correct pronunciation of words. (See, for example, generalizations 19, 35, and 36.)

A group of generalizations seem to be useful only after the pupil can pronounce the word. Generalizations which specify vowel pronunciation in stressed syllables require that the pupil know the pronunciation of the word before he can apply the generalization. (See, for example, generalization 33.) This criticism assumes, of course, that the purpose of a generalization is to help the child unlock the pronunciation of unknown words.

The usefulness of certain generalizations depends upon regional pronunciations. While following Webster's markings, generalization 34 is rejected. Midwestern pronunciation makes this generalization rather useful, although we reject it because we used Webster as the authority. Such problems are natural, and we should not hold it against Mr. Webster that he came from New England.

If we adhere to the criteria set up at the beginning of the study, of the forty-five generalizations only eighteen, numbers 5, 8, 10, 16, 20, 21, 22, 23, 25, 28, 29, 30, 31, 32, 40, 41, 44, and 45, are useful. Some of the generalizations which failed to met our criteria might be useful if stated in different terms or if restricted to certain types of words. We are studying these problems at the present time. We are also examining other generalizations which we did not test in this study.

Conclusion

In evaluating this initial venture in testing the utility of phonic generalizations, it seems quite clear that many generalizations which are commonly taught are of limited value. Certainly the study indicates that we should give careful attention to pointing out the many exceptions to most of the generalizations that we teach. Current "extrinsic" phonics programs which present large numbers of

The utility of forty-five phonic generalizations			
*Generalization	No. of words conforming	No. of exceptions	Per cent of utility
1. When there are two vowels side by side, the long sound of the first one is heard and the second is usually silent.	309 (bead) †	377 (chief) †	45
2. When a vowel is in the middle of a one-syllable word, the vowel is short.	408	249	62
middle letter	191 (dress)	84 (scold)	69
one of the middle two letters in a word of four letters	191 (rest)	135 (told)	59
one vowel *within* a word of more than four letters	26 (splash)	30 (fight)	46
3. If the only vowel letter is at the end of a word, the letter usually stands for a long sound.	23 (he)	8 (to)	74
4. When there are two vowels, one of which is final e, the first vowel is long and the e is silent.	180 (bone)	108 (done)	63
*5. The r gives the preceding vowel a sound that is neither long nor short.	484 (horn)	134 (wire)	78
6. The first vowel is usually long and the second silent in the digraphs *ai*, *ea*, *oa*, and *ui*.	179	92	66
ai	43 (nail)	24 (said)	64
ea	101 (bead)	51 (head)	66
oa	34 (boat)	1 (cupboard)	97
ui	1 (suit)	16 (build)	6
7. In the phonogram *ie*, the i is silent and the e has a long sound.	8 (field)	39 (friend)	17
*8. Words having double e usually have the long e sound.	85 (seem)	2 (been)	98
9. When words end with silent e, the preceding a or i is long.	164 (cake)	108 (have)	60
*10. In *ay* the y is silent and gives a its long sound.	36 (play)	10 (always)	78
11. When the letter i is followed by the letters gh, the i usually stands for its long sound and the gh is silent.	22 (high)	9 (neighbor)	71
12. When a follows w in a word, it usually has the sound a as in *was*.	15 (watch)	32 (swam)	32
13. When e is followed by w, the vowel sound is the same as represented by oo.	9 (blew)	17 (sew)	35
14. The two letters ow make the long o sound.	50 (own)	35 (down)	59
15. W is sometimes a vowel and follows the vowel digraph rule.	50 (crow)	75 (threw)	40
*16. When y is the final letter in a word, it usually has a vowel sound.	169 (dry)	32 (tray)	84
17. When y is used as a vowel in words, it sometimes has the sound of long i.	29 (fly)	170 (funny)	15
18. The letter a has the same sound (ô) when followed by l, w, and u.	61 (all)	65 (canal)	48
19. When a is followed by r and final e, we expect to hear the sound heard in *care*.	9 (dare)	1 (are)	90
*20. When c and h are next to each other, they make only one sound.	103 (peach)	0	100
*21. Ch is usually pronounced as it is in *kitchen*, *catch*, and *chair*, not like sh.	99 (catch)	5 (machine)	95
			(continued)

The utility of forty-five phonic generalizations (continued)

*Generalization	No. of words conforming	No. of exceptions	Per cent of utility
*22. When c is followed by e or i, the sound of s is likely to be heard.	66 (cent)	3 (ocean)	96
*23. When the letter c is followed by o or a, the sound k is likely to be heard.	143 (camp)	0	100
24. The letter g often has a sound similar to that of j in jump when it precedes the letter i or e.	49 (engine)	28 (give)	64
*25. When ght is seen in a word, gh is silent.	30 (fight)	0	100
26. When a word begins with kn, the k is silent.	10 (knife)	0	100
27. When a word begins with wr, the w is silent.	8 (write)	0	100
*28. When two of the same consonants are side by side only one is heard.	334 (carry)	3 (suggest)	99
*29. When a word ends in ck, it has the same last sound as in look.	46 (brick)	0	100
*30. In most two-syllable words, the first syllable is accented.	828 (famous)	143 (polite)	85
*31. If a, in, re, ex, de, or be is the first syllable in a word, it is usually unaccented.	86 (belong)	13 (insect)	87
*32. In most two-syllable words that end in a consonant followed by y, the first syllable is accented and the last is unaccented.	101 (baby)	4 (supply)	96
33. One vowel letter in an accented syllable has its short sound.	547 (city)	356 (lady)	61
34. When y or ey is seen in the last syllable that is not accented, the long sound of e is heard.	0	157 (baby)	0
35. When ture is the final syllable in a word, it is unaccented.	4 (picture)	0	100
36. When tion is the final syllable in a word, it is unaccented.	5 (station)	0	100
37. In many two- and three-syllable words, the final e lengthens the vowel in the last syllable.	52 (invite)	62 (gasoline)	46
38. If the first vowel sound in a word is followed by two consonants, the first syllable usually ends with the first of the two consonants.	404 (bullet)	159 (singer)	72
39. If the first vowel sound in a word is followed by a single consonant, that consonant usually begins the second syllable.	190 (over)	237 (oven)	44
*40. If the last syllable of a word ends in le, the consonant preceding the le usually begins the last syllable.	62 (tumble)	2 (buckle)	97
*41. When the first vowel element in a word is followed by th, ch, or sh, these symbols are not broken when the word is divided into syllables and may go with either the first or second syllable.	30 (dishes)	0	100
42. In a word of more than one syllable, the letter v usually goes with the preceding vowel to form a syllable.	53 (cover)	20 (clover)	73
43. When a word has only one vowel letter, the vowel sound is likely to be short.	433 (hid)	322 (kind)	57
*44. When there is one e in a word that ends in a consonant, the e usually has a short sound.	85 (leg)	27 (blew)	76
*45. When the last syllable is the sound r, it is unaccented.	188 (butter)	9 (appear)	95

†Words in parentheses are examples—either of words which conform or of exceptions, depending on the column.
*Generalizations marked with an asterisk were found "useful" according to the criteria.

generalizations are open to question on the basis of this study.

This study does not, of course, answer the question of which generalizations primary children can apply in working out the pronunciation of unknown words. The answer to the question of the primary child's ability to apply these and other generalizations will come only through classroom experimentation. Also, this study does not establish the per cent of utility required for a generalization to be useful. The percentage suggested here (75) may be too high. Classroom research might reveal that generalizations with lower percentages of utility should be taught because they encourage children to examine words for sound and letter relationships.

The most disturbing fact to come from the study may be rather dismal failure of generalization 1 to provide the correct pronunciation even 50 per cent of the time. As one teacher remarked when this study was presented to a reading methods class, "Mr. Clymer, for years I've been teaching 'When two vowels go walking, the first one does the talking.' You're ruining the romance in the teaching of reading!"

This paper is an extension of a report given at a joint meeting of the International Reading Association and the National Conference of Research in English, May 1961. Thomas Barrett, Harriette Anderson, Joan Hanson, and David Palmer provided invaluable assistance in various phases of the study.

Saying the "p" Word:
Nine Guidelines for Exemplary Phonics Instruction

Steven A. Stahl

Phonics, like beauty, is in the eye of the beholder. For many people, "phonics" implies stacks of worksheets, with bored children mindlessly filling in the blanks. For some people, "phonics" implies children barking at print, often in unison, meaningless strings of letter sounds to be blended into words. For some people, "phonics" implies lists of skills that must be mastered, each with its own criterion-referenced test, which must be passed or the teacher is "in for it." For some people, "phonics" somehow contrasts with "meaning," implying that concentrating on phonics means that one must ignore the meaning of the text. For others, "phonics" is the solution to the reading problem, as Flesch (1955) argued and others have concurred (see Republican Party National Steering Committee, 1990), that if we just teach children the sounds of the letters, all else will fall in place.

Because "phonics" can be so many things, some people treat it as a dirty word, others as the salvation of reading. It is neither. With these strong feelings, though, extreme views have been allowed to predominate, seemingly forcing out any middle position that allows for the importance of systematic attention to decoding in the context of a program stressing comprehension and interpretation of quality literature and expository text. The truth is that some attention to the relationships between spelling patterns and their pronunciations is characteristic of all types of reading programs, including whole language. As Newman and Church (1990) explain:

No one can read without taking into account the graphophonemic cues of written language. As readers all of us use information about the way words are written to help us make sense of what we're reading.... Whole language teachers do teach phonics but not as something separate from actual reading and writing.... Readers use graphophonic cues; whole language teachers help students orchestrate their use for reading and writing. (pp. 20–21)

"Phonics" merely refers to various approaches designed to teach children about the orthographic code of the language and the relationships of spelling patterns to sound patterns. These approaches can range from direct instruction approaches through instruction that is embedded in the reading of literature. There is no requirement that phonics instruction use worksheets, that it involve having children bark at print, that it be taught as a set of discrete skills mastered in isolation, or that it preclude paying attention to the meaning of texts.

In this article, I want to discuss some principles about what effective phonics instruction should contain and describe some successful programs that meet these criteria.

Why Teach Phonics at All?

The reading field has been racked by vociferous debates about the importance of teaching phonics, when it is to be taught, and how it is to be taught. The interested reader can get a flavor of this debate by reviewing such sources as Adams (1990), Chall

Reprinted from *The Reading Teacher*, 45(8), pp. 618–625. © 1992 by the International Reading Association.

(1983a, 1989), Carbo (1988), and so on. To rehash these arguments would not be useful.

The fact is that all students, regardless of the type of instruction they receive, learn about letter-sound correspondences as part of learning to read. There are a number of models of children's initial word learning showing similar stages of development (e.g., Chall, 1983b; Frith, 1985; Lomax & McGee, 1987; McCormick & Mason, 1986). Frith, for example, suggests that children go through three stages as they learn about words. The first stage is *logographic* in which words are learned as whole units, sometimes embedded in a logo, such as stop sign. This is followed by an *alphabetic* stage, in which children use individual letters and sounds to identify words. The last stage is *orthographic* in which children begin to see patterns in words, and use these patterns to identify words without sounding them out. One can see children go through these stages and begin to see words orthographically by the end of the first grade. Following the orthographic stage children grow in their ability to recognize words automatically, without having to think consciously about word structure or spelling patterns.

These stages in the development of word recognition take place while children are learning about how print functions (what a written "word" is, directionality, punctuation, etc.), that it can signify meanings, about the nature of stories, and all of the other learnings that go on in emergent literacy (see Teale, 1987). Learning about words goes hand in hand with other learnings about reading and writing.

All children appear to go through these stages on their way to becoming successful readers. Some will learn to decode on their own, without any instruction. Others will need some degree of instruction, ranging from some pointing out of common spelling patterns to intense and systematic instruction to help them through the alphabetic and orthographic stages. I want to outline some components of what exemplary instruction might look like. These components could be found in classrooms based on shared reading of literature, as in a whole language philosophy, or in classrooms in which the basal reader is used as the core text.

Exemplary Phonics Instruction...

1. Builds on a child's rich concepts about how print functions. The major source of the debates on phonics is whether one should go from part to whole (begin by teaching letters and sounds and blend those into words) or from whole to part (begin with words and analyze those into letters). Actually, there should be no debate. Letter-sound instruction makes no sense to a child who does not have an overall conception of what reading is about, how print functions, what stories are, and so on, so it must build on a child's concept of the whole process of reading.

A good analogy is baseball. For a person learning to play baseball, batting practice is an important part of learning how to play the game. However, imagine a person who has never seen a baseball game. Making that person do nothing but batting practice may lead to the misconception that baseball is about standing at the plate and repeatedly swinging at the ball. That person would miss the purpose of baseball and would think it a boring way to spend an afternoon.

Adams (1990) points out that children from homes that are successful in preparing children for literacy have a rich idea of what "reading" is before they get to school. They are read to, play with letters on the refrigerator door, discuss print with their parents, and so on. Other children may have had only minimal or no exposure to print prior to school. The differences may add up to 1,000 hours or more of exposure to print.

For the child who has had that 1,000 hours or more, phonics instruction is grounded in his or her experiences with words. Such a child may not need extensive phonics instruction. Good phonics instruction should help make sense of patterns noticed within words. Just "mentioning" the patterns might suffice. However, for the child with little or no exposure, phonics instruction would be an abstract and artificial task until the child has additional meaningful encounters with print.

To develop this base of experience with reading, one might begin reading in kindergarten with activities such as sharing books with children, writing down their dictated stories, and engaging them in authentic reading and writing tasks. Predictable books work especially well for beginning word recognition (Bridge, Winograd, & Haley, 1983). Stahl and Miller (1989) found that whole language programs appeared to work effectively in kindergarten. Their effectiveness, however, diminished in first grade, where more structured, code-emphasis approaches seemed to produce better results. In short, children benefited from the experiences with reading that a whole language program gives early on, but, once they had that exposure, they benefit from more systematic study.

2. Builds on a foundation of phonemic awareness.

Phonemic awareness is not phonics. Phonemic awareness is awareness of sounds in *spoken* words; phonics is the relation between letters and sounds in *written* words. Phonemic awareness is an important precursor to success in reading. One study (Juel, 1988) found that children who were in the bottom fourth of their group in phonemic awareness in first grade remained in the bottom fourth of their class in reading four years later.

An example is Heather, a child I saw in our clinic. As part of an overall reading assessment, I gave Heather a task involving removing a phoneme from a spoken word. For example, I had Heather say *meat* and then repeat it without saying the /m/ sound (*eat*). When Heather said *chicken* after some hesitation, I was taken aback. When I had her say *coat* without the /k/ sound, she said *jacket*. Looking over the tasks we did together, it appeared that she viewed words only in terms of their meaning. For her, a little less than *meat* was *chicken*, a little less than *coat* was *jacket*.

For most communication, focusing on meaning is necessary. But for learning to read, especially learning about sound-symbol relations, it is desirable to view words in terms of the sounds they contain. Only by understanding that spoken words contain phonemes can one learn the relationships between letters and sounds. The alternative is learning each word as a logograph, as in Chinese. This is possible,

up to a certain limit, but does not use the alphabetic nature of our language to its best advantage.

Heather was a bright child, and this was her only difficulty, but she was having specific difficulties learning to decode. Other children like Heather, or children with more complex difficulties, are going to have similar problems. We worked for a short period of time on teaching her to reflect on sounds in spoken words, and, with about 6 weeks of instruction, she took off and became an excellent reader. The moral is that phonemic awareness is easily taught, but absence of it leads to reading difficulties.

3. Is clear and direct. Good teachers explain what they mean very clearly. Yet, some phonics instruction seems to be excessively ambiguous.

Some of this ambiguity comes from trying to solve the problem of pronouncing single phonemes. One cannot pronounce the sounds represented by many of the consonants in isolation. For example, the sound made by *b* cannot be spoken by itself, without adding a vowel (such as /buh/).

To avoid having the teacher add the vowel to the consonant sound, however, some basals have come up with some terribly circuitous routes. For example, a phonics lesson from a current basal program begins with a teacher presenting a picture of a key word, such as *bear*, pronouncing the key word and two or three words with a shared phonic element (such as *boat*, *ball*, and *bed*). The teacher is to point out that the sound at the beginning of each word is spelled with a B. The teacher then might say some other words and ask if they, too, have the same sound. Next, written words are introduced and may be read by the whole class or by individuals. After this brief lesson, students might complete two worksheets, which both involve circling pictures of items that start with *b* and one which includes copying upper- and lowercase *b*'s.

In this lesson, (a) nowhere is the teacher supposed to attempt to say what sound the *b* is supposed to represent and (b) nowhere is the teacher directed to tell the children that these relationships have anything to do with reading words in text. For a child with little phonemic awareness, the instructions, which require that the child segment the initial phoneme from a word, would be very confusing. Children such as Heather view the word *bear* not as a combination of sounds or letters, but identical to its meaning. For that child, the question of what *bear* begins with does not make any sense, because it is seen as a whole meaning unit, not as a series of sounds that has a beginning and an end.

Some of this confusion could be alleviated if the teacher dealt with written words. A more direct approach is to show the word *bear*, in the context of a story or in isolation, and pointing out that it begins with the letter *b*, and the letter *b* makes the /b/ sound. This approach goes right to the basic concept, that a letter in a word represents a particular phoneme, involving fewer extraneous concepts. Going the other direction, showing the letter *b* and then showing words such as *bear* that begin with that letter, would also be clear. Each of these should be followed by having children practice reading *words* that contain the letter *b*, rather than pictures. Children learn to read by reading words, in stories or in lists. This can be done in small groups or with pairs of children reading with each other independently. Circling pictures, coloring, cutting, and pasting, and so on wastes a lot of time.

4. Is integrated into a total reading program. Phonics instruction, no matter how useful it is, should never dominate reading instruction. I know of no research to guide us in deciding how much time should be spent on decoding instruction, but my rule of thumb is that at least half of the time devoted to reading (and probably more) should be spent reading connected text—stories, poems, plays, trade books, and so on. No more than 25% of the time (and possibly less) should be spent on phonics instruction and practice.

Unfortunately, I have seen too many schools in which one day the members of the reading group do the green pages (the skills instruction), the next day they read the story, and the third day they do the blue pages. The result is that, on most days, children are not reading text. Certainly, in these classes, children are going to view "reading" as filling out workbook pages, since this is what they do most of the time. Instead, they should read some text daily, preferably a complete story, with phonics instruction integrated into the text reading.

In many basals, the patterns taught in the phonics lessons appear infrequently in the text, leading students to believe that phonics is somehow unrelated to the task of reading (Adams, 1990). What is taught should be directly usable in children's reading. Juel and Roper/Schneider (1985) found that children were better able to use their phonics knowledge, for both decoding and comprehension, when the texts they read contained a higher percentage of words that conformed to the patterns they were taught. It is best to teach elements that can be used with stories the children are going to read. Teachers using a basal might rearrange the phonics lessons so that a more appropriate element is taught with each story.

Teachers using trade books might choose elements from the books they plan to use, and either preteach them or integrate the instruction into the lesson. A good procedure for doing this is described by Trachtenburg (1990). She suggests beginning by reading a quality children's story (such as *Angus and the Cat*, cited in Trachtenburg, 1990), providing instruction in a high-utility phonic element appearing in that story (short *a* in this case), and using that element to help read another book (such as *The Cat in the Hat* or *Who Took the Farmer's Hat?*). Trachtenburg (1990) provides a list of trade books that contain high percentages of common phonic elements.

Reading Recovery is another example of how phonics instruction can be integrated into a total reading program. Reading Recovery lessons differ depending on the child's needs, but a typical lesson begins with the rereading of a familiar book, followed by the taking of a "running record" on a book introduced the previous session (see Pinnell, Fried, & Estice, 1990, for details). The phonics instruction occurs in the middle of the lesson and could involve directed work in phonemic awareness, letter-sound correspondences using children's spelling or magnetic letters, or even lists of words. The teacher chooses a pattern with which the child had difficulty. The "phonics" instruction is a relatively small component of the total Reading Recovery program, but it is an important one.

5. Focuses on reading words, not learning rules. When competent adults read, they do not refer to a set of rules that they store in their heads. Instead, as Adams (1990) points out, they recognize new words by comparing them or spelling patterns within them to words they already know. When an unknown word such as *Minatory* is encountered, it is not read by figuring out whether the first syllable is open or closed. Instead most people that I have asked usually say the first syllable says /min/ as in *minute* or *miniature*, comparing it to a pattern in a word they already know how to pronounce. Effective decoders see words not in terms of phonics rules, but in terms of patterns of letters that are used to aid in identification.

Effective phonics instruction helps children do this, by first drawing their attention to the order of letters in words, forcing them to examine common patterns in English through sounding out words, and showing similarities between words. As an interim step, rules can be useful in helping children see patterns. Some rules, such as the silent *e* rule, point out common patterns in English. However, rules are not useful enough to be taught as absolutes. Clymer (1963) found that only 45% of the commonly taught phonics rules worked as much as 75% of the time.

A good guideline might be that rules be pointed out, as a way of highlighting a particular spelling pattern, but children should not be asked to memorize or recite them. And, when rules are pointed out, they should be discussed as tentative, with exceptions given at the same time as conforming patterns. Finally, only rules with reasonable utility should be used. Teaching children that *ough* has six sounds is a waste of everyone's time.

6. May include onsets and rimes. An alternative to teaching rules is using onsets and rimes. Treiman (1985) has found that breaking down syllables into onsets (or the part of the syllable before the vowel) and rimes (the part from the vowel onward) is useful to describe how we process syllables in oral language. Teaching onsets and rimes may be useful in written language as well.

Adams (1990) points out that letter-sound correspondences are more stable when one looks at rimes than when letters are looked at in isolation. For example, *ea* taken alone is thought of as irregular. However, it is very regular in all rimes, except *-ead* (*bead* vs. *bread*), *-eaf* (*sheaf* vs. *deaf*), and *-ear* (*hear* vs. *bear*). The rime *-ean*, for example, nearly always has the long *e* sound. Of the 286 phonograms that appear in primary grade texts, 95% of them were pronounced the same in every word in which they appeared (Adams, 1990).

In addition, nearly 500 words can be derived from the following 37 rimes:

-ack	-ain	-ake	-ale	-all	-ame
-an	-ank	-ap	-ash	-at	-ate
-aw	-ay	-eat	-ell	-est	-ice
-ick	-ide	-ight	-ill	-in	-ine
-ing	-ink	-ip	-ir	-ock	-oke
-op	-or	-ore	-uck	-ug	-ump
-unk					

Rime-based instruction is used in a number of successful reading programs. In one such program, children are taught to compare an unknown word to already known words and to use context to confirm their predictions (Gaskins et al., 1988). For example, when encountering *wheat* in a sentence, such as *The little red hen gathered the wheat*, a student might be taught to compare it to *meat* and say "If m-e-a-t is *meat* then this is *wheat*." The student would then cross-check the pronunciation by seeing if *wheat* made sense in the sentence. This approach is comprehension oriented in that students are focused on the comprehension of sentences and stories, but it does teach decoding effectively (see also Cunningham, 1991).

7. May include invented spelling practice. It has been suggested that when children work out their invented spellings, they are learning phonic principles, but learning them "naturally." For this reason, many whole language advocates suggest that practice in writing with invented spelling might be a good substitute for direct phonics instruction. Practice with invented spelling does improve children's awareness of phonemes, which, as discussed earlier, is an important precursor to learning to decode.

However, there is very little research on the effects of invented spelling. That research is positive, but I know of only one study that directly addresses the question. Clarke (1989) found that children who were encouraged to invent spelling and given additional time for writing journals were significantly better at decoding and comprehension than children in a traditional spelling program. However, the classes she studied used a synthetic phonics program as their core reading program. These results may not transfer to a whole language program or even to a more eclectic basal program. An evaluation of the Writing-to-Read program, a computer-based program incorporating writing, found that it had little effect on children's reading abilities (Slavin, 1991).

We need not wait for the research needed to evaluate the use of invented spelling. Writing stories and journal entries using invented spelling does not seem to hurt one's reading or spelling abilities and may help them, and it certainly improves children's writing.

8. Develops independent word recognition strategies, focusing attention on the internal structure of words. The object of phonics instruction is to get children to notice orthographic patterns in words and to use those patterns to recognize words. Effective strategies, whether they involve having a child sound a word out letter by letter, find a word that shares the same rime as an unknown word, or spell out the word through invented or practiced spelling, all force the child to look closely at patterns in words. It is through the learning of these patterns that children learn to recognize words efficiently.

Good phonics instruction should help children through the stages described earlier as quickly as possible. Beginning with bookhandling experiences, storybook reading and "Big Books," and other fea-

tures of a whole language kindergarten support children at the logographic stage. Frith (1985) suggests that writing and spelling may aid in the development of alphabetic knowledge. This can be built upon with some direct instruction of letters and sounds, and showing students how to use that knowledge to unlock words in text. Sounding words out also forces children to examine the internal structure of words, as does rime-based instruction. These can help children make the transition to the orthographic stage. In the next stage, the child develops automatic word recognition skills, or the ability to recognize words without conscious attention.

9. Develops automatic word recognition skills so that students can devote their attention to comprehension, not words. The purpose of phonics instruction is *not* that children learn to sound out words. The purpose is that they learn to recognize words, quickly and automatically, so that they can turn their attention to comprehension of the text. If children are devoting too much energy sounding out words, they will not be able to direct enough of their attention to comprehension (Samuels, 1988).

We know that children develop automatic word recognition skills through practicing reading words. We know that reading words in context does improve children's recognition of words, an improvement which transfers to improved comprehension. There is some question about whether reading words in isolation necessarily results in improved comprehension. Fleisher, Jenkins, and Pany (1979–1980) found that increasing word recognition speed in isolation did not result in improved comprehension; Blanchard (1981) found that it did. Either way, there is ample evidence that practice reading words in text, either repeated readings of the same text (Samuels, 1988) or just reading of connected text in general (Taylor & Nosbush, 1983), improves children's comprehension.

Good phonics instruction is also over relatively quickly. Anderson, Hiebert, Wilkinson, and Scott (1985) recommend that phonics instruction be completed by the end of the second grade. This may even be too long. Stretching phonics instruction out too long, or spending time on teaching the arcane aspects of phonics—the schwa, the silent *k*, assigning accent to polysyllabic words—is at best a waste of time. Once a child begins to use orthographic patterns in recognizing words and recognizes words at an easy, fluent pace, it is time to move away from phonics instruction and to spend even more time reading and writing text.

The "Politics" of Phonics

Given that all children do need to learn about the relationships between spelling patterns and pronunciations on route to becoming a successful reader, why all the fuss about phonics?

Part of the reason is that there is confusion about what phonics instruction is. A teacher pointing out the "short *a*" words during the reading of a Big Book in a whole language classroom is doing something different from a teacher telling her class that the short sound of the letter *a* is /a/ and having them blend in unison 12 words that contain that sound, yet both might be effective phonics instruction. The differences are not only in practice but in philosophy.

In discussions on this issue, the philosophical differences seem to predominate. These exaggerated differences often find people arguing that "phonics" proponents oppose the use of literature and writing in the primary grades, which is clearly false, or that "whole language" people oppose any sort of direct teaching, also clearly false. The truth is that there are commonalities that can be found in effective practices of widely differing philosophies, some of which are reflected in the nine guidelines discussed here.

In this article, I have proposed some characteristics of exemplary phonics instruction. Such instruction is very different from what I see in many classrooms. But because phonics is often taught badly is no reason to stop attempting to teach it well. Quality phonics instruction should be a part of a reading program, integrated and relevant to the reading and writing of actual texts, based on and building upon children's experiences with texts. Such phonics instruction can and should be built into all beginning reading programs.

REFERENCES

Adams, M.J. (1990). *Beginning to read: Thinking and learning about print*. Cambridge, MA: M.I.T. Press.

Anderson, R.C., Hiebert, E.F., Wilkinson, I.A.G., & Scott, J. (1985). *Becoming a nation of readers*. Champaign, IL: National Academy of Education and Center for the Study of Reading.

Blanchard, J.S. (1981). A comprehension strategy for disabled readers in the middle school. *Journal of Reading, 24,* 331–336.

Bridge, C.A., Winograd, P.N., & Haley, D. (1983). Using predictable materials vs. preprimers to teach beginning sight words. *The Reading Teacher, 36,* 884–891.

Carbo, M. (1988). Debunking the great phonics myth. *Phi Delta Kappan, 70,* 226–240.

Chall, J.S. (1983a). *Learning to read: The great debate* (Rev. ed.). New York: McGraw-Hill.

Chall, J.S. (1983b). *Stages of reading development*. New York: McGraw-Hill.

Chall, J.S. (1989). Learning to read: The great debate twenty years later. A response to "Debunking the great phonics myth." *Phi Delta Kappan, 71,* 521–538.

Clarke, L.K. (1989). Encouraging invented spelling in first graders' writing: Effects on learning to spell and read. *Research in the Teaching of English, 22,* 281–309.

Clymer, T. (1963). The utility of phonic generalization in the primary grades. *The Reading Teacher, 16,* 252–258.

Cunningham, P.M. (1991). *Phonics they use*. New York: HarperCollins.

Fleisher, L.S., Jenkins, J.R., & Pany, D. (1979–1980). Effects on poor readers' comprehension of training in rapid decoding. *Reading Research Quarterly, 15,* 30–48.

Flesch, R. (1955). *Why Johnny can't read*. New York: Harper & Row.

Frith, U. (1985). Beneath the surface of developmental dyslexia. In K.E. Patterson, K.C. Marshall, & M. Coltheart (Eds.), *Surface dyslexia: Neuropsychological and cognitive studies of phonological reading*. Hillsdale, NJ: Erlbaum.

Gaskins, I.W., Downer, M.A., Anderson, R.C., Cunningham, P.M., Gaskins, R.W., Schommer, M., & The Teachers of Benchmark School. (1988). A metacognitive approach to phonics: Using what you know to decode what you don't know. *Remedial and Special Education, 9,* 36–41.

Juel, C. (1988). Learning to read and write: A longitudinal study of fifty-four children from first through fourth grade. *Journal of Educational Psychology, 80,* 437–447.

Juel, C., & Roper/Schneider, D. (1985). The influence of basal readers on first grade reading. *Reading Research Quarterly, 20,* 134–152.

Lomax, R.G., & McGee, L.M. (1987). Young children's concepts about print and reading: Toward a model of reading acquisition. *Reading Research Quarterly, 22,* 237–256.

McCormick, C.E., & Mason, J.M. (1986). Intervention procedures for increasing preschool children's interest in and knowledge about reading. In W.H. Teale & E. Sulzby (Eds.), *Emergent literacy: Writing and reading* (pp. 90–115). Norwood, NJ: Ablex.

Newman, J.M., & Church, S.M. (1990). Commentary: Myths of whole language. *The Reading Teacher, 44,* 20–27.

Pinnell, G.S., Fried, M.D., & Estice, R.M. (1990). Reading Recovery: Learning how to make a difference. *The Reading Teacher, 43,* 282–295.

Republican Party National Steering Committee. (1990). *Position paper on teaching children to read.* Washington, DC: Author.

Samuels, S.J. (1988). Decoding and automaticity: Helping poor readers become automatic at word recognition. *The Reading Teacher, 41,* 756–760.

Slavin, R.E. (1991). Reading effects of IBM's "Writing to Read" program: A review of evaluations. *Educational Evaluation and Policy Analysis, 13,* 1–11.

Stahl, S.A., & Miller, P.D. (1989). Whole language and language experience approaches for beginning reading: A quantitative research synthesis. *Review of Educational Research, 59,* 87–116.

Taylor, B.M., & Nosbush, L. (1983). Oral reading for meaning: A technique for improving word identification skills. *The Reading Teacher, 37,* 234–237.

Teale, W.H. (1987). Emergent literacy: Reading and writing development in early childhood. In J.E. Readence & R.S. Baldwin (Eds.), *Research in literacy: Merging perspectives, Thirty-sixth Yearbook of the National Reading Conference* (pp. 45–74). Rochester, NY: National Reading Conference.

Trachtenburg, P. (1990). Using children's literature to enhance phonics instruction. *The Reading Teacher, 43,* 648–653.

Treiman, R. (1985). Onsets and rimes as units of spoken syllables: Evidence from children. *Journal of Experimental Child Psychology, 39,* 161–181.

Where's the Phonics?
Making the Case (Again)
for Integrated Code Instruction

Diane Lapp and James Flood

Last week a friend called and invited us to join her for a round of golf. We were excited because we played our first round of golf with her a few weeks before and had a wonderful experience. The par three course was green and lush and set in beautiful surroundings. We accompanied our friend from hole to hole where she explained to us what she was doing as she did it. For example, when we were putting she said, "Kneel down close to the ground and look toward the hole so you'll be able to get a feel for the path your ball has to follow." It was a lovely day. We left with a little knowledge, limited skill, but a feeling of excitement and a belief that if we wanted to we could become Tiger Woods. Our friend had done a terrific job of introducing us to golf.

So you can see why we were so excited when our second invitation came from the same person. This time she told us to meet her at a golf driving range. We knew it was a different place with a different name, but we expected a similarly delightful experience.

Our expectations were immediately modified when, upon her arrival, our friend told us that today we would each be getting a large bucket of balls so that we could practice our swings. She modeled, we watched, we practiced, she praised and reinforced, and we *did* improve. However, we thought we would never reach the bottom of the bucket. We could hardly wait for the session to end. We hope that our next golf invitation will combine the first

two experiences. If the second experience had preceded the first, neither of us would have made it to lesson two.

Our experience serves as a commonplace for considering a complex and controversial topic: phonics. Although most teachers agree that phonics, which is the relationship between letters and their corresponding sounds, is very much a part of learning how to read, ideas about exactly how and when to teach phonics are recurring points of contention. Many educators today are being pressured by hysteria from the media, parents, and legislators to teach phonics systematically and explicitly, separate from rather than as an integrated segment of a text. But there is no strong research base to support this practice. In fact, as observed by Chall (1967/83), systematic, decontextualized phonics in comparison with traditional contextualized approaches, as in basal readers prior to the mid-1990s, may at best produce better reading comprehension scores on tests (certainly a limited view) and only through Grade 3.

Despite the hysteria, many eager children, excited about learning to read, are being taught to do so every day by very good teacher readers who model, instruct, encourage, assist, practice, and praise until the children learn. One such teacher is Kelly Goss, a first-grade teacher at Oak Park Elementary School in San Diego, California, USA. Oak Park is a racially balanced, multiethnic urban public school directed by Juel Moore. We spend a great deal of

Reprinted from *The Reading Teacher*, 50(8), pp. 696–700. © 1997 by the International Reading Association.

time there, since it is a partner school site with San Diego State University.

Today Goss begins by talking with the children about how much fun she has when she and her dog, Clifford, go walking. She named her dog after the storybook *Clifford*, which first graders love to explore. During the discussion, Goss encouraged the children to think about taking walks (see Figure 1).

After a very engaging conversation, she told the children that they were going to read a story about a boy and what he saw on his walk, entitled *I Went Walking*, written by Sue Williams and illustrated by Julie Vivas (1997). They mused about the pictures and made predictions before she launched into a read-aloud of the book.

After reading, the children talked about their responses to the book, wrote, shared their thoughts about the boy's experiences, and retraced to see how closely their predictions had matched what had really happened on the boy's walk. Goss then reread the story and asked the children to listen for all of the color words. She also encouraged them to join in the reading whenever they wanted to do so. Next she and the children wrote a list of the color words with the corresponding crayons. They also discussed the story and the use of the color words as a technique designed by the illustrator to help them "see" the story.

Goss and the children also looked at the sentences and identified the number of words in each; they noted punctuation, directionality, capitaliza-

tion; they matched the sight words (*I, the, see, you, me*) in the book with the ones on the sight words section of their word wall. Goss also isolated the words *at* and *cat* in the book and asked the children to raise their hands when they saw one of these words on another page in the story. After noting the words on the pages, Goss told the children that sometimes when words rhyme it's because they end in the same letters. She asked them to think of all of the other words they knew that rhymed with *cat* and *at*. They developed a list that included *cat, at, hat, sat, mat, pat, that, bat, fat, rat, tat, vat*. Goss and the children read the list together while listening for the sound of a in these words. Goss targeted the sound of a in *at* because she and the children had been focusing in other similar lessons on the many sounds of a in various phonogram families. She and the children chose *cat* for the common spelling pattern to be added to the word wall.

The children and Goss then reread the story together and shared additional thoughts about the story. Then the children copied the lists of at words onto 3" (5" cards and placed them in the a section of their word rings. They took turns reading the word cards to a partner. They also took turns reading the story to each other. When they finished reading their words and the story, they were able to visit the drama center to put together a costume, from a collection of garments Goss kept there, that the boy in the story could wear on various walks. The children

---

FIGURE 1
Thinking about walking

Walking
Where can we go? What can we see?

Places to walk	Things to see while walking		Things to do while walking
Neighborhood	Houses	Stores	Sing songs
Zoo	Animals	Trees	Talk to a friend
Park	Swings	People	Skip
School	Apartment buildings		Smell the air
Mall			Think about things

were encouraged to role play how the boy and anyone he met along the way might act. They knew that when Goss finished working with small groups of students they would get a chance to share their acting with the whole class.

While the children were busy doing these things, Goss called homogeneous groups to the teacher center to read the story with them and to reinforce their comprehension of it as well as their knowledge of sequential story development; directionality; the sight and color words; their concepts of print; and their awareness of letters, phonograms, and the related sounds they make in words. She asked them to retell the story and to tell her if they were having any trouble reading the story. What she chose to explicitly teach and share with each small homogeneous group was related to their reading performance.

Once the group finished meeting with Goss, the members were encouraged to read their word rings, their practice books, and I Went Walking together or alone or to complete the earlier assigned activities or other extension activities including word matching, retellings with story strips, cloze sentences, writing additional sentences that fit the pattern of the book, playing "I went walking and I saw _____" (each pair must give two clues via pantomime), role playing, and drawing and writing about what they would like to see on a walk. In addition, after meeting with all of the children in groups, Goss called several children to her teacher center one at a time and worked with them individually at the text, sentence, word, or letter level.

Children need exposure to great literature because it enables them to experience new ways of thinking and knowing. Goss's conversations with the class, groups, and individuals were always designed to develop story understanding. She encouraged the children to pause if they were not able to read a word and to try to say the first sound, to check to see if it contained a phonogram that was similar to one on the word wall, to look for picture clues, or to read ahead to see if the other words could help give them the meaning.

Watching Goss and noting how engaged all of the children were, we couldn't help but reflect on

our earlier golf lessons and wonder what might have happened if the reading lesson had begun with the children being shown an *a*, being told that *a* says /aw/ and /a/, and being asked to practice these decontextualized sounds. Would they have eventually become uninterested and perhaps confused readers?

This is a critical question at the heart of many conversations about phonics today. In attempting to answer the *when* and *how* of phonics we believe that one of the first goals of literacy instruction must be to quickly provide children with the skills they will need to read the texts that surround them. Children need to develop ability to decode printed words.

Many different terms have been used to describe the way that children learn to recognize words. In the past, confusion about some of these terms has led to misunderstandings about best practices. The following six terms are at the core of decoding: *code, decode, word attack, word recognition, phonics,* and *sight word method* (see Figure 2).

Code is a system of signals used to represent meaning. These signals become meaningful when an individual knows the meaning that has been assigned to them. When children apply meaning to signals they have learned to decode. In learning to decode the words of English, which has an alphabetic system, children have to learn to map letters and sounds. When children learn these mappings, they have "broken the code," and this enables them to figure out plausible pronunciations for the words they will meet in print. Even adult competent readers who have automated their word recognition skills use their knowledge of the code when they encounter new words.

All readers use a different level of attention to apply their knowledge of the code as they read. At one extreme, when they encounter familiar, well-practiced words, they apply their knowledge without any apparent attention; this phenomenon has been labeled word recognition, word identification, and/or sight word recognition. At the other extreme, readers need to consciously apply their knowledge; this happens when they encounter new words they know and they have to work to produce plausible pronunciations for the new words. The

FIGURE 2
Glossary of reading terms for code instruction

Code	A system of symbols used to represent assigned meanings
Decode	Applying meaning to signals
Word recognition/ word identification/ sight word recognition	Applying knowledge of the code with little conscious attention because the word(s) have been previously "read" many times
Word attack	A system in which readers consciously apply their knowledge of the code by "attacking" the word in order to approximate pronunciation
Sight word method	An approach in which words are introduced to readers as whole words without attention to subword parts
Phonics	A set of instructional strategies that bring the child's attention to parts of words including syllables, phonograms (*at*, *ick*), and single letters

term that best describes this phenomenon is word attack. By noting spelling patterns in the words the children were meeting in their reading, Goss was helping them develop word attack strategies. Readers at both ends of the continuum are decoding even though they are doing it at different levels of consciousness. In both instances they are using symbols to interpret a unit that has meaning.

Sight word recognition and sight word method have also been confused in the past. Sight word recognition (in which the child builds a sight word vocabulary) is an important goal of reading instruction. However, this goal should not be confused with instructional procedures called "sight word method," "whole word method," or "look-say method" in which words are introduced to children as whole units without subword parts. Goss and the children shared the sight words found in the story (*I, the, see, you, me*).

Phonics embraces many instructional strategies that help children attend to parts of words, including syllables, phonograms (the *at* in *cat*), and single letters (the *b* in *bat*). The goal of phonics is to help children learn with the mappings between letters and sounds, but it is not a goal unto itself. Phonics merely provides children with the knowledge needed to decipher a word in order to approximate pronunciation.

Helping Children Learn the Code
Many researchers have argued for the importance of early acquisition of decoding skills. Stanovich (1986) found convincing evidence that children who start slowly in acquiring decoding skills rarely become strong readers throughout their academic careers, and Juel (1988) found that early acquisition of decoding skills leads to wider reading in and out of school, which, in turn, provides abundant opportunities for growth in vocabulary, concepts, and general knowledge.

Learning to read is made much easier when children have acquired three prerequisite understandings about print: print carries messages, printed words are composed of letters, and letters correspond to the sounds in spoken words. Many children learn these prerequisites from having been read to in and out of school settings by adults who routinely note and explain correspondences between letters and sounds. However, many children come to school without these prerequisites and need direct instruction in them. Goss attempted to develop these strategies contextually as she and the children previewed and discussed the book, read, reread and retraced the book together, met in homogeneous groups to note various print and message elements, and finally shared these understandings through extension activities.

Printed Words Carry Meaning: Understanding Concepts of Print

Young children need to understand that there is a systematic relationship between printed symbols and spoken messages and that they need to "look at" the print in texts to interpret the messages. Although this idea might seem obvious, it is not always apparent to new readers because storybooks are often filled with colorfully engaging pictures that capture their interest and attention. In contrast, the printed marks at the bottom of the page often seem uninteresting and unengaging. Print may be ignored when illustrations overwhelm it. Children need to be directed to letters and words if they are to understand that print carries meaning. Children should be taught phonics contextually when they are learning to read and enjoy literature and when they are emerging as writers.

The understanding that messages are found in the printed words can also be modeled in classrooms through morning messages. A message Goss put on her board after she and the children had, through a variety of activities, explored the *a* sound in words that contained the *at* phonogram was

> Happy Wednesday. Today is September 18, 1996. The weather is very sunny. Monday we read *I Went Walking* (Williams, 1997). On Tuesday we read *Who Is That?* (Lewis, 1997). Please reread these books. Also read all of the *at* words in your word rings. Today we are going to read a wonderful book titled *The Cat in the Hat* by Dr. Seuss (1957).

Words Are Composed of Letters

As children first attempt to decode print, they often find distinctive features of words that act as cues that help them identify the words (Gough & Hillinger, 1980). Frequently the distinctive feature that the child attends to will be tied to a picture.

In other instances, children will remember a word because of some distinctive visual configurations like the beginning and ending letters of *bat* (*b* and *t*), which may seem to frame the word for some children. Initial letters or clusters of letters are also frequently used to recall words by young children (e.g., they might remember the word *duck* by its initial letter *d* or *chick* by the *ch* or *that* by the *th* combination of letters). As children see more new words, they often encounter problems because they cannot find a single distinctive cue that is reliable. At this point in their development, reading can become very frustrating because their cueing systems are so completely inadequate.

Words Are Composed of Sounds

After children understand that words are composed of letters, they need to be able to make correspondences between printed letters and sounds. In order to do this children must hear sounds in spoken words. For example, they need to hear the /at/ sound in *cat*, *hat*, and *bat* and to perceive that the differences between these words is in the initial sound in each. Goss attempted to illustrate this by having children note the short /a/ sound in *cat*, *hat*, and *bat*, and the *at* sound in these words. After recognizing these features, she also illustrated that these sounds were part of the words found in the books they were reading.

If children cannot perceive sound segments they will have difficulty when they try to sound out words in both reading and writing (Beck & Juel, 1995). This understanding that words are composed of sounds is called *phonemic awareness*. It is not a single ability; rather, it includes the ability to rhyme words (as in *cat*, *hat*, *bat*) and the understanding that *bat* has three distinctive sounds that are overlapping and abstract. This awareness comes to children gradually because phonemes in the speech they hear are difficult to perceive individually. For example, we begin saying the /a/ sound while we are still saying the /b/ sound. Beck and Juel (1995) maintain that we don't clearly know how phonemic awareness is acquired, but we do know that certain activities seem to foster its development.

These activities need to become part of early reading instruction. Phonemic awareness can be taught and will help young children decode words as they immerse themselves in the process of learning to read (Lundberg, Frost, & Peterson, 1988). Such instruction should not occur in isolation from books, since, as noted by Carbo (1987), most emergent readers are unable to learn through analytic, abstract, or auditory experiences. They are better able to learn to read through whole-to-part (books then phonics skills) experiences than through part-to-whole (explicit phonics first, books later) experiences. This is why Goss connected quality patterned stories and explicit phonics and comprehension instruction.

Teaching Explicit Phonics

Many researchers have recommended the teaching of phonics as an important aid in helping children learn the code (Adams, 1990; Anderson, Hiebert, Scott, & Wilkinson, 1985). There are two approaches to phonics: explicit phonics and implicit phonics. In explicit phonics children are told the sounds of individual letters (e.g., the letter *b* represents the /b/ sound in *bat*). In implicit phonics children are expected to induce the sounds that correspond to the letters based upon their accumulated exposure to words that have contained these letters. While there is not a definitive answer about which of these is a better approach, a trend in the data favors explicit phonics because it provides children with close approximations between letters and sounds. In addition to learning the code, children need to make meaning as they read—they need to comprehend what they are reading. Proficient readers have thoroughly integrated strategies since they use prior knowledge, context, and letter/sound relationships (phonics) as needed to identify words and to construct meaning. In contrast, less proficient readers are often the victims of isolated phonics instruction that is devoid of strategies, including phonics, designed to help one make meaning while reading (Chomsky, 1976).

Goss teaches phonics explicitly and contextually. She teaches all of the letters and phonogram families explicitly, but she also contextualizes this instruction because she believes that children come to school wanting to hold, touch, and read books. She believes that motivation to read is enhanced as children are taught strategies while exploring many

wonderful age-appropriate books. When phonics is taught devoid of books, children are asked to postpone their excitement for literacy. Overemphasized, isolated phonics instruction encourages many children to rely on "sounding it out" as their only meaning-making strategy (Applebee, Langer, & Mullis, 1988). A child in this situation is like some adults who practice their golf swings without understanding the relationship of the swing to the game—they may improve their swings but never become proficient golfers. Attitude and enthusiasm matter.

Balance and Harmony

As evidenced by Goss's instruction, a balanced approach toward literacy instruction creates harmony in the learner's and the teacher's mind. This approach helps children integrate what they already know with new strategies, skills, and content that will best serve their new and developing reading interests. A balanced approach ensures that this can become a reality when children are taught language arts skills and strategies in a context that invites them to explore the wonderful world of books. Figure 3 illustrates the language arts skills/strategies Goss explicitly taught as she worked with a heterogeneous whole class, heterogeneous and homogeneous pairs, individuals, and small homogeneous groups. As Goss continues to approach the task of helping young readers and writers grow, she needs to be sure that her methods are worthy of her students' time and effort. She and all other teachers must be certain that they are adding to students' understanding in a way that will make them lifelong independent learners who are able and excited readers, writers, and literate communicators.

REFERENCES

Adams, M.J. (1990). *Beginning to read: Thinking and learning about print.* Cambridge, MA: MIT Press.
Anderson, R.C., Hiebert, E.H., Scott, J.A., & Wilkinson, I.A.G. (1985). *Becoming a nation of readers: The report of the commission on reading.* Washington, DC: National Institute of Education.

FIGURE 3
Language arts strategies

Strategy	Language arts				
	Reading Comprehension	Reading Word analysis	Writing	Listening	Speaking
Inferring	X			X	X
Synthesizing	X			X	X
Understanding	X			X	X
Creating	X		X		X
Drawing/illustrating			X		
Predicting	X				
Comparing	X		X	X	X
Identifying	X				
Matching	X		X		
Developing concepts of print	X	X			
Noting grammar/mechanics		X	X		X
Noting punctuation/mechanics		X	X		
Recognizing sounds made by letters in words		X			
Recognizing spelling patterns		X	X		
Recognizing letters		X			
Dramatizing			X		X
Analyzing plot/story	X		X		
Noting/developing characterization	X		X		
Evaluating	X				
Responding	X			X	X
Noting/developing supporting details	X		X		X
Role playing	X		X	X	X

Applebee, A.N., Langer, J.A., & Mullis, I.V.S. (1988). *Learning to be literate in America: Reading, writing and reasoning.* Princeton, NJ: National Assessment of Educational Progress, Educational Testing Service.

Beck, I., & Juel, C. (1995, Summer). The role of decoding in learning to read. *American Educator, 8,* 8–23.

Carbo, M. (1987). Reading style research: "What works" isn't always phonics. *Phi Delta Kappan, 68,* 431–435.

Chall, J. (1967/1983). *Learning to read: The great debate.* New York: McGraw-Hill.

Chomsky, C. (1976). After decoding: What? *Language Arts, 53,* 288–296, 314.

Gough, P.B., & Hillinger, M.L. (1980). Learning to read: An unnatural act. *Bulletin of the Orton Society, 30,* 171–176.

Juel, C. (1988). Learning to read and write: A longitudinal study of fifty-four children from first through fourth grade. *Journal of Educational Psychology, 80,* 437–447.

Lewis, K.E. (1997). *Who is that?* New York: Macmillan/McGraw-Hill.

Lundberg, I., Frost, J., & Peterson, O. (1988). Effects of an extensive program for stimulating phonological awareness in preschool children. *Reading Research Quarterly, 23,* 263–284.

Seuss, Dr. (1957). *The cat in the hat.* New York: Random House.

Stanovich, K.E. (1986). Matthew effects in reading: Some consequences of individual differences in the acquisition of literacy. *Reading Research Quarterly, 21,* 360–406.

Williams, S. (1997). *I went walking.* New York: Macmillan/McGraw-Hill.

What Can I Say Besides "Sound It Out"? Coaching Word Recognition in Beginning Reading

Kathleen F. Clark

It's 9:20 in the morning. Five first graders are reading *Cave Boy* (Dubowski, 1988) with their teacher. After they read from the text, "He gets lots of presents. A rock, some wood, a fish, a bone" (p. 19), the following interaction takes place:

Student: "He gets lots of presents and...." [a rock]

Teacher: And....

Student: [no response]

Teacher: Let's see. Have we done everything we know how to do? We can look at the picture. We can take a running start. Think of all the things you can do.

Student: Hope? [rock]

Teacher: Can you say the sounds?

Student: /r/ /o/ /k/

Teacher: Now take a running start.

Student: Rock.

Teacher: Works every time.

In a classroom in another state, four second graders are reading *The Color Wizard* (Brenner, 1989) with their teacher. After they read, "'What we need around here is a little red. Red is bright!' So he painted his coach" (pp. 4–5), a similar interaction takes place:

Student: "So he painted...his...." [coach]

Teacher: Good job. Now just follow your rules. What's that [coach] going to say? Follow your rules. What vowel will you hear?

Student: [no response]

Teacher: Will you hear the *o* or the *a*?

Student: *o*

Teacher: And now what does *ch* say?

Student: /ch/

Teacher: So what's the word? The *c* is making the hard sound.

Student: Cuch...coach!

Teacher: Coach is right! Did you see Cinderella? She had a beautiful coach. That's what this is [picture of a coach].

These interactions illustrate a highly effective instructional technique, that of coaching. In the interactions, knowledgeable teachers have crafted just the right cues for readers to apply their developing knowledge of word-recognition strategies. In doing so, the teachers have incrementally fostered students' ability to become strategic and independent readers. The purpose of this article is to describe the technique of coaching word recognition. I review the reading process, elaborate on coaching, present examples of coaching, share elements to consider when preparing to coach, discuss implications for practice, and offer conclusions about the nature of effective coaching.

The Reading Process: An Overview

Reading is a complex problem-solving process in which readers actively pursue meaning (Graves,

Reprinted from *The Reading Teacher*, 57(5), pp. 440–449. © 2004 by the International Reading Association.

Juel, & Graves, 2001). It is a "message-getting" activity (Clay, 1991, p. 6) in which readers draw on multiple interacting knowledge sources to construct meaning. Readers use these sources as they engage in basic (i.e., word-recognition and syntactic) and higher order (i.e., inferring and reasoning) processes (van den Broek & Kremer, 2000). As educators, we seek to develop students' knowledge of these sources and their ability to coordinate and apply them flexibly as they read.

The challenges readers face as they work to construct meaning vary with skill and experience. In early primary grade classrooms, word recognition presents a significant challenge for students. While they work to construct meaning, they must devote considerable attention to activating, coordinating, and applying their developing knowledge of word-recognition strategies. That so much attention be allocated to acquiring and refining word-recognition strategies is no insignificant matter. Word recognition is a necessary but insufficient condition for comprehension: It alone does not guarantee comprehension, but without it comprehension cannot occur (van den Broek & Kremer, 2000).

Coaching: The Concept

Coaching is a technique with roots in the work of Marie Clay. Clay (2001) viewed young readers as active learners working to construct a self-extending system—a system that "bring[s] about new forms of mediation," "alter[s] an existing working system to become more effective," and "compile[s] more effective assemblies of systems" (p. 136). One way children develop this system is through "powerful interactions with teachers" during reading (p. 136). Teachers closely observe students and intervene to support their developing strategic processes. Clay described this approach as an interactive option. Others have referred to it as coaching (Taylor, Pearson, Clark, & Walpole, 2000) and scaffolding (Pressley et al., 2001). Recent studies have identified the technique as characteristic of accomplished classroom teachers (Pressley et al., 2001; Taylor et al., 2000) and Reading Recovery teachers (Rodgers,

2000) and as a technique that distinguishes more effective teachers from their less effective peers (Taylor et al.).

The following discussion is derived from my case study (Clark, 2000) of the instructional talk of a subset of teachers identified as most accomplished in a large-scale study of effective practice (Taylor et al., 2000). The case study inquiry occurred after the original study in which the teachers participated and yielded a unique data set and analysis. All teacher and student names used in this discussion are pseudonyms.

All teachers grouped their students homogenously for guided reading instruction based on their perceptions of students' abilities, and each teacher altered the composition of these groups as necessary to meet student needs. I first describe the nature of teachers' instructional cues, then I provide examples of their coaching as it occurred in context.

The Nature of Teachers' Instructional Cues

In the case study (Clark, 2000), I qualitatively analyzed teachers' instructional cues using the constant-comparison method (Glaser & Strauss, 1967). In coding the cues, I engaged in an iterative process in which categories emerged from the data. As successive transcripts were coded, and additional categories emerged and were refined, I returned to previously coded cues and adjusted my analysis. In addition, I used two independent coders to validate my structure.

Teachers' cues to students were of two broad types: general cues to prompt thought and more focused cues to prompt specific action. The cues took the form of either questions or statements to students. The particular characteristics of these cues are as follows.

General cues to promote thought. General cues to promote thought are nonspecific in nature. They prompt readers to think about their knowledge of word-recognition strategies and how to apply this knowledge to the word-recognition task (e.g., How are you going to figure that out? What can you do?).

They do not, however, point readers in any one direction. The responsibility for thinking is with the reader. Examples of these cues are presented in Table 1.

Cues to prompt specific action. Cues to prompt specific action provide readers with more detailed information about the word-recognition task. They focus readers' attention on graphophonic knowledge, word-part identification strategies, and contextual supports.

Cues that focus readers' attention on grapheme-phoneme correspondences direct them to consider individual letters and sounds (e.g., It's a soft *c*. The *y* is acting like an *i*) and multiple-letter phonic elements such as blends (e.g., What does *spr-* say?), digraphs (e.g., What does *ch* say? Remember, *gh* can make an *f* sound), and r-controlled vowels (e.g., Does the *-or* sound like *-or* in *corn* or in *actor*?).

Other specific cues direct readers' attention to larger word-part identification strategies. They encourage readers to locate phonograms (e.g., I see one of our word families), known smaller words (e.g., Is there a little word in there? It's a compound word; the first word is....), and inflected (e.g., Take off the *-es/-ed/-ing*) and derivational (e.g., Take off the *-ly*) endings in an unfamiliar print word.

Cues that make use of contextual supports focus readers' attention on the inappropriateness of a miscue (e.g., You said *taking* [thinking] of ways.), the possibilities given the sentence (e.g., What _____ are you counting?), and picture supports (e.g., Use pictures and words). I summarize these cues in Table 2 to illustrate their specific characteristics.

The Nature of Coaching as It Occurred in Context

The following dialogues illustrate the manner in which coaching occurred within the context of guided reading lessons. In the dialogues, teachers cue students as they apply their knowledge of word-recognition strategies during reading. The cues reflect multiple instructional focuses.

Grade 1

Mrs. Fry taught first grade in a rural school. There were 22 children in her classroom (20 European American and 2 Hispanic children). Mrs. Fry had a master's degree in elementary education and 11 years of experience, all in grade 1. Mrs. Wilson taught first grade in an urban school. There were 18 students in her classroom, all of whom were African American. She had 10 years of experience, 7 in kindergarten and 3 in first grade. She had a master's degree in curriculum and instruction.

In these teachers' classrooms, leveled texts were used. These are sets of texts that move from simpler to more complex reading and can be matched to students' abilities (Brabham & Villaume, 2002). Mrs. Fry's students read texts she believed would enable them to practice previously taught phonic elements

TABLE 1 General cues to prompt thought	
Questions	Statements
What do you know about that?	Look for something you already know how to do.
What are you going to do to help yourself out?	Look and think what you need to do.
If you're stuck, what can you do?	
What do you think?	
How are you going to figure that out?	

TABLE 2
Cues to prompt specific action

Grapheme-phoneme correspondences	Word-part identification strategies	Use of contextual supports (sentence structure or picture supports)
The first g is hard; the second g is soft.	Is there a chunk you know?	This is what you said: Brer Fox is *taking* [thinking] of ways....
It's a soft c.	Can you take something off?	Does that sound right?
Throw away the g-h.	Take off or cover up the ending and see what the word is.	What _____ are you counting? What would make sense there?
Remember, g-h can make an f sound.	Look for a little word.	
It's a double vowel.	It's a compound word. What's the first or second word?	Let's read to the end and see what makes sense.
It's an r-controlled vowel.		Use pictures and words.
What do you think that e sounds like?		What in the picture starts with the letter you see?
Put an /h/ sound in front of is.		
The y is acting like an i.		
It's a blend. I see a blend.		

and orthographic patterns. Mrs. Wilson's students read books that came with a reading series.

In the following example, Mrs. Fry's first graders are reading *"Not Now!" Said the Cow* (Oppenheim, 1989), when a child has difficulty recognizing the word *grunted*. The text reads, "'I can't do that!' meowed the cat. 'Not my job!' grunted hog" (p. 24).

Student:	"'I can't do that!' meowed the cat. 'Not my job!' grunt...grunt....'"
Teacher:	If there were an *-ed* at the end of that word, how would you say that?
Student:	Grundable?
Teacher:	Say it again?
Student:	Grunded.
Teacher:	Okay, cover up the *-ed* and see what the word is.
Student:	Grund.
Teacher:	Is it *grund* or *grunt*?
Student:	Grunt.... "Grunted hog."

In this dialogue, the reader's first attempt to recognize *grunted* results in *grunt*. The child recog-

nizes the root of the unfamiliar word *grunted*. Mrs. Fry prompts her to call to mind her knowledge of how to pronounce *-ed* at the end of a word. The reader responds with two inaccurate attempts, *grundable* and *grunded*, in which she has both applied incorrect word endings and replaced the /t/ with /d/. Mrs. Fry then becomes more directive. She tells the reader to cover up the confusing word part and note the remaining word. The reader identifies the root as *grund*. Mrs. Fry repeats the inaccurate partial word identification and presents it with the correct root, emphasizing the ending consonant in each. The reader is then able to identify the correct root, *grunt*, and the unfamiliar word, *grunted*. Mrs. Fry began this coaching episode by being less directive in her cueing of the child. When the child was unsuccessful, Mrs. Fry became more directive and specific in her cueing.

In Mrs. Wilson's first-grade class, the students have difficulty decoding the word wind during a choral reading of *Where Does Everybody Go?* (Dodds, 1996). The text reads, "When rain falls hard and cold wind blows, where does everybody go?" (p. 2).

All:	"When rain falls hard and cold...wuh...wuh...." [wind]
Teacher:	Let's look for a chunk in there.
Student 1:	Can I sound it out?
Student 2:	Here's a chunk.
Teacher:	Where's a chunk?
Student 2:	[no response]
Teacher:	What is this word right here? [Teacher frames *in* within *wind*]
All:	[chorally] In.
Student 2:	That's what I said.
All:	Wind.
Teacher:	Okay. Let's start from the beginning.
All:	"When rain falls hard and cold wind blows, where does everybody go?"

In response to the students' attempt to decode the word, Mrs. Wilson cues them to look for a known word part (Let's look for a chunk in there). When the students are unsuccessful, she frames the known word *in* within the unknown word *wind*. With these two cues of increasing support, the students are able to decode the word and continue choral reading.

Grade 2

Mrs. Green taught second grade in a suburban school. She had a master's degree in curriculum development and four years of experience, with two of those years at grade 2. There were 17 students in her classroom (16 European American and 1 Korean American). Mr. Turner taught second grade in an urban school. He had three years of experience, all at grade 2, and he was completing his master's degree. He taught 22 students, all of whom were African American.

These second-grade teachers' coaching proceeded in a similar manner. In their classrooms, leveled texts as well as more literary texts are used during guided-reading lessons.

In Mr. Turner's class, a small group of students is reading *Red Riding Hood* (Marshall, 1987). The text reads, "Beyond the forest, they came to a patch of sunflowers. 'Why not pick a few?' suggested the wolf" (p. 12). One reader has difficulty with the word *suggested*.

Student:	"'Why not pick a few?' snuggled [suggested] the wolf."
Teacher:	Okay, try it again. Sug....
Student:	[no response]
Teacher:	The first *g* is hard. The second *g* is soft. *Sug-juh....*
Student:	"Suggested the wolf."

In this exchange, the reader has miscued the word *suggested*. Mr. Turner models the first part of the word, but the child is unable to use this information to recognize the word. Mr. Turner then cues the child to the different sounds the two *gs* make in the word and models each. With this support, the child is able to recognize the word and continue reading. In this dialogue, Mr. Turner models pronunciation of the first syllable. This proves insufficient, so he intervenes with very focused cues.

When another small group of Mr. Turner's students is reading *The Color Wizard* (Brenner, 1989), a reader encounters difficulty when she comes to the word *fence*. The text reads, "So he painted his castle and his fence all blue" (p. 8).

Student:	"So he painted his...castle blue."
Teacher:	Use your strategies.
Student:	"So he painted his castle and his...." [fence]
Teacher:	Use pictures and words.
Student:	His fuh...flll...fountain.
Teacher:	Pictures and words—*f-e-n-c-e.*
Student:	Faces.
Teacher:	Look, *f-e-n,* you all should know says *fen.* That *c,* you could either make it a /k/ or /s/. *Fenk,* is that a word?
All:	[shake heads negative]
Teacher:	So what's left? Look at the picture there [points to the picture of a fence].
All:	Fence.
All:	"So he painted his castle and his fence all blue."

In this dialogue, Mr. Turner encourages the focal reader and her groupmates to use their knowledge of graphophonic and picture cues to recognize the unfamiliar print word *fence*. The readers are unable to systematically think through the application of their developing strategic knowledge, so Mr. Turner demonstrates the process, becoming more specific in his coaching as he proceeds. He indicates their familiarity with the spelling pattern that comprises the first part of the word (Look, *f-e-n*, you all should know says *fen*). Then he highlights the two sounds the letter c can make (That *c*, you could either make it a /k/ or /s/) and models the incorrect choice (*Fenk*, is that a word?). He then directs their attention to the illustration (So what's left? Look at the picture there). With this support, the children are able to recognize the word.

A reader in Mrs. Green's second-grade class has difficulty decoding the word *semisalted* (a word the child reports he has never seen) when reading *My Visit to the Aquarium* (Aliki, 1993). The text reads, "In the coastal stream exhibit, we saw fish that travel. They live in fresh and salt water, and in semisalted coastal streams that lead to the sea" (p. 23).

Student:	"In the coastal stream exhibit, we saw fish that travel. They live in fresh and salt water, and in....solt...."
Teacher:	Okay, break it up into two parts.
Teacher:	[points to a word in the book and sequentially covers the word parts *semi-* and *salted* with her finger] The *i* is long. Just *s-e-m-i*....
Student:	Sem....
Teacher:	Sem...and then a long *i*.
Student:	Semi...salt.... Semisalted.

In this interaction, Mrs. Green directs the child to break the word into two parts and cues him to the vowel sound (The *i* is long). She leads him through the process, and he decodes the first syllable. Mrs. Green confirms the partial decoding and restates the graphophonic cue (and then the long *i*). With this support, the reader is able to recognize the word. Mrs. Green began the interaction by identifying a possible strategy and cueing a relevant sound, and

then she became more specific by guiding the student through the strategy.

Eliciting Student Coaching

In Mrs. Fry's classroom, students had learned to contribute cues during coaching episodes. Mrs. Fry described her rationale for student coaching and how it came to occur in her classroom.

> I think you have to have everybody involved when you're just addressing one child. So one day, I just started saying, "What does everybody else think?" and "Let's give some clues. How could you help her? What are some ways we could get unstuck?" And so then they're just thinking about it. Well, I could cover up that *s*. Oh look! There's a family there. What family is it? Oh, it's the *-at* family. And so everybody just became engaged in the conversation. (Clark, 2000, p. 105)

The following dialogue is representative of such a coaching episode. The students are reading *The Carrot Seed* (Krauss, 1945). The text reads, "But he still pulled up the weeds around it every day and sprinkled the ground with water" (p. 17). Multiple students join Mrs. Fry in coaching a child struggling with *every*.

Student 1:	"But he...still pulled up the weeds around the...it...a...a...." [every]
Teacher:	What do you think? Can you please touch the letters and say those sounds for me?
Student 1:	Eh...vuh...er...ever....
Teacher:	There's a little word isn't there? What's the little word?
Student 1:	Ever.
Teacher:	Ever.... Now, slide to the end.
Student 1:	Oh.
Teacher:	Jim [another student with raised hand] thinks he knows.
Teacher:	What about the *y*? Ever...ever.... What's [the original reader] going to do?
Student 2:	I know.
Teacher:	You know?
Student 2:	The *y* acts like an *i*.
Teacher:	Are you sure? Then it would say evri [long *i*].

Student 3: No—*e* [long *e*].

Teacher: E [long *e* sound].

Student 1: "Every...day and sprinkled the ground with water."

When the reader encounters difficulty, Mrs. Fry initially intervenes with a general cue (What do you think?) and a directive to apply a strategy (Can you please touch the letters and say those sounds for me?). With this support, the reader recognizes the first two syllables in the word. The final *y* proves difficult, however. At this point, Mrs. Fry provides a more specific cue that directs the reader's attention to a known word part (There's a little word there. What's the little word?). The reader identifies the little word (*ever*), and Mrs. Fry then gives another directive (Now, slide to the end). The child remains unsuccessful, and another child raises his hand and provides a clue, albeit an inaccurate one (The *y* acts like an *i*). Mrs. Fry highlights the inaccuracy (Then it would say evr*i* [long *i*]). In so doing, she focuses the children's attention on the sound in question and implies they should try the other sound for *y*—a strategy she has taught them to apply. Another child then identifies the correct sound, and Mrs. Fry confirms it. With this support, the focal reader recognizes the word *every* and continues reading.

Preparing to Coach Word Recognition

In coaching word recognition, a teacher crafts cues that enable readers to think to the edge of their knowledge as they attempt to recognize unfamiliar words. To coach successfully, one must be aware of the knowledge sources available for word recognition, have specific knowledge of students' word-recognition abilities, be able to analyze a word, and generate appropriate cues.

Factors to Consider

In discussing coaching, the teachers highlighted factors they considered when crafting cues:

- The sounds the vowels or vowel teams (e.g., *oa, ea, oi, ay, ou*) make in the word
- The sound the *y* makes when it is a vowel (e.g., *e* or *i*)
- The sounds consonants make, such as *c, s,* or *g*
- The presence of blends (e.g., *cr, fl, sk, spr, scr*) or digraphs (e.g., *ch, sh, th, wh, gh*)
- The presence of *r*-controlled vowels (e.g., *ur, ir, er, or, ar*)
- The presence of silent letters (e.g., *e, gh*)
- The presence of known word parts, such as phonograms (e.g., *-ake, -at, -ame*); smaller words within a word; or affixes (e.g., *re-, un-, -ment, -ly, -ed, -ing*)
- The context in which a word occurs

Generating Cues: Two Textual Examples

The teachers all said that coaching was critical to their success in helping children learn to read, and they indicated it was a technique they acquired after completing their teacher certification programs. Intrigued by this, I now include coaching in reading methods courses I teach. Following are examples of cues my preservice teachers generated.

The first example is from *Lon Po Po* (Young, 1989). The three children menaced by the wolf in the story have climbed a gingko tree to escape and outwit the wolf. He waits below, expecting to be furnished with gingko nuts. The text reads, "'But Po Po, gingko is magic only if it is plucked directly from the tree'" (p. 18).

Our hypothetical reader is unable to recognize the word *gingko*. The following cues will support the reader as he or she works to decode the word.

- Think what two sounds *g* can make (/g/ and /j/).
- What sound does *-ing* make?
- Break it into two parts (*ging* and *-ko*).

The second example is from *My Visit to the Aquarium* (Aliki, 1993). The text reads, "Turtles and other reptiles share the leafy habitat" (p. 22). Our hypothetical student is unable to recognize the word *reptiles*. The following cues might help the reader.

- Cover up the *s*.
- There is a word family (*-ile*).
- The first *e* is short.
- Break it into two parts (*rep* and *-tiles*).
- What kind of animals are turtles and alligators? Think about the picture and the first part of the word (*rep*). What would make sense?

Implications for Practice

Coaching word recognition. Three points should be made when crafting cues to support word recognition. First, it is crucial to understand word recognition in beginning reading. While readers draw on multiple knowledge sources to understand what they read (Clay, 2001), not all knowledge sources contribute equally to word recognition. Word recognition relies heavily on graphophonic knowledge (Pressley, 1998). Further, a developmental process is involved in learning to read words, and at different stages of development children read words in qualitatively different ways (Ehri, 1991; Juel, 1991).

Juel (1991) summarized three stages of word recognition: the selective-cue stage, the spelling-sound stage, and the automatic stage. In the selective-cue stage, children recognize words by attending to the environment in which words are placed (e.g., a red hexagon) or to selected print but nonalphabetic features (e.g., the two circles in *moon*). In this stage, children rely heavily on picture and semantic context clues to recognize words; their challenge is to acquire the alphabetic principle and to learn to attend to the letters and spelling patterns in words (Lipson & Wixson, 2003).

In the spelling-sound stage (Juel, 1991), children primarily use letter-sound relationships in their word recognitions and approximations. The challenge at this stage is to fully analyze the letters in words, paying particular attention to vowels and to the spelling patterns that represent the larger parts of words (Lipson & Wixson, 2003).

In the automatic stage (Juel, 1991), children are able to recognize most words they read without conscious attention to spelling-sound relationships. This ability to read words at sight enables children to allocate more attention to higher level meaning-making processes (van den Broek & Kremer, 2000).

We must recognize these developmental differences as we craft instructional cues, and the cues we craft should support students' movement through the stages of word learning. Children at the selective-cue stage should be cued to attend to print information to build their awareness and knowledge of letter-sound relationships. Those at the spelling-sound stage should be cued to fully analyze the constituent letters and orthographic patterns in words. This is not to suggest that there is no place for syntactic and semantic cues in word-recognition instruction. Rather, such cues should follow students' initial print-driven approximations (Juel, 1991). Once children have achieved automaticity of word recognition, they are beyond the stage at which they can benefit from word-level cues. Cues should address other areas of the reading process, unless a specific word-level need arises.

Second, it is important to craft cues that reflect contemporary understandings of phonics instruction. Two teachers whose practice is shared in this discussion encouraged children to use phonic rules to recognize words. I agree with Cunningham and Allington (2003) and Stahl (2002); we should not emphasize the use of phonic rules with students. As Stahl (2002) noted, Theodore Clymer found that "only 45% of the commonly taught phonics rules worked as much as 75% of the time" (p. 65). The guidelines for exemplary phonics instruction Stahl offered in this article can guide the construction of phonic cues. Cues should be "clear and direct," should focus on "reading words, not learning rules," may "include onsets and rimes," and should develop "independent word recognition strategies, focusing attention on the internal structure of words" (Stahl, 2002, pp. 63–66).

Third, it is important to consider the language we use to convey our assistance. That is, the language of phonics and orthography need not necessarily be the language of phonics and orthographic instruction. It is critical that children develop facility with orthographic patterns and phonic elements (e.g., *ake*, *sh*, *oi*). It is much less important that they become facile with the terms associated with these patterns and elements (i.e., rime, digraph, diphthong). This is not to say discipline-specific language should not be used, merely that we should be mindful of its use. The teachers whose practice is represented in this article used specific phonic terms with students. The terms they used were consistent with their knowledge and philosophies, and they were terms they had taught and reinforced throughout the year. Other teachers may choose different terms or choose not to use specific terms at all.

Coaching across the reading process. The first- and second-grade teachers in this article coached word recognition. This is not surprising; learning to recognize words is extremely important for first- and second-grade readers. However, coaching can and should be applied to other reading processes in the early primary years as well as in later years. Cunningham and Allington (2003) presented one instructional format designed specifically to support coaching across the reading process. They recommended coaching groups—small, flexible groups with whom the teacher meets for 10–15 minutes a few times a week to coach word-recognition and comprehension strategies per students' changing needs. In the groups, students of somewhat varied abilities are coached and learn to coach themselves and others. They then apply their knowledge of coaching in other instructional contexts. These groups seem an ideal way to make coaching a part of an instructional program.

Learning to coach. It is of note that the teachers whose practice is shared in this article reported learning to coach while engaged in professional development efforts in early reading intervention. The Early Intervention in Reading (EIR) training in which Mr. Turner, Mrs. Wilson, and Mrs. Green participated involved an initial half-day workshop, monthly meetings in which they analyzed their

videotaped practice, and regular classroom visits by mentors. The Right Start training in which Mrs. Fry participated involved an initial two-day workshop, monthly meetings in which participants analyzed videotapes of their practice, and ongoing observation and support by project staff (Hiebert & Taylor, 2000). A primary focus of these efforts was the development of a strategic stance toward reading. Coaching reflects this stance. Teachers learned to support students on a moment-to-moment basis as they applied strategic knowledge while reading connected text. The teachers completed this professional development within one (Mrs. Wilson, Mr. Turner, Mrs. Green) and five (Mrs. Fry) years of the inquiry from which this discussion is drawn.

Because coaching is such an effective technique, it would make sense to include it in university reading methods courses. This is likely happening in some teacher education programs, particularly in light of recent discussions of the importance of scaffolding students' learning (Pressley et al., 2001; Taylor et al., 2000) and of the provision of a viable model for engaging in such instruction (Cunningham & Allington, 2003). I envision instruction in which preservice teachers in methods courses invoke, build, and make explicit their understanding of our graphophonic system and English orthography, use this understanding to craft cues for words with which their students struggle, and apply these cues as they read one-on-one with students. As in the EIR and Right Start intervention efforts, ongoing analysis and discussion of taped practice are critical to development.

Coaching Is a Powerful Technique

The teachers in this article are highly skilled educators. Close examination of their interactions with children led me to believe three factors contributed to their coaching effectiveness. First, the teachers had considerable explicit knowledge of phonics and English orthography. They understood the relationships between graphemes and phonemes and knew how English words are put together. Second, they maintained a conscious awareness of students' instructional histories. They kept anecdotal records of what they had taught and whom they had taught, and they referred to these records to plan instruction. Third, the teachers were aware of students' individual strengths and weaknesses. When coaching, they drew on their knowledge of phonics, orthography, instructional history, and students' abilities in a coordinated manner to provide tailored, moment-to-moment cues that helped students to identify and apply their knowledge of word-recognition strategies as they read. Strickland (2002) stated that young readers need to view learning to read as "a problem-solving activit[y] that they are increasingly equipped to handle on their own" (p. 80). Coaching is a powerful technique that supports young readers as they problem solve during meaningful reading experiences and develop reading independence.

REFERENCES

Brabham, E.G., & Villaume, S.K. (2002). Leveled text: The good news and the bad news. *The Reading Teacher, 55,* 438–441.

Clark, K.F. (2000). Instructional scaffolding in reading: A case study of four primary grade teachers. *Dissertation Abstracts International, 61,* 06A.

Clay, M.M. (1991). *Becoming literate: The construction of inner control.* Auckland, New Zealand: Heinemann.

Clay, M.M. (2001). *Change over time in children's literacy development.* Portsmouth, NH: Heinemann.

Cunningham, P.M., & Allington, R.L. (2003). *Classrooms that work: They can all read and write.* Boston: Allyn & Bacon.

Ehri, L.C. (1991). Development of the ability to read words. In R. Barr, M.L. Kamil, P.B. Mosenthal, & P.D. Pearson (Eds.), *Handbook of reading research* (Vol. 2, pp. 383–417). Mahwah, NJ: Erlbaum.

Glaser, B.G., & Strauss, A.L. (1967). *The discovery of grounded theory: Strategies for qualitative research.* New York: Aldine Press.

Graves, M.F., Juel, C., & Graves, B.B. (2001). *Teaching reading in the 21st century.* Boston: Allyn & Bacon.

Hiebert, E.H., & Taylor, B.M. (2000). Beginning reading instruction: Research on early interventions. In M.L. Kamil, P.B. Mosenthal, P.D. Pearson, & R. Barr (Eds.), *Handbook of reading research* (Vol. 3, pp. 455–482). Mahwah, NJ: Erlbaum.

Juel, C. (1991). Beginning reading. In R. Barr, M.L. Kamil, P.B. Mosenthal, & P.D. Pearson (Eds.), *Handbook of reading research* (Vol. 2, pp. 759–788). Mahwah, NJ: Erlbaum.

Lipson, M.Y., & Wixson, K.K. (2003). *Assessment & instruction of reading and writing difficulty: An interactive approach.* Boston: Allyn & Bacon.

Pressley, M. (1998). *Reading instruction that works: The case for balanced teaching.* New York: Guilford.

Pressley, M., Wharton-McDonald, R., Allington, R., Block, C.C., Morrow, L., Tracey, D., et al. (2001). A study of effective first-grade literacy instruction. *Scientific Studies of Reading, 5*(1), 35–58.

Rodgers, E.M. (2000). Language matters: When is a scaffold really a scaffold? In T.S. Shanahan & F.V. Rodriguez-Brown (Eds.), *49th yearbook of the National Reading Conference* (pp. 8–90). Chicago: National Reading Conference.

Stahl, S.A. (2002). Saying the "p" word: Nine guidelines for exemplary phonics instruction. In International Reading Association (Ed.), *Evidence-based reading instruction: Putting the National Reading Panel report into practice* (pp. 61–68). Newark, DE: International Reading Association.

Strickland, D.S. (2002). The importance of effective early intervention. In A.E. Farstrup & S.J. Samuels (Eds.), *What research has to say about reading instruction* (pp. 69–86). Newark, DE: International Reading Association.

Taylor, B.M., Pearson, P.D., Clark, K.F., & Walpole, S. (2000). Effective schools and accomplished teachers: Lessons about primary-grade reading instruction in low-income schools. *Elementary School Journal, 101*(2), 121–165.

van den Broek, P., & Kremer, K.E. (2000). The mind in action: What it means to comprehend during reading. In B.M. Taylor, M.F. Graves, & P. van den Broek (Eds.), *Reading for meaning: Fostering comprehension in the middle grades* (pp. 1–31). New York: Teachers College Press.

CHILDREN'S BOOKS CITED

Aliki. (1993). *My visit to the aquarium.* New York: HarperCollins.

Brenner, B. (1989). *The color wizard.* New York: Bantam.

Dodds, D.A. (1996). *Where does everybody go?* St. Charles, IL: Houghton Mifflin.

Dubowski, C.E. (1988). *Cave boy.* New York: Random House.

Krauss, R. (1945). *The carrot seed.* New York: HarperCollins.

Marshall, J. (1987). *Red Riding Hood.* New York: Dial.

Oppenheim, J. (1989). *"Not now!" said the cow.* New York: Bantam.

Young, E. (1989). *Lon Po Po: A Red-Riding Hood story from China.* New York: Penguin Putnam.

Reading Comprehension

Reading is responding. The response may
be at the surface level of "calling" the word.
It may be at the somewhat deeper level of
understanding the explicit meaning of
sentence, paragraph or passage. Sometimes
reading may be at a third level. It may
involve going beyond the facts to the
discovery of new and personal meanings. It
may be a stimulus to images, memories,
identification or fresh and creative thoughts.

—DAVID H. RUSSELL (1958, p. 3)

Those [literacy educators] who are
helping to push the new era that is on
its way are urging vigorously that we
couple thought and reading, that we
go far beyond the stage of picking up
what the book says and use our higher
mental processes in thinking about
what it says.

—NILA BANTON SMITH (1969, p. 249)

Comprehension strategies can be
important to a reader because they
have the potential to provide access
to knowledge that is removed from
personal experience.

—KATHERINE A. DOUGHERTY STAHL
(2004, p. 598)

Issues and Innovations in Literacy Education: Readings From The Reading Teacher, edited by Richard D. Robinson. © 2006 by the International Reading Association.

The foundation of all successful reading is effective comprehension of what is being read. On the surface, what may seem to be a relatively easy concept is in reality a very difficult component of literacy education. There are many questions in the study of comprehension that remain unanswered today. Issues related to the effective teaching of understanding, as well as its accurate assessment, currently remain unresolved.

Throughout the long history of *The Reading Teacher*, there has been a continual thread relating to the various aspects of reading comprehension. Leading reading authorities such as William S. Gray, Helen Robinson, and David Russell, as well as countless classroom teachers, have provided a wide variety of articles on both theory and practice related to comprehension. This section provides only a sampling of the rich legacy on the topic of reading understanding from past issues of *The Reading Teacher*.

As you read the following articles on reading comprehension that span 50 years, note the common themes that appear, such as the basic nature of understanding, the role of the teacher in comprehension instruction, and various related teaching techniques.

Section Readings

Section Three opens with an article by Helen M. Robinson, who was a national leader in the field of literacy education for many years, during which time she authored many articles in *The Reading Teacher*. Consider the discussion of what constitutes effective comprehension and how this fundamental aspect of literacy develops over time. This relatively short article, published in 1954, was certainly relevant to teachers then, as well as for today's literacy instruction.

The second article in this section was written for the classroom teacher, illustrating common problems faced daily in the teaching of literacy comprehension. Emphasis is placed on the importance of higher levels of understanding as opposed to what author Helen J. Caskey identifies as "passive reading." Throughout this article, the role of the classroom teacher is stressed as critical in the successful teaching of effective comprehension strategies.

Dixie Lee Spiegel continues the discussion of comprehension as being much more than just the "teaching of skills." Her article is one of the early discussions of encouraging the reader to become, in the author's words, "a risk-taker" in terms of understanding of text. Importantly, there is the emphasis on readers "monitoring their own responses" or, in more modern terms, using metacomprehension in their reading.

The discussion continues with an article by Linda K. Crafton addressing a number of specific comprehension issues for classroom instruction. As the author notes, "comprehension is not static and...'out of sight' does not necessarily mean 'out of mind' when it comes to print." A critical aspect of this discussion is that understanding is a dynamic active process that for readers takes place at all stages of effective instruction. The key implication for classroom teachers is to consider carefully comprehension strategies that are most appropriate for each individual reader throughout the entire reading experience. It is of great importance to extend these activities beyond the classroom setting into student lives.

Next is an article by P. David Pearson, who has a long and distinguished career as a literacy educator. His writing has been extensive, including significant articles and books on a wide range of topics of interest to both reading researchers as well as classroom practitioners. Pearson's article is considered one of the key discussions of comprehension. He provides an excellent overview of the history of the teaching of comprehension and then reflects on how these experiences have shaped current attitudes and classroom teaching experiences. Particular strengths of his discussion are the implications of this work in reading comprehension and for the classroom teacher.

Finally, the article by Laura S. Pardo is an excellent summary of the latest thinking related to various aspects of comprehension. Many of the themes present in the previous articles in this section are stressed again here as being of particular importance in the understanding process. These include the various roles of the classroom teacher in helping students with the comprehension process, the transaction between reader and text, and the importance of the reader monitoring his or her own understanding.

REFERENCES

Russell, D.H. (1958). Personal values in reading. *The Reading Teacher*, 12(1), 3–9.
Smith, N.B. (1969). The many faces of reading comprehension. *The Reading Teacher*, 23(3), 249–259, 291.
Stahl, K.A.D. (2004). Proof, practice, and promise: Comprehension strategy instruction in the primary grades. *The Reading Teacher*, 57(7), 598–609.

For Further Reading on Reading Comprehension

The articles listed here have been included because they reflect some of the best material on this topic from past issues of *The Reading Teacher*. These references will help to broaden your understanding of the role of reading comprehension.

Russell, D.H. (1951). The mature reader. *Bulletin*, IV(2), 1, 13.
Defines the significant characteristics of the mature reader with emphasis on the role of effective comprehension in the literacy process.

McCullough, C.M. (1958). Context aids in reading. *The Reading Teacher*, 11(4), 225–229.
Describes the role of context clues and how they are important in the effective development of comprehension from kindergarten through all grades.

Niles, O.S. (1963). Comprehension skills. *The Reading Teacher*, 17(1), 2–7.
Stresses the importance of comprehension as the major component of successful reading at all levels of literacy instruction.

Smith, N.B. (1969). The many faces of reading comprehension. *The Reading Teacher*, 23(3), 249–259, 291.
Presents a detailed discussion of the principle components of comprehension with particular emphasis on the thinking process as a critical aspect of understanding.

Singer, H. (1978). Active comprehension: From answering to asking questions. *The Reading Teacher*, 31(8), 901–908.
Describes the importance for readers to take active leadership in the development of effective questions as they read various types of text material.

Villaume, S.K., & Brabham, E.G. (2003). Comprehension instruction: Beyond strategies. *The Reading Teacher*, 55(7), 672–675.

Describes the role of effective comprehension strategies in relation to explicit and systematic instruction.

Stahl, K.A.D. (2004). Proof, practice, and promise: Comprehension strategy instruction in the primary grades. *The Reading Teacher*, 57(7), 598–609.

Discusses the most current research on reading comprehension and provides specific teaching strategies based on this information.

What Research Says to the Teacher of Reading

Helen M. Robinson

COMPREHENSION

It seems trite to state that the end result of all reading is comprehension. Yet isolated examples reveal that some teachers become so involved in the "means to the end", that they lose sight of the final goal. Assuming that we may all agree that comprehension is essential, we may consider several crucial questions. What is the nature of the process of comprehension? What are its components? How and when does this reading skill develop? What means do we have for evaluating comprehension?

The remainder of this paper will consider briefly each of the questions listed above.

The Nature of Comprehension

The dictionary defines comprehension as the ability to grasp meaning or to understand. Durrell[1] suggests that it is the ability to translate printed symbols into images, ideas, emotions, plans, and action. Others might add the ability to evaluate for accuracy and bias.

Research in this area has been limited by inadequate techniques to explore the process. As early as 1917, Thorndike[2] concluded that reasoning was im-portant to understanding the printed page. Subsequent research has agreed that reasoning is essential. It has also suggested that comprehension requires active participation on the part of the reader. Furthermore, comprehension is enhanced by the fund of information and experience which the reader brings to the printed page.

A number of peripheral studies have explored isolated factors which influence comprehension. For example, intelligence, attitude, interest, and purpose have been shown to be related, but no single factor describes the process *per se*.

Some recent attempts to explore the process of comprehension have used retrospective verbalization. An example is the study by Piekarz[3] who recorded the oral responses of superior Grade VI pupils as they reread, and answered questions about, a selection. The analysis of the transcribed recordings afforded some new insights, and suggested that this technique offers promise for further studies into the nature of comprehension. It is quite likely that techniques for research in this area will be expanded rapidly in the near future.

The Components of Comprehension

Some research has produced evidence that reading comprehension is a unitary or single trait which does

---

[1]Donald D. Durrell, *Reading in the Elementary School*, p. 194, The Forty-Eighth Yearbook, Part II, National Society for the Study of Education. Chicago: University of Chicago Press, 1949.

[2]Edward L. Thorndike, "Reading as Reasoning: A Study of Mistakes in Paragraph Reading," *Journal of Educational Psychology*, VIII, (June, 1919), 323–32.

[3]Josephine A. Piekarz, "Individual Differences in Interpretive Responses in Reading," Unpublished Doctor's dissertation, University of Chicago, 1954.

Reprinted from *The Reading Teacher*, 8(2), pp. 116–118. © 1954 by the International Reading Association.

not lend itself to separation. Other studies, such as that of Davis[4], identify as many as nine separate components. Briefly, they were: word knowledge (ability to recognize words and know their meanings); reasoning in reading; understanding the writer's explicit statements; ability to identify the writer's intent, purpose, and point of view; ability to select word meanings from context; the grasp of detailed statements; following the organization of a passage; knowledge of literary devices and techniques; and the ability to select the main thought of a passage. Davis identified this array of abilities through the use of a statistical device called factor analysis. Many others have used the same technique, often based on the results of different tests, and have identified fewer factors. It is significant that the greatest number of the factor studies have been done at the college level. Here the process of comprehension should be more highly developed so that it may appear to be a single ability. In the earlier stages, where skills are maturing, it may be possible to identify separate components.

While the components of comprehension are being studied further, teachers can successfully develop many aspects of comprehension through direct instruction.

How and When Comprehension Develops

Studies of reading readiness reveal that children comprehend spoken language before they begin to read. In the initial stages of learning to read, the teacher who places emphasis on reading as a means of getting ideas and information lays a solid foundation for growth in this area. Proficiency in word recognition which is gained in the early school years enables the pupil to give increased attention to meaning. A thoughtful attitude toward reading may be developed from experiences (either real or vicarious), through oral discussions, and by setting the purpose. One means is to use carefully formulated questions. Holmes[5] found that students comprehended more, and remembered better what was read when guiding questions were given as a part of the assignment.

In general, children develop skill in answering the kinds of questions posed. Therefore, the teacher who wishes to insure growth in all aspects of comprehension should not rely on factual questions alone. Questions answered directly in the text are easy to formulate and to score, but those calling for the main idea, conclusions, implications and evaluation, must also be used.

Research has also revealed that children do not reach maturity in comprehension of what is read by the end of the elementary school. Studies show clearly that with carefully planned instruction, students develop increased power of comprehension throughout the secondary school, and during the early college years. The implication is that comprehension begins before school entrance and that every teacher is responsible for building systematically upon the foundation.

Furthermore, surveys of achievement reveal a wide range in comprehension at any given level in school. The individual differences in this area are as great as in any academic or personal ability. This finding implies that the teacher must be prepared to begin where each student is in comprehension and direct his growth in harmony with his potentiality. Teachers may anticipate individual differences among students in rate of growth, and in the final level of attainment.

Evaluating Comprehension

Comprehension may be evaluated by the answers to questions, by solving problems, by oral discussions, or in many instances by less direct means. Many teachers have come to depend upon the results of standardized tests. Careful appraisal of the questions reveal that factual information is strongly emphasized. An analysis of the standardized read-

---

[4]Frederick B. Davis, "Fundamental Factors of Comprehension in Reading", *Psychometrika*, IX, (September, 1944), 185–97.

[5]Eleanor Holmes, "Reading Guided by Questions versus Careful Reading and Rereading Without Questions", *School Review*, XXXIX, (May, 1931), 361–71.

ing tests commonly used in the elementary schools was made by Traxler.[6] He concluded that the skills appearing most frequently in the tests represent a good starting point in analysis of interpretation. The implication is clear that until standardized tests include the broader and more complex comprehension skills, elementary teachers must depend on less formal techniques of evaluation. Even at the secondary and college levels, care must be exercised in selecting a test which will evaluate the many facets of comprehension.

One of the difficulties in this area of evaluation is the inconclusive evidence concerning the components of comprehension, discussed earlier in this paper. While further explorations and refinements are being made, teachers should use standardized tests with full regard for their values and limitations. In addition, the ability of each individual to comprehend may be constantly appraised as he carries on his usual activities.

Concluding Statement

The complexity of our society demands, as never before, that readers understand the printed page. They must comprehend the literal meaning, but must also be able to read between the lines, derive inferences, evaluate, accept and reject ideas presented, and use the information gained to improve personal and social affairs. The need is urgent for greater insights into many aspects of comprehension of the printed page, but teachers, who are on the frontier of education, must continue to accept the challenge to use all that is now known in this area.

---

[6]Arthur E. Traxler, "Critical Survey of Tests for Identifying Difficulties in Interpreting What is Read" in *Promoting Growth toward Maturity in Interpreting What is Read*, William S. Gray, Editor, p. 195–200. Supplementary Monographs, No. 74. Chicago: University of Chicago Press, 1951.

Guidelines for Teaching Comprehension

Helen J. Caskey

The importance of developing pupils' abilities in reading comprehension is not questioned. There may well be uncertainties about the contributions of this or that approach to beginning reading, or differences of opinion among those who support programmed texts, teaching machines, individualized reading, or ability grouping, early or delayed instruction. Few persons question that the ultimate objective of teaching a child to read is to make him able to read with maximum power to comprehend what the writer intended to have understood by his readers.

Teachers are generally aware that comprehending a given passage, or indeed an entire book, can be on different levels. At a simpler level, the reader is expected to recall the facts given in the selection he has read, and to make a decently accurate summary of the gist of the passage. He is expected to tell how many boys in the troop went on the overnight hike, and to tell in his own words what happened after they reached their destination. This level of comprehension has sometimes been referred to as passive understanding (Covington, 1967). At another level reading comprehension which involves making evaluative judgments, making inferences about what is not directly stated in the selection, and drawing conclusions based upon the information given has been referred to as critical reading or active reading, or creative reading, or more simply as a higher level of comprehension skill. As far as teachers are concerned, the nomenclature used it not of great importance. Whether these aspects of comprehension are termed critical, active, or creative, some kind of reading activity exists which goes beyond both the grasp of literal meaning of the passage and the recall of specific details. Of course, the grasp of the central idea and the clear understanding of basic details is essential; no analytical or evaluative procedures by the reader are possible without such basic understanding. The important consideration is to decide whether or not more than passive understanding is to be developed, and how the development of such higher levels of understanding is to be brought about. The choice is an important one and is based upon the values held concerning reading, and concerning education of the young.

In the present state of society the choice to develop the highest possible level of comprehension seems inescapable. Problems of stunning magnitude press for effective solutions if man is to survive, let alone prevail, and a good deal of the information needed on which to base decisions is found in print. Thus the passive reader who is limited to simple recall of detail, or even the recognition of the main content of a message is not able to cope with the reading tasks he is likely to face. The good reader, perhaps even more in the future than at present, will be the one who is able to hold a sort of "summit meeting" with the writer, engaging in an alert dialogue as he encounters an author through the printed page.

Achieving Higher Levels of Comprehension

It is one thing, of course, to indicate an ideal outcome for teaching, and another thing to accomplish

Reprinted from *The Reading Teacher*, 23(7), pp. 649–654, 669. © 1970 by the International Reading Association.

it. Two questions particularly come to mind. First, are the higher levels of comprehension in reading teachable? Does such comprehension depend almost completely upon the reader's background of experience (about which the teacher can do some things, but certainly not all things), or the intellectual ability of the learner (about which the teacher can do considerably less). For children limited in these areas, must teaching of necessity be limited largely to developing a more passive kind of reading? Secondly, if higher levels of comprehension are thought to be desirable, what factors in the reading situation should be of chief concern to the teachers? Reduced to its simplest terms, the problem of improving comprehension involves three interrelated factors: the pupil himself, the items he reads, and the kind of instruction in reading which he receives. The teacher in any subject area, as well as the teacher of reading, is vitally concerned with all three of these if power in comprehending is to be enhanced.

With respect to the pupil himself, it is clear that there are some fundamental skills that are basic to his effective comprehension. These include sufficient skill to handle word recognition problems, experiences which he can relate to meanings of words in their present context, and a meaning vocabulary sufficiently accurate and extensive to enable him to cope with his reading materials. Further, he is helped by having a disposition to seek additional information when he feels uncertain as to the accuracy of his present interpretations. These factors influencing power of comprehension are evident both in research and in everyday teaching experience.

There is, however, some uncertainty respecting the relationship of mental abilities and higher levels of comprehension. A high level of comprehension involves thinking activities that are more complex than those required in passive reading. Assume that you as a reader are at some time asked to respond to such questions as: "Why do you think the author repeated the word *green* in this description of the fields and mountains?" or, "If the person in this story of colonial times were living today, how do you think he would earn his living?" or, "How do you think Jim felt when Mr. Jones discovered the missing boat?" or, "What did Launcelot mean when he said, 'Diamond me no diamonds'?" In responding you are evidently expected to go beyond what is specifically given in the selection in order to project the ideas into a different setting, to relate what is said there to what you already know, or what you have felt yourself in a similar circumstance. You are asked to infer why a deliberate choice of words was made, and are expected to expand or to translate a cryptic remark into language which reveals the same idea, put into idioms equally revealing, but in a currently conversational tone. Perhaps Launcelot in a baseball uniform, and putting on a catcher's mitt instead of an azure and silver shield might well have said, "Don't give me any of that stuff!"

It is possible that many teachers feel that questions like these may be suggested only for the most able pupils, since they obviously require ability to take a kind of forward mental leap, and to perceive relationships that are far from obvious. Should those of us who teach the "average" or the "below average" pupils in any age group be discouraged from making efforts to help these children to comprehend in this more complex set of situations?

Fortunately, there is evidence that achievement in higher level comprehension skills is not limited to gifted pupils only. The nature of the stimulation and guidance which has been received by the pupil appears to be more important. In the teaching of critical reading at the elementary level Wolf, *et al.* (1968) noted, for example, the importance of the teacher in "determining the depth of pupils' thinking." In comparing the responses of two subgroups of good and poor readers in a twelfth grade to questions posed by the investigator, Smith (1967) found that subjects whose intelligence quotients were within approximately the same range differed in success in reading, and that difference appeared to be more closely related to reading achievement than to the mental ability of the students. Covington (1967) reported that a group of pupils in grade five with lower I.Q. scores (below 100) was not specifically handicapped in what was termed "creative understanding." The conclusion drawn was that: "the fact that these same low I.Q. children were reading on the average almost two years below grade level strongly suggests that students can benefit from such instruction (in creative understanding) in reading proficiency, provided, of course, that the reading level of the materials is adjusted accordingly."

Thus it appears that if the pupil has skills adequate for dealing with the material at his level, a higher level of comprehension is dependent not so much upon intellectual ability as it is upon the kind of instructional assistance that is given him.

Guiding Pupils' Reading

What kinds of instruction and guidance are most likely to be helpful in bringing about higher levels of comprehension? The first step is to note the range of skills involved in comprehending. Fortunately, information on this point is readily available; lists of comprehension skills exist in abundance, as every teacher who has used a workbook, looked into a teacher's manual for a reading series, or consulted a book on the teaching of reading at any level will quickly tell you. A helpful recent analysis of eight comprehension skills by Davis (1968) showed two significant and independent abilities: "memory of word meanings," and "drawing inferences about the content of material read." While no aspect of reading skill necessary to the best development of the reader may be neglected, here are two particular reading abilities in which specific help given the pupil will be likely to yield results in development of comprehension at higher levels.

Acquiring a broad and accurate vocabulary, one rich in depth and range of meanings is a life-time job. The language grows, new terms are added and meanings shift, or become current in a new context. Yesterday *Medicare* came into the language and the words to be used wherever possible were *charisma* and *relevant*. Tomorrow—who knows what words will be in a newly minted, or repolished, verbal currency? The speaker and listener, the writer and reader, will have to know them and to use them in their new settings.

Field trips call attention to new words, and develop concepts, particularly if both planning for the

experience and subsequent discussion are assured. Such experiences give pupils at all levels a chance to learn new terms and to use them with precision and accuracy. Such first hand experience can also lend vitality to the "book bait" that teachers have used for a long time: "You were interested in the fossils we saw yesterday...here are some books you might like to read that tell a good bit more about fossils."

Self-help devices also help the learner to acquire greater precision in using words. Many teachers and pupils develop class word lists to help with words they are likely to need in their writing at a given time. A pupil's own word list is also useful. Furthermore, wide reading has a great deal to offer in this area. The reader finds many words which have recently been introduced to him, and meanings are more likely to be retained than would be the case with one or two exposures. Also, words are used in instruction and in general conversation for the express purpose of adding to the pupils' stock of word meanings. The youngster who hears quite frequently such transitional phrases as "on the other hand," "on the contrary," "in addition to," especially if attention is called to them specifically, finds that he can use them as aids in structuring his own ideas in speaking or in writing.

Word meanings, important as they are in developing higher levels of comprehension that go beyond remembering and restating factual details of the content, need to be supplemented by additional learnings. What do teachers consider important respecting levels of thinking and reading in elementary and secondary classroom? Guszak (1967) examined nearly two thousand questions asked by a dozen teachers in grades four, five, and six. Over one-half of the questions asked required the pupils to recall some specific detail mentioned in the selection. This proportion may not reflect the situation in classrooms familiar to the reader, but it tallies pretty closely with the candid evaluations of many teachers with whom the writer has worked during recent years.

Since pupils master early the art of doing what they think teachers are going to ask them to do in class, or more particularly on written examinations, it appears that many of them stand a good chance of getting thorough preparation in avoiding any kind of thinking that would lead to habits of judging, evaluating, or drawing inferences or conclusions from their reading. The secondary pupils are also likely to be in the same condition. Smith (1967) comments that: "This study showed that the teachers' questions and examinations are important determinants of the manner in which students read. It further pointed out that the preponderance of questions asked by teachers were those requiring students to recall details or factual information."

It is not too helpful to say merely "Don't ask so many questions requiring the recall of specific details." A more positive approach is called for. If pupils are to increase their power in making inferences, they must have guided practice in doing so.

It is especially useful to think about the kinds of assignments that are made in any subject area involving reading. They can be managed so as to set up situations that require judging, evaluating and making inferences. For example, pupils may be asked to respond to this situation: "Many people who have read this short story consider the author a master in choosing and describing incidents which add, bit by bit, to our understanding of the character. Do you agree? Can you give some examples of how the author proceeds to make us better understand the persons in the story?" Or another: "Is there any indication in this story as to what season of the year it is? Does the time of year make any particular difference in the story? Why do you think so?"

A social studies class is challenged to discover what is involved in the statement "The frontier had ceased to be a factor in American life." A science class may try to describe a plan for a simple, workable, and easily visible demonstration of convection.

Another fruitful area for development of thinking is in guided classroom discussion, or in individual conferences that are a planned part of instruction. A good "first step" may be to seek a cure for the "right answer syndrome"—the hardened conviction that any question must have a quite visible answer directly stated in the text. There are two reasons why such a fixed idea needs to be overcome.

First, reliance upon questions of such factual nature establishes the habit of the teacher's preparing evaluations which rely solely upon easily verifiable questions. Such items can be undeniably right or wrong, with no possibility of haggling argument, a thing to be dreaded as papers are returned to their writers. Admittedly, it is difficult to phrase questions which require judgment, evaluation, and inference, and still avoid ambiguities.

In the second place, pupils thoroughly conditioned to responding with an easily verifiable "right answer" are likely to be afraid to make any bolder attempts to speculate, to inquire, to test out the possibilities of understandings that go beyond involvement in the literal sense meaning. The final results of such conditioning appear in college students who complain bitterly that they "don't make the grades" because their responses do not exactly agree with those expected by their instructors.

Furthermore, the learner can acquire an unfortunate habit of needing to lean on the teacher's question. "Don't you think the boy felt lonely?" or, "Look again; that's not what the story tells us." There is not very much to be done in situations like this other than to guess as quickly as possible the response that will meet with approval.

A possibility for the more fruitful guidance of development in reading comprehension is in the use of a question that widens the range of possible response. "Did Jim feel different, in some way, at the end of the story?" may induce some pupils to think whether there was or was not a difference. Once this small response is unearthed another probing must follows. "How different?" "Why?" Good enough, but perhaps a better tool would be a question that tickles the imagination, as well as calls for recall of a set of related circumstances. "Suppose you were the illustrator for this story. What expression would you show on Jim's face as the story ends?" The "Why," of course, follows as a most important adjunct. Hopefully, the net result of such stimulation is to involve all children in the group in the thinking that must accompany any reasoned responses. There is a strong temptation, however, to feel that the situation will be challenging to Bob and Sue and

Harry, but that it is not really right for poor Jane and Willard. They, it is feared, will be left out entirely as unequal to the task of what is hoped to be some fairly high-powered thinking. These pupils who are "slower" than others can also be a part of the thinking and responding. Any experience background possessed by any in the group can also be Jane's or Willard's if they share the same conversations and discussions, if they see the same pictures, and talk about them, or if they manipulate the same tools, or hold the same objects in hand.

All our concern for the individual and his guidance will be of little help if materials read are not chosen wisely and carefully. The level of difficulty of a given reading selection can be lowered markedly, while the level of thinking about it can be genuinely evaluative and interpretive. Beginners can cope with such problems as "Does this story have too many persons in it to make a good dramatization for our small group?" "Would this be a good story to read aloud? Do you think other children would enjoy hearing the parts we think are especially funny?" Older pupils can deal with such questions as: "Is the author accurate and realistic in describing a tense moment in the bas-

ketball game?" "How does the author foreshadow the tragic ending of the play?" Any of these questions can be considered about relatively short and easy selections and in all of them the implicit next item is "Why?" The objective is not only to respond in some fashion. To be "involved" is commendable, but to sort out reasons, to note relationships, to predict consequences and to substantiate judgments with a statement of the reasons why they are held is indeed to grow in the acts of reading and thinking.

REFERENCES

Covington, M.V. Some experimental evidence on teaching for creative understanding. *The Reading Teacher*, 1967, *20*, 390–96.

Davis, F.B. Research in comprehension in reading. *Reading Research Quarterly*, 1968, 499–543.

Guszak, F.J. Teacher questioning and reading. *The Reading Teacher*, 1967, *21*, 227–234.

Smith, Helen K. The responses of good and poor readers when asked to read for different purposes. *Reading Research Quarterly*, 1967, 53–83.

Wolf, Willavene, King, Martha L., and Huck, Charlotte. Teaching critical reading to elementary school children. *Reading Research Quarterly*, 1968, 495.

Meaning-Seeking Strategies for the Beginning Reader

Dixie Lee Spiegel

uch attention is given to the teaching of skills to beginning and intermediate level readers. However, children must also develop a set of reading strategies that are just as important as specific reading skills. These strategies both cause and reflect the child's perception of what reading is and of his or her own role in the reading process.

Does the child see reading as a mystical process, so complex that he or she has no hope of mastering it? As one child expressed this feeling to me recently, "Why should I guess at the word? I'll just get it wrong." Is reading perceived as merely saying the words and not as communication that must be meaningful? Does the child see himself or herself as a passive decoder who makes one guess at a word and then races on? Too often beginning readers do have misperceptions such as these, and the teacher must guard against these distorted notions.

Goodman (1967, 1976) has suggested a set of strategies that fluent readers follow. The following set of strategies for the beginning reader may help prepare a child to become an interactive, fluent reader.

Perhaps the most basic strategy that the teacher of reading must develop in children is one of risk-taking. Risk-taking is rooted in the reader's self-confidence. Beginning readers must realize that reading is not an arbitrary or esoteric system of squiggles on a page. They must believe that they *can* learn to deal with words and ideas in print. Too often children have become overwhelmed by having

made errors and have lost their initial belief that they can learn to read.

Biemiller's research (1970) supports this contention. In analyzing the oral reading errors of first graders, Biemiller found that these errors could be categorized into three successive stages. In the first phase, the beginning readers primarily used context clues to guide their guesses. Then in the next phase, the children frequently would not even make a guess at an unknown word. In the third phase, the readers began to use both graphic and contextual restraints to aid them in word identification, and the number of non-response errors decreased.

Biemiller's study shows that the children initially approached the reading task with confidence and with a set for getting meaning. However, as they became aware of the many constraints placed upon their guesses, they became less willing to risk errors. Eventually, as the children were introduced to more and more clues to guide their guesses, they were able to overcome this hesitancy, use multiple cues to word meaning, and make intelligent guesses.

Unfortunately, too many children have difficulty escaping from the second phase. These children need a great deal of encouragement and training in order to develop the confidence to take risks, to make the educated guesses that all successful readers make.

A second important strategy for beginning readers is that of monitoring what they decode. A reader who blithely reads "Ben went to the birthday pretty," "This is the rig-hut (for *right*) answer," or "The

Reprinted from *The Reading Teacher*, 31(7), 772–776. © 1978 by the International Reading Association.

owl coaches mice and eats them" is not doing any self-monitoring and is not demanding meaning from the words. Young readers must develop the habit from the very beginning of "listening" to what they are reading and of stopping when their self-monitor has sounded the alarm for a meaningless response.

A third strategy to be encouraged is that of self-correction. When the self-monitor alarm has rung, something must be changed. Some poor readers will read "Ben went to the birthday pretty" and will realize that something is wrong, but then respond only with a bewildered expression, a pause, and a determined attack on the next sentence. Children must be taught from the beginning to use correction strategies. They must develop a set of skills that enable them to look at the words in a sentence in several different ways, gaining clues not only from sounds but also from meaning and syntax. Skill at using correction strategies will improve as the children learn more ways to identify words, but the basic concept of trying alternative strategies should be taught as soon as the children learn more than one cue to word meaning.

The development of confidence and risk-taking strategies within children can only evolve in a climate of acceptance and encouragement in which the students are rewarded for a good try. Children should be encouraged to take a risk and to make a "good guess," using all the data that are available and that they know how to use. They should receive praise for a good guess even though it is not completely accurate. For example, if a child read "I like to eat carrots" as "I like to eat cake," praise should be given for supplying a word that makes sense and follows at least some of the phonics cues. The teacher may also choose to supply the correct response in an offhand and uncritical manner. If the child read the sentence as "I like to eat cars," the teacher should remind the reader that that does not make sense.

Oral reading of material that has been well rehearsed privately or with a partner can also lead to improved self-confidence. Choral reading, in which hesitant readers are carried along by the melody of the language and of the group, can help children develop a feeling of success. Willingness to take risks at identifying words can be encouraged by oral language activities, such as completion of riddles for which the child may suggest several meaningful answers.

Tangible evidence of progress can help some children become more confident. Word banks that grow in bulk as a child learns more and more words can help the child to read with more confidence because he or she is aware that many of the words that might be met are in that word bank and are already known. Charts that reward children for progress, not perfection, may be used.

Reward Improvement

This last point needs to be emphasized. None of us attains perfection consistently, especially when learning a new task. To reward a struggling reader only for a perfect performance, either oral or written, is to break down the child's self-confidence. A mother once related the sad story to me of her eight-year-old son who had received "happy faces" from his second grade teacher for work that showed improvement, but received such rewards only for flawless work in the third grade. In reviewing the child's workbook one day the mother noted that he was drawing his own happy faces because he was never able to reach the third grade teacher's standard of excellence.

After children have gained enough confidence to risk guesses at words, they need to learn to monitor those guesses for meaning. Self-monitoring will not help readers to identify all inappropriate responses, for many of these miscues will fit semantically and syntactically into the surrounding context. But children can learn to identify responses that don't make sense. One activity that can help develop this habit is to have children identify "senseless" words in oral sentences and to suggest more appropriate responses. When a child has read a sentence that does not make sense, the teacher should repeat the sentence exactly as the child said it. The child should be asked to tell which part of the sentence didn't make sense and then to return to the printed sentence and try to correct the miscue.

To reinforce the concept that reading must make sense, children might construct meaningful sentences by choosing from three phrase pools.

Example: Make a sentence by choosing one phrase from 1, one from 2, and one from 3. Make three sentences altogether. A phrase may be used more than once.

1
The little dog
The big monster
A milk shake

2
is made with ice cream
bit the mailman
scared me

3
when he yelled.
in the arm.
and milk.

For more practice in monitoring meaning in written sentences, the students might be presented with a list of written sentences and a pool of words. The children are to replace *poison* in each sentence with a word that makes sense, choosing from the word pool. (To make the game more challenging, a different incorrect word could be provided for each sentence. In this way the students would have both to identify the meaningless word and supply the correct one.)

Example:

The poison ate my lunch.
I put on my red poison.
Dad drove his new poison.

Pool: coat, car, dog

All of the activities just described have a common goal: to encourage children to see reading as a meaning-getting experience. If children understand that reading must be meaningful, self-monitoring should follow automatically.

Once children have learned to monitor their own responses, they must have a repertoire of strategies that enable them to make different informed guesses about words. Many children stop reading as soon as they come to a troublesome word. When they do this, they are cutting themselves off from all of the context cues that come after the problem word. Children should be encouraged to use the following strategies each time they encounter an un-

known word in context or when they know they have miscalled a word.

1. First read the rest of the sentence, skipping the troublesome word. If that word is at the end of the sentence, reread the entire sentence (and even the sentence before it). In this way readers will have available to them all of the clues contained in the context.

2. Next use phonics cues to attempt to sound out the word. The word should both make sense and fit the phonics cues.

3. If neither of these strategies works, ask for help or put in a word that makes sense even though it does not match the phonics cues and go on.

Many children may need to be shown step-by-step how they should narrow down guesses to a specific right answer. Brainstorming activities may help. For example, the children could be presented orally with the sentence "I love to eat_____." They could be asked to suggest 10 words that would make sense in the blank. These words should be written on the board. Then the choice could be narrowed by identifying the initial consonant of the missing word. If several of the suggested words are still appropriate, an additional context clue could be provided.

Example:
First stimulus
I love to eat _____.

Sample responses
peanuts, cake, carrots, spinach, apples

Narrowed stimulus
I love to eat c_____.

Responses still appropriate
cake, carrots

Further narrowed stimulus
I love to eat chocolate _____.

Only appropriate response left
cake

To encourage the children to finish a sentence before guessing at an unknown word, they could be asked to fill in the blanks in written sentences in which they have to read the entire context before they can make a correct choice.

Examples:

My (nose, dog, apple) is black, brown, and white.
The (car, cookie, leaf) fell off the tree.

To provide more help in using meaning cues to narrow down answers, the children might be asked to guess answers to riddles, making more precise guesses after each line of the riddle has been given.

Example:

This is something to eat.
Sometimes you eat it on bread or sometimes on crackers.
It is brown and sticky and sometimes it has chunks in it.
You usually eat it with jelly.

When the children have identified *peanut butter*, they could be asked to tell which clues led them to the right answer.

Taking children through the steps of using different word identification strategies, with an emphasis on meaning, can help them become more able readers. Teachers need to plan activities that will help their students become confident readers who are willing to risk an educated guess at an unknown word and who have a set of strategies for noting and correcting responses that do not make sense.

REFERENCES

Biemiller, A. "The Development of the Use of Graphic and Contextual Information as Children Learn to Read." *Reading Research Quarterly*, vol. 6, no. 1 (Fall 1970), pp. 75–96.

Goodman, K. "Reading: A Psycholinguistic Guessing Game." *Theoretical Models and Processes of Reading*, 2nd ed., H. Singer and R.B. Ruddell, Eds., pp. 497–508. (Reprinted from *Journal of the Reading Specialist*, 1967.) Newark, Del.: International Reading Association, 1976.

Comprehension Before, During, and After Reading

Linda K. Crafton

As part of a graduate course called "Linguistics and Reading," my students are asked to set up an informal experiment to observe some aspect of reading or writing as they occur naturally. This summer one of my students decided to ask subjects of different ages to read orally to see if she could find a developmental pattern in their miscues. In addition, she wanted to see how well they comprehended what they read.

One of the subjects was Christina, five and a half years old. She read aloud "The Boy Who Cried Wolf" and then was asked to tell the story in her own words.

> It was a sad story. A little boy and a sheep were friends all the time. The wolf was going to eat the sheep up. He liked sheeps. And the boy said, "Please don't eat my sheep. There's more food around here."

When my student said, "Christina, what else happened?" Christina replied, "I don't know, I forgot." When asked "Do you know why the man did not come to help the boy?", she said, "No."

It appeared that Christina had missed the point of the story. However, the next day her mother reported that Christina had told her, "Did you know if you lie all the time no one will ever believe you?"

Comprehension as an Extended Process

Christina's story gives insight into the comprehension process and helps to lay a theoretical framework for considering the nature of understanding. Christina showed clearly that comprehension is not static and that out of sight does not necessarily mean out of mind when it comes to print.

Even though Christina's initial retelling would cause many of us to shake our heads and say, "She didn't understand. It must have been too difficult for her," Christina had not closed her mind to the author's message—just because the reading was finished did not mean that her comprehension was complete (or incomplete, as her retelling indicated). Christina must have been actively dealing with the story's content between the time she read it and the time she drew a conclusion about its message. Comprehension can best be described here as an extended process. Defining comprehension as an ongoing mental activity not only addresses the postreading phase but prereading and in-process behavior as well.

According to schema-theorists (Anderson, 1977, 1978; Adams and Collins, 1977; Neisser, 1976) and sociopsycholinguists (Carey, Harste, and Smith, 1980; Harste and Burke, 1978), those variables which greatly influence the meaning any reader can give to a text are brought to the reading process as part of the reader's cognitive makeup. Anderson et al. (1976) have demonstrated that readers' background experiences profoundly influence their interpretation of text. Crafton (1981) has shown the influence one text has on the reading of another when the topic is the same. Harste and Carey (1979) refer to the reader's mental setting as a way of highlighting the importance of reader

Reprinted from *The Reading Teacher*, 36(3), pp. 293–297. © 1982 by the International Reading Association.

contribution to the process. Factors which have become part of the reader and which affect mental setting include past experiences, expectations for print based on natural encounters with it, strategies developed for use during reading, and reader purpose. All of this information can be mobilized by the reader before reading starts, used during the process, and developed further after reading. Readers, then, do not naturally treat one text as an end in itself (Burke, 1980).

As current insights into the reading process allow us to consider comprehension before, during, and after, how can teachers facilitate these ongoing phases of coming to know?

Comprehension: Before Reading

Comprehension before reading begins means comprehension without print. What we begin with—the reader—is perhaps the most important part of the transaction. The information and perceptions readers bring with them to the reading process can literally make or break the experience. Those components of the reader's mental setting are all organized and available to assist comprehension. However, even at this early stage, problems can arise.

For example, if readers cannot or do not know how to mobilize what they already know about a topic so they can relate it to what they're reading, comprehension will suffer. I recently observed a young girl reading aloud a story about an Indian brave trying to kill a buffalo. While she knew much about American Indian culture, she could not deal with such items as *tipi* and *bows and arrows*. She did little predicting as she read, and her comprehension of the story, not surprisingly, was poor. A meaningful reading event was destroyed because the reader was not aware of how information in her head could make information on the page meaningful.

Students at all grade levels should be encouraged to anticipate what they are going to meet in text before they start reading. Anticipation allows them to begin with what they know and to proceed from that point, with the reading experience acting as a real learning experience. Anticipation of con-

tent should have a positive effect on further concept development due to the use of prior knowledge to help propel the reader from one state of understanding to another.

Anticipation should occur not only with text content but text organization as well. If students have read a narrative or similar informational piece before, then calling to mind that organization should facilitate comprehension of the current text.

Another prereading problem is a lack of relevant background information—knowing little about the topic. One way to develop some background knowledge is to read other materials on the same topic. Conceptually related texts (Watson, 1980; Burke, 1979) are a way to get students to prepare independently for an upcoming reading experience. Learning about a topic occurs over time as readers have multiple experiences—linguistic and alinguistic—with the concept. Reading related texts hastens schematic development through the reading process itself. Consequently, not only are readers developing background information but they are strengthening their reading capabilities as well. Related-texts libraries are a wonderful addition to the classroom. Topics can be organized in sections with varying readability levels, and students may read multiple texts on the same topic in order to acquire adequate background information.

Comprehension: During Reading

Once readers have mentally prepared for reading, how can we best facilitate comprehension during the reading process?

All readers need to develop flexible reading strategies which will allow the process to move in a fairly smooth and uninterrupted fashion. The strategies mentioned here are general comprehension techniques. More specific in-process problems call for more specific strategies.

As students are reading, encountering unknowns as all readers do, they need to understand that they can put difficult items on hold as they continue to read for meaning. If those items seem significant to what they are reading, they can go back and deal with them later. If they no longer seem important, readers should feel free to ignore them without feeling guilty. The compulsion to understand every bit of information has made control of the reading process impossible for many students. One way to help them focus on overall comprehension is to guide them as they learn to judge significant from insignificant information.

Learning to gather clues to meaning is another in-process strategy. Authors usually provide adequate information for readers to construct a working interpretation. The reader's responsibility, then, is to refine and modify interpretations as information is continually gathered and explained in light of what has come before.

Readers can be guided in this process by materials which clearly demonstrate how this part of reading works. For example, a well known concept can be replaced with a nonsense word as in the following example. (See Goodman and Burke, 1980, p. 159, for an excellent discussion of this strategy.)

The Little Green Sory

It was fall. The leaves were many colors. Some were yellow, some were red and some were bright orange. But one little sory was still green. "I wish I had bright leaves," she thought. "The sories are beautiful." Then the snow came and all the pretty leaves fell. Now the other sories were not beautiful. But one little sory was still green. She would always been green! "Now I'm glad!" thought the sory. "I'll be beautiful all winter."

(Adapted from "The Little Green Tree," Brandzel, 1961.)

An unknown concept to a reader is, after all, so much nonsense until s/he can combine prior knowledge with incoming clues to produce a state of comprehension.

Comprehension: After Reading

As students continue to think about prose after it's read, there are procedures which can further this phase of learning to help solidify the information and to make it an integral part of their cognitive network. This stage of comprehension is the one

we've tended to neglect. Even though teachers are frequently encouraged to consider postreading activity as part of reading to learn, it's often treated cursorily at best and is usually aimed at comprehension assessment rather than a way to influence students' understanding. The classroom scenario too often takes the form of students reading, teachers questioning and then moving on.

We have to ask ourselves what intellectual purpose is served when students are asked to answer questions unique to one text. It's *using* the information learned from reading that counts. What is the value of asking students questions when they could be generating their own questions, determining what else they would like to know about a topic and where and how they can find it.

A particular topic may come up as part of a basal series, but rather than being merely a lesson to be taught and completed, it becomes the foundation for student generated learning. It becomes an exciting topic to be pursued through reading, writing, reporting, and sharing.

The focus, then, should rightly be on expanding, sharing, and exchanging information as we consider comprehension as an extended process rather than a point in time. This phase of comprehension can no longer be ignored if our goal is real learning and language growth.

Extending Classroom Learning

That learning takes time is an accepted premise, but too often students are allowed only a glimpse of a topic before they are asked to consider something else. Teachers who feel satisfied that real learning has occurred when students are able to answer questions immediately after reading or when they can perform well on a test may need to reconsider the nature of learning and comprehension.

One extended strategy that encompasses the notion of comprehension as an ongoing process is a procedure Burke (1979) calls Shared Books. Books built around the same characters or whose chapters are related in theme yet can be read as independent units are used for this strategy. Examples of this type of book include Judy Blume's *Tales of a Fourth Grade Nothing* (1972) and *Superfudge* (1970), Beverly Cleary's *Ramona* series (1968, 1975, 1981), *Animals Do the Strangest Things* (Hornblow and Hornblow, 1964), and, for adults, James Herriot's (1972) *All Creatures Great and Small*. Understanding one part of these books does not depend on understanding what came before or what comes after.

Once the characters or topic has been established, individual students can be given one chapter to read independently. After reading, students come together as a group to share and to make personal contributions. No one has all the information, so there is a reason to exchange what is known.

Whole series of books can be pursued in a similar fashion with one text serving as preparation for the next. Comprehension is extended in a very real sense, and individual contribution is capitalized on at the same time. With this strategy, every student can share what s/he has learned from reading without fear of someone else coming up with a "better" interpretation.

It's this type of long-term learning setting that allows for modification and extension of ideas just beginning to take root with one reading. It may be that we are currently sacrificing synthesis of information in an effort to expedite instruction. We have to begin to value the time it takes to learn.

REFERENCES

Adams, Marilyn, and Allan Collins. *A Schema-Theoretic View of Reading*. Technical Report Number 32. Urbana, Ill: Center for the Study of Reading, University of Illinois, 1977.

Anderson, Richard. "The Notion of Schemata and the Educational Enterprise: General Discussion of the Conference." In *Schooling and the Acquisition of Knowledge*, edited by Richard Anderson, Rand Spiro, and William Montague. Hillsdale, N.J.: Lawrence Erlbaum Associates, 1977.

Anderson, Richard. "Schema-directed Processes in Language Comprehension." In *Cognitive Psychology and Instruction*, edited by Alan M. Lesgold, J. Pelligreno, S. Fokkema, and Robert Glaser. New York, N.Y.: Plenum Press, 1978.

Anderson, Richard, Ralph Reynolds, Diane Schallert and Ernest T. Goetz. *Frameworks for Comprehending Discourse*. Technical Report Number 12. Urbana, Ill: Center for the Study of Reading, University of Illinois, 1976.

Blume, Judy. *Superfudge*. New York, N.Y.: E.P. Dutton, 1970.

Blume, Judy. *Tales of a Fourth Grade Nothing*. New York, N.Y.: E.P. Dutton, 1972.

Brandzel, Elizabeth. "The Little Green Tree." In *Science Research Associates Reading Laboratory*, Lab 1a, aqua. Chicago, Ill.: Science Research Associates, 1961.

Burke, Carolyn. Unpublished reading strategy. Indiana University, Bloomington, Indiana, 1979.

Burke, Carolyn. Personal communication, 1980.

Carey, Robert, Jerome Harste, and Sharon Smith. "Contextual Constraints and Discourse Processes: A Replication." *Reading Research Quarterly*, vol. 16 (1980), pp. 201–12.

Cleary, Beverly. *Ramona Quimby, Age 8*. New York, N.Y.: William Morrow, 1981.

Cleary, Beverly. *Ramona the Brave*. New York, N.Y.: William Morrow, 1975.

Cleary, Beverly. *Ramona the Pest*. New York, N.Y.: William Morrow, 1968.

Crafton, Linda. "The Reading Process as a Transactional Learning Experience." Doctoral dissertation, Indiana University, Bloomington, 1981.

Goodman, Yetta, and Carolyn Burke. *Reading Strategies: Focus on Comprehension*. New York, N.Y.: Holt, Rinehart, and Winston, 1980.

Harste, Jerome, and Carolyn Burke. "Toward a Sociopsycholinguistic Model of Reading Comprehension." In *Viewpoints in Teaching and Learning*, vol. 45 (July 1978), pp. 9–34.

Harste, Jerome, and Robert Carey. "Comprehension as Setting." In *Monograph in Language and Reading Studies: New Perspectives in Comprehension*, edited by Jerome Harste and Robert Carey. Bloomington, Ind.: Indiana University School of Education, 1979.

Herriot, James. *All Creatures Great and Small*. Boston, Mass.: G.K. Hall, 1972.

Hornblow, Leonora, and Arther Hornblow. *Animals Do the Strangest Things*. New York, N.Y.: Random House, 1964.

Neisser, Ulrich. *Cognition and Reality*. San Francisco, Calif.: W.H. Freeman, 1976.

Watson, Dorothy. "Learning About the Reader." In *Reading Comprehension: An Instructional Videotape Series*, edited by Beverly Farr and Daryl A. Strickler. Bloomington, Ind.: Indiana University Printing, 1980.

Changing the Face of Reading Comprehension Instruction

P. David Pearson

There can be no doubt that children's reading comprehension performance concerns educators at all levels today. More than ever before, we are devoting much intellectual and emotional energy to helping students better understand the texts we require them to read in our schools. There are, I think, three reasons why comprehension has achieved this dominant position.

The first reason is that we no longer spend much energy on issues that once dominated the reading field. Reflecting upon the past 15 years in reading education, I am impressed by some significant changes in our concerns about reading instruction.

When I first entered the field, the issues of debate were:

1. What's the best way to teach beginning reading?
2. Should the alphabet be taught as a prerequisite to reading instruction?
3. How can a school build a sound individualized reading program?

Even at that time only a few of my colleagues believed that our energies and efforts should be focused on the comprehension issue. Some even thought that there was little one could do to train comprehension (believing, I suppose, that it was a matter properly left to the fates of intelligence and experience).

But the times have changed. For better or worse, at least if one regards available instructional materials as a barometer of practice, the issue of early reading seems settled, with most commercial programs teaching phonics early and intensively. Also it is hard to find commercial programs that do not teach the alphabet early on, most often in kindergarten readiness programs.

I mean neither to celebrate nor condemn the broad consensus on these issues; rather, I only make the observation that broad consensus frees psychic energy to examine other issues that may have gone unexamined previously.

Regarding individualization, two kinds of conclusions were reached: (1) that progress in reading should be monitored frequently, minutely (note the myriad of specific skills tests at the end of every unit and level in most commercial programs), and individually; (2) that individualized instruction meant offering practice materials for children to complete individually and independently. Unlike the consensus on early phonics and the alphabet, however, I detect serious discontent in the field about our current practices of individualization.

A second reason for the new interest in comprehension comes directly from concerns of practitioners. All too frequently, when meeting with administrators or committees from school districts, I have encountered this scenario. The group expresses the dilemma of their reading program's test results, which goes like this:

> You know, when we look at our primary grade results we feel good about our program. Our kids are scoring above national norms, which is more than we have a right to expect. Then we look beyond Grade 3 and what

Reprinted from *The Reading Teacher*, 38(8), pp. 724–738. © 1985 by the International Reading Association.

we find is a gradual slide in those scores, relative to national norms, all the way into high school.

This observation is usually followed by the conclusion that:

> We must be doing a good job of teaching the decoding skills that characterize the primary grades and a mediocre job of teaching the comprehension skills that characterize the intermediate grades. What can we do about it?

Data from National Assessment should reinforce this concern. The assessment (NAEP, 1981) indicates that during the 70s American education made excellent progress for 9-year-olds; however, we did not fare well in helping 13-year-olds or 17-year-olds, particularly in test items requiring inferential and interpretive comprehension.

A third factor promoting comprehension concerns stems from a renaissance in psychology. From 1920 to 1965, psychologists, wedded as they were to their behavioristic models, did not study reading. Reading was generally regarded as too complex a process to examine, given the constraints of the behavioral perspective. But the past decade has witnessed a redirection of perspective among psychologists. Indeed the relatively new field of cognitive psychology considers the reading process to be one of its most precious objects of study, encompassing as it does subprocesses like attention, perception, encoding, comprehension, memory, information storage, and retrieval.

As a result, psychology has returned to one of its rightful homes—the study of reading. Reading education has benefitted greatly from the return, for new insight into cognition has provided a wealth of ideas and hypotheses worthy of testing in the ultimate laboratory—the classroom.

These three forces (consensus on other matters, heightened concern about comprehension failures, and a new set of intellectual challenges), then, have converged to create an atmosphere in which the psychic energy of the reading field has been unleashed toward the study of comprehension.

The challenge we must meet is the question posed by the school reading committees: "What can we do about it?" Though there may be others, at this time I believe that we have gathered enough research, theory, and practical wisdom to support these six changes.

1. We must accept comprehension for what it is.
2. We must change the kinds of questions we ask about selections children read.
3. We must change our attitude toward and practices of teaching vocabulary.
4. We must change the way we teach comprehension skills.
5. We must begin to develop curricular materials that recognize the fact that comprehension and composition are remarkably similar in process.
6. We must change our conception of the teacher's role in the reading program.

The Truth About Comprehension

Prior to 1970, our view of the comprehension process was driven by our fixation upon the text as an object of study. Comprehension was viewed as some degree of "approximation" to the text read. And, if we had any notion that readers build mental models as they read, then our standard for what a mental model should look like was the text itself.

For a variety of historical, political, and theoretical reasons too detailed to elucidate here, our views of comprehension and text have changed dramatically. No longer do we regard text as a fixed object that the reader is supposed to "approximate" as closely as possible as s/he reads. Instead we now view text as a sort of blueprint for meaning, a set of tracks or clues that the reader uses as s/he builds a model of what the text means (see Collins, Brown, and Larkin, 1980).

In this new view, we recognize that no text is ever fully explicit, no text ever specifies all the relationships among events, motivation of characters, and nuances of tone and style that every author hopes readers will infer as they read. Instead, authors omit from their texts exactly those relationships and nuances they expect (and hope) readers can figure out for themselves. As readers, we would be bored to death if authors chose to specify these matters, saying to ourselves "Well, I knew that!"

In short, this new view suggests that readers play a much more active-constructive role in their own comprehension than our earlier passive-receptive views dictated.

An active-constructive model of comprehension has enormous implications for the role of the classroom teacher in promoting comprehension. A teacher can no longer regard the text as the ultimate criterion for defining what good comprehension is; instead s/he must view the text, along with students' prior knowledge, students' strategies, the task, and the classroom situation, as one facet in the complex array we call comprehension. Now a teacher must know as much about the influence of these other facets (prior knowledge, strategies, task, situation) as s/he knows about the text itself. In fact, these other facets—especially prior knowledge, strategies, and task—form the basis for the remaining five changed outlines in this presentation.

Changing Questions

Durkin (1978–79) and her coworkers, after some 17,997 minutes observing intermediate grade reading lessons, concluded that teachers devote much of their reading class time to asking students questions about stories they have just read. Students, conversely, spend lots of time answering questions, or listening to classmates' answers. Furthermore, these sessions (described by Durkin as assessment rather than teaching) tended to be characterized by relatively low-level, literally-based questions in search of single correct answers.

We have all seen this; probably most of us, myself included, have done it ourselves. I ask a question. I call upon Suzie. She gives an answer other than the one I had in mind. I turn toward Tommy. He gives a second answer, but still not the one I had in mind. My head bobs from student to student until someone finally gives the answer I was looking for. It is a game we play called "Guess what's in my head."

When Durkin (1981) turned from classroom observation to teachers' manuals, she discovered a remarkably similar situation—lots of space devoted to story questions, lots of literal-level questions in search of single correct answers (*and manuals provided correct answers to each comprehension question*, save those that invited almost any and every response, coded as "answers will vary").

Beck and her colleagues (1979) have also examined teacher's manual questions. Reading their analysis, one is struck by another facet of the questions in manuals: They represent a random barrage of questions that do not cohere with one another. They do not form a *line of questions* to lead children through the main crises and events of a story so they can build their own coherent representation of its meaning.

The story map. After examining recent research about story comprehension, Beck (1984) suggested that, prior to question generation, teachers need to develop an outline of the important ideas in the story, what Beck has come to call a "story map." A story map specifies the main character's problem in the story and then attempts to solve that problem, leading eventually to a resolution, and perhaps a moral or lesson about life. Beck suggests that, having generated such a map, teachers should develop questions that elicit major components of the story map. Questions that elicit either too general or too specific responses should not be used during initial guided reading discussions. The flow of the story, from inception to resolution, serves as the paramount criterion for question selection or creation.

Translated into practical issues regarding basal reading questions, this analysis suggests that in addition to developing questions that go beyond the literal text, guided reading questions should be limited to eliciting only those details that drive the flow of the story, that is, problems, goals, attempts to solve problems, characters' reactions, resolution, and theme (or moral).

Recent research evidence (Beck, Omanson, and McKeown, 1982; Gordon and Pearson, 1983; Singer and Donlan, 1982) validates exactly such a notion. Questions that focus student attention on salient story elements elicit better comprehension and recall of the story in which such questions are embedded as well as better recall of new stories for which no questions are asked. Apparently, the systematic application of such a framework for story comprehension helps students develop their own frameworks for understanding stories; such a framework may well serve as a strategic device for understanding and recalling what is read.

Prereading questions. In addition to guided reading questions, researchers have examined prereading questions intended to build background for story comprehension. Here considerable evidence suggests that it matters a great deal what kind of questions we use: A set for predicting, relating text to prior knowledge, and evaluating predicted outcomes is superior to more literal/factual orientation.

For example, Hansen and Pearson (Hansen, 1981; Hansen and Pearson, 1980, 1983) have done several studies on the effect of story questions, particularly with reference to enhancing children's ability to answer inferential comprehension questions. Two of their findings are relevant to our concerns.

First, simply making sure that guided reading questions (asked either during or after stories) include a lot of inference questions enhances both story specific inferential comprehension and comprehension of new stories. Second, they found that adding a prereading set for invoking relevant prior knowledge and predicting what will happen in a story coupled with discussion of why it is important to do so results in even better inferential comprehension and even helps literal comprehension.

Developing questions to invoke prior knowledge and engage in prediction is not difficult (see Hansen and Hubbard, 1984, for details on this technique). Basically, a teacher must:

1. Read the text.
2. Decide on a few (2–4) key ideas, ideas which usually represent the theme or moral, the main character's basic problem, or a key action, event, or feeling.

3. For each key idea, ask "Have you ever...?" and "What do you think X will do...?"
4. Before reading, spend a few minutes discussing each of the two questions for each key idea.
5. (Optional) After reading, return to the predictions to discuss reason for differences or similarities between predictions and what actually happened.
6. Somewhere discuss why you are doing all this.

In trying to reconcile the available data on what promotes better understanding of textbook selections with conventional practices, I have derived the following instructional guidelines for asking questions. (For a more complete treatment, see Pearson, 1982.)

1. Ask questions that encourage children to relate the story to prior experiences.
2. Then, try to elicit predictions about what story characters will do in similar circumstances.
3. Ask purpose setting questions that persist as long as possible throughout the reading of a selection.
4. Immediately after reading, return to the purpose.
5. Use a story map to generate guided reading questions.
6. Include follow-up tasks that encourage synthesis of the entire story (retelling, dramatizing, summarizing).
7. Reserve comparison questions (with prior knowledge and other stories) for a second pass through.
8. Reserve author's craft questions (e.g., techniques for persuasion) for a second (even a third) pass.

Vocabulary Instruction

Dale Johnson and I have been so concerned about vocabulary instruction that we have written two books devoted exclusively to the topic (Johnson and Pearson, 1978, 1984). Our main concerns in those books are twofold: (1) that people will recognize the primacy of *meaning* vocabulary over *word recognition* vocabulary, and (2) that they will embrace our philosophy of *ownership of a word's meaning* over *facility at defining the word.* Let me explain with an anecdote.

Several years ago a student teacher brought in to my colleague, Robert Schreiner (University of Minnesota), a lesson plan and some student papers from a reading lesson he had taught to some fifth grade students, remarking "Let me tell you about my great vocabulary lesson."

"What did you do?"

"Well, first I had them look up the new words in their pocket dictionaries..."

"And then?..."

"I knew you'd ask that," he added firmly. "And then I asked them to write the words in sentences."

"Can I see some students' papers?" The first word on the first paper was *exasperated.* The student had written, for a definition, *vexed.* And her accompanying sentence was *He was exasperated.*

At that point, all the student teacher knew was that (1) the child could find the word in the dictionary, (2) she could copy the first available definition, and (3) she recognized that a word ending in *-ed* could serve in the past participle slot in a sentence. He knew nothing about whether the child knew the meaning of the word, or whether the child *owned* the word, to use Beck's (1984) term for knowing a new word in its fullest sense.

The problem illustrated here is similar to the dilemma faced by teachers each time they find a new list of vocabulary for a new reading selection (or when they come to a new chapter in a social studies or science textbook). How much concept development needs to be done *before* children will be able to understand the text at hand and use that new vocabulary when they read different texts?

While we do not have the final answer on these questions, we do have some guidelines derived from recent research on the relationship between knowledge about a topic and comprehension of texts related to that topic. First, there is no question about that relationship: A reader's knowledge about a topic, particularly key vocabulary, is a better predictor of comprehension of a text than is any measure of reading ability or achievement (Johnston and Pearson, 1982; Johnston, 1984).

Second, several studies point to the advantage of a fullblown concept development approach to vocabulary over a more conventional definition and sentence approach. Particularly useful have been semantic mapping and semantic feature analysis approaches (Johnson, Toms-Bronowski, and Pittleman, 1982; Johnson, 1983; Johnson and Pearson, 1984), as well as other approaches that emphasize semantic elaboration (Beck, Perfetti, and McKeown, 1982; Kameenui, Carnine, and Freschi, 1982). What these more useful approaches have in common is that they emphasize where a word fits in children's semantic repertoire rather than what it means or how it is used in sentences. That's what it means to own a word—to know what it is like and how it differs from other words that a child knows.

To accomplish this goal for vocabulary, we must alter our stance toward vocabulary instruction (for a more complete treatment of these issues, see Johnson 1983, or Johnson, Toms-Bronowski, and Pittleman, 1982). We must change the questions we ask when we get ready to help a child acquire a new concept. Too often we have asked "What is it that children do not know and how can I get that into their heads?" The better question is "What is it that children *do* know that is enough like the new concepts so that I can use it as an anchor point?"

We can learn new concepts only in relationship to concepts we already possess. This is a principle that we, as considerate adults, use all the time with our peers when we explain a new phenomenon. We say "Well, it is sort of like X...but..." We establish a contact between the new and the known, then we explain how the new concept is different.

We must extend the same courtesy to children. We must refocus our vocabulary efforts on techniques emphasizing semantic elaboration and semantic fit rather than definition and usage. Only then will we achieve the goal of *ownership* we would all like to achieve.

Comprehension Skill Instruction

In Durkin's (1978–79) classroom observations, one of her goals was to determine when, how, and how often teachers engaged in direct, explicit instruction for comprehension skills; that is, what did teachers tell students about *how* they should perform the various comprehension tasks assigned on the myriad of worksheets and workbook pages in their reading programs? Of 17,997 minutes, she found precisely 45 minutes devoted to this kind of direct instruction in comprehension (and some 11 minutes of that was on the influence of punctuation).

She found lots of what she labeled mentioning —saying just enough about an assignment so that students understood the formal requirements of the task, but stopping short of demonstrating how to solve the task cognitively or what to look for as clues for generating a solution.

Durkin (1981) conducted a similar analysis of basal manuals, looking for instances of comprehension instruction. While the manuals fared somewhat better than the teachers, they still fell woefully short of what we might call substantive instruction. Most of their instructional directives consisted of a single sentence, perhaps something like "Tell the students that the main idea is the most important idea in the paragraph." Rarely was much in the way of modeling, guided practice, or substantive feedback suggested.

Again, Durkin felt that "mentioning" better characterized what the manuals were offering in the way of instructional directives to teachers.

One can argue that the reason both teachers and manuals offer little explicit instruction in how to solve comprehension tasks is that comprehension is such a complex interactive process, influenced by so many situational and individual factors. Until recently we simply have not understood the process well enough to be able to identify and define basic and distinct comprehension skills, let alone determine strategies that teachers could use to help students apply these skills consistently across the range of texts and practice activities they encounter.

Recent researchers, however, have been successful in helping students develop strategies for dis-covering some regularities across different texts, tasks, and situations.

Questions. Hansen (1981) tried to determine whether she could improve second graders' ability to answer questions that did not have explicit answers in the texts (what we usually call inferential comprehension). She found that giving students several opportunities to respond to inferential guided reading and follow-up questions or employing a prereading strategy that encouraged students to use their own experiences to predict and evaluate story characters' problems and actions both produced reliable increases in the children's ability to answer inferential comprehension questions, at no loss to their performance on literal tasks.

Apparently, what happened was that students *either* exposed to lots of questions requiring answers from prior knowledge *or* encouraged to use prior knowledge to predict and evaluate story events learned that it was legitimate to invoke one's prior knowledge in answering questions. Several students actually volunteered that, prior to the training, they did not know that it was "OK" to use "their own words" to answer questions.

In a related study, Hansen and Pearson (1983) combined the two treatments (strategy training and lots of inferential postreading questions) and compared the hybrid to a "business as usual" control group (do whatever the Teacher's Manual says) for both good and poor fourth graders. They also trained teachers to administer the treatments instead of having the experimenters do so and stressed the metacognitive dimension (self-awareness of the strategy) in this training. Before each training session, they discussed with students what it was they were doing before each story (using prior knowledge to predict story events) and why.

After 10 weeks of training, few differences emerged among good readers; however, strong and reliable differences surfaced among the poor readers, favoring the hybrid inference training group. In fact, on one measure, the poor experimental students performed as well as the good control students despite a 3-year grade norm difference in average reading test scores. Differences in performance were observed on both literal and inferential measures but were more striking on the inferential measures.

Hansen and Pearson concluded that the training was most effective for precisely those students who typically exhibit frustration on comprehension tasks. The lack of consistent reliable differences among good readers might be attributed to the fact that many good readers often discover such strategies on their own through sheer exposure to various tasks. Poor readers appear to require more and more careful guidance from a teacher.

Teachers who participated in the study expressed great satisfaction with the experimental treatment, stating that their reading group discussions were more lively and interesting. They also expressed some concern in getting used to the treatment, the variety of responses offered (they had to learn to live with the fact that answers *do* vary), and the difficulty of generating good inference questions.

Inference training. Gordon and Pearson (1983), continuing this general line of inference training research, developed and evaluated an even more explicit technique for helping children become better at drawing inferences. As a first step, they established four subtasks that ought to be completed for every inference task: (1) ask the inference question, (2) answer it, (3) find clues in the text to support the inference, and (4) tell how to get from the clues to the answer (i.e., give a "line of reasoning").

In their 8-week training procedure, they led fourth graders through stages varying along a continuum of responsibility for task completion (Table 1).

In Stage 1, the teacher takes all the responsibility. By Stage 4, the student takes most of the responsibility. In a sense, Stage 1 represents modeling and Stage 4, independent practice or application; Stages 2 and 3 represent guided practice. Instruction is what happens in those intermediate stages between total teacher responsibility (modeling) and total student responsibility (practice or application). (See Gordon, 1985, for a detailed description of this technique.)

In fact, the whole procedure can be depicted graphically, as in the Figure (from Pearson and Gallagher, 1983, after Campione, 1981). In this model, the assumption is that the completion of any task can be conceptualized as requiring some varying proportion of responsibility from the teacher and the students. The diagonal line from upper left to lower right depicts such varying degrees, ranging from all teacher (i.e., modeling) in the upper left corner to all students in the lower right corner. What ensues between these extremes is guided practice, or the "gradual release of responsibility" from teacher to student.

Question-answer relationships. In another example of the model, Raphael (Raphael and Pearson, in press; Raphael and Wonnacutt, in press) has conducted several studies that focus students' attention on how they should vary their strategies for answering questions. Raphael contends that they should

---

TABLE 1
Stages of responsibility in inference training task

Stages	Subtasks			
	Ask question	Answer question	Find clues	Line of reasoning
1. Modeling	T	T	T	T
2. Guided practice	T	T	S	S
3. Guided practice	T	S	T	S
4. Independent practice	T	S	S	S

After Gordon and Pearson, 1983.
Note: T = Teacher does subtask, S = Student does subtask

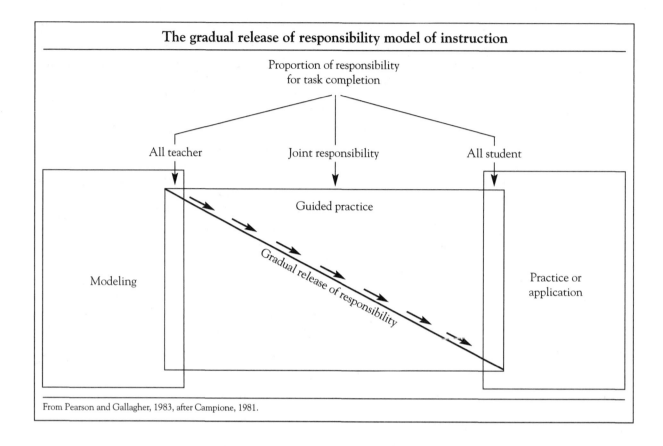

The gradual release of responsibility model of instruction

Proportion of responsibility
for task completion

All teacher   Joint responsibility   All student

Guided practice

Modeling

Gradual release of responsibility

Practice or
application

From Pearson and Gallagher, 1983, after Campione, 1981.

vary strategies as a function of the task demands of the question (*Does it look like I should go to the text or to my head for an answer?*) in relationship to the information available (*What does the text say about this?* and *What do I already know about this issue?*).

Using Pearson and Johnson's (1978) trichotomy for classifying question-answer relations (text-explicit, text-implicit, and script-implicit), Raphael has taught fourth, sixth, and eighth graders to discriminate among three response situations, as illustrated in relation to Text 1 below. Under (a), both the question and the answer come from the same sentence in the text; under (b) the question and answer come from different parts of the text; under (c) the question is motivated by the text but the answer comes from the reader's prior knowledge.

> Text: (1) Matthew was afraid Susan would beat him in the tennis match. He broke both of Susan's rackets the night before the match.

(a) Who was afraid? *Matthew*

(b) Why did Matthew break both of Susan's rackets? *He was afraid Susan would beat him.*

(c) Why was Matthew afraid? *Maybe Susan was a better player.*

Raphael and Pearson (in press) and Raphael and Wonnacott (in press) taught the students to label these three strategies *right there, think and search,* and *on my own,* respectively, as they answer the questions. In their work, they have found that students of all ability groups and all grade levels who receive systematic and directed instruction in this technique were better able to comprehend new texts and to monitor their own comprehension. Like students in the Hansen and Pearson (1983) study, one student said, "I never knew I could get answers from my head before."

Raphael's procedure (see Raphael, 1982 or 1984, for complete details) can also be viewed as an application of the model in the Figure. Think of the entire procedure as requiring the completion of four tasks (in Table 2), consisting of (1) asking a question, (2) answering it, (3) classifying the Question-Answer relationship, and (4) telling why it deserves that classification.

Notice how Stages 1–4 represent the same sort of logic present in the Gordon and Pearson (1983) work. Raphael, however, has added a Stage 5, one in which students generate their own questions and then apply the other subtasks. I regard this additional step as representing "true ownership" of the strategy because, at this point, it comes under complete student control.

Reciprocal teaching. Palincsar and Brown (1984) have developed a somewhat different application of this model for helping remedial junior high students improve their comprehension of content area materials. Particularly interesting in this work is the interaction between teacher and student in the small group training. Using reciprocal teaching, the teacher meets with a small group (5 to 15 students) and models four tasks for them to perform over each paragraph or segment read from their content area (science and social studies) materials.

1. Summarize the paragraph or segment in a sentence.

2. Ask a good question or two.

3. Clarify hard parts.

4. Predict what the next paragraph or segment will discuss.

Initially, the students' role is to concur on the summary and the quality of the questions, to answer the questions, and to help clarify unclear text segments. After a few models by the teacher, the students take over the role of teacher. Whoever plays teacher must generate the summary, ask a few questions, lead a discussion of unclear words or parts, and predict the next subtopic. Whoever is playing student must help revise the summary, answer the questions (or suggest alternative questions), clarify unclear parts, and concur in (or disagree with) the prediction.

After turning over the reins to the students, the teacher:

1. takes a regular turn as "teacher,"

2. provides feedback about the quality of summaries or questions,

3. provides encouragement to students playing "teacher" ("you must feel good about the way you generated that summary!"),

4. keeps the students on track, and

	TABLE 2 Stages of responsibility in question-answer relationship task			
	Subtasks			
Stages	Ask question	Answer question	Assign QAR classification	Justify classification
1. Modeling	T	T	T	T
2. Guided practice	T	T	T	S
3. Guided practice	T	T	S	S
4. Independent practice	T	S	S	S
5. True ownership	S	S	S	S

After Raphael, 1982, 1984.
Note: T = Teacher does subtask, S = Student does subtask

5. encourages each student playing the teacher role to take *one* step beyond their present level of competence (based upon individual diagnosis about where each student is operating).

Additionally, at the end of each 25–30 minute reciprocal teaching period, students receive a completely novel passage for which they must generate a summary or answer several questions independently.

Palincsar and Brown have applied this technique to triads (1 teacher, 2 students), small groups conducted by volunteer remedial reading teachers, and intermediate grade teachers working with regular reading groups. In all cases student gains have been dramatic.

Typically students scores went from less than 40% correct on the daily independent exercises to over 80% correct on questions or summaries. The effects lasted anywhere from 8 weeks to 6 months. And students receiving this training made gains in their social studies and science classwork that moved them, on average, from the 20th to the 60th or 70th percentile.

Referring back to the model in the Figure, reciprocal teaching may provide the clearest and most readily implementable example of gradually releasing task responsibility from teacher to student.

This group of studies provides evidence that comprehension can be taught after all. They also suggest that what is missing in our current milieu (what I like to call our practice-only approach to comprehension) is the critical element of the teacher interacting with groups of students to help them gain more personal control over the instructional environment in which we place them and the tasks we require them to perform in that environment (see Pearson and Leys, in press, for further examples of application of this model).

Comprehending and Composing

The May 1983 issue of *Language Arts*, the elementary school journal of the National Council of Teachers of English, was devoted to explicating the theoretical and practical interfaces between reading and writing.

In reading the issue, one soon discovers that the authors are *nor* writing about similarities in phonics for reading and phonics for spelling! Instead, the broad points of similarity are to be found in considering the basic similarity between composing a text and comprehending a text. Several authors, in fact, make the point that readers, at least metaphorically, have to compose their own texts as they read.

Whether this metaphor of a reader as a writer holds up point for point is not really the issue. Truly at issue here is that modern theories of comprehension (as in the first change I suggest) require us as educators to realize that the whole process of comprehension is much more *active, constructive*, and *reader-based* than our older theories suggested. No longer can we think of comprehension as *passive, receptive*, and *text-based*. No longer can we think of meaning as residing "in the text." Instead, we must regard each and every text students read as a blueprint to guide them in building their own model of what the text means. The text sets some broad boundaries on the range of permissible meanings, but it does not specify particular meanings. Particular meanings are negotiations between an author and a reader, with a teacher playing the role of a guide in helping students negotiate a meaning.

To realize the truth of this perspective, all one has to do is to watch a teacher and some students read and discuss a typical preprimer story—a 6-page story of 80 words with 4 to 6 pictures and 20 comprehension questions in the teacher's manual.

The key question is why are there 20 comprehension questions and what are they about? A few, we know, are about the words in the text. A few more, perhaps, are about the pictures. But many are really about students' prior knowledge of the scenarios only hinted at by the text and the pictures.

Why are they there? They are there because the people who wrote them realize (most likely intuitively and unconsciously) that a complete understanding of the story could not occur without providing cues to help fill in the gaps left in the combination of text and pictures on the page. To corroborate for yourself that even a novice reader's understanding is richer than the explicit message on the page, ask a student who has just read and discussed one of these "stories" to retell it to you. You'll likely find rich elaborations, indicating that he or she has added much in building a personal model of what the text means.

Tierney and Pearson (1983) have noted the similarity of several subprocesses in composing and comprehending. The writing process, they note, entails planning, composing, and revising. Writers gather information (from their own knowledge or from reading designed to bolster their own knowledge), establish a purpose, and hypothesize an audience when they *plan* their writing. They begin to set pen to paper (or with modern technology to create dots on a cathode ray tube) as they compose. And they can revise the text they have created during and after composing. Tierney and Pearson also note that these subprocesses are not necessarily distinct stages—that one can, for example, revise one's plans or composition, plan one's revisions.

Then they argue that good reading entails exactly the same sort of subprocesses. Good readers will plan their reading (note the kinds of prereading activities described in the earlier section on vocabulary), compose at least a tentative meaning as they read, and constantly revise that meaning in accordance with new information they gain from the text's blueprint or from new insight from their own store of knowledge.

Also, revision can and does occur when a teacher guides students in a discussion. In fact, the real purpose of a story discussion may be to help students revise their models of what a text means, to help them take new perspectives and align themselves to characters and events in ways they have not yet considered.

The difficulty in separating comprehension and composition can also be seen in certain activities teachers may ask students to do. For example, suppose a teacher gives some fourth graders an assignment in which they are told that a writer was careless in composing a news article and inadvertently included some irrelevant information. The students' task is to edit out that irrelevant information and replace it with better information. Is this an act of composition or comprehension? I cannot tell.

Or suppose a third grade teacher, concerned about figurative language, asks a group of students to replace certain literal expressions with figurative paraphrases (or vice versa). Is this composition or comprehension? I cannot tell.

Or suppose a group of seventh graders rewrites a part of a chapter in their science text to make it more understandable to a group of sixth graders. Is this composition or comprehension? I cannot tell.

Or suppose a teacher, conducting a writing conference with a first grade student, asks that student whether the audience would like to know or needs to know the information contained in a particular paragraph. Is this composition or comprehension? Again, I cannot make the distinction.

Teachers who choose to accept this basic process similarity between comprehension and composition will discover that their role in teaching is not so much to sit in judgment about what is right or wrong in an essay, a story, or an answer to a question, but to act as a sort of tour guide to help students see richness and possibility with different language, different interpretations, different perspectives cued by different questions. (For a more complete treatment of these issues and more specific suggestions on teaching reading and writing together, see *Language Arts*, May 1983, and Indrisano, 1984.)

Were I to make a prediction about the single most important change in language instruction that will take place in the next decade, it would be that we will no longer separate instruction and reading and writing. It is one of the most exciting prospects I can think of.

Changing Role for Teachers

Taken together, these first five changes that I am advocating imply a sixth more pervasive change in our prevailing model of the role of the teacher. The model implicit in the practices of the 70s was that of a manager—a person who arranged materials, tests, and the classroom environment so learning could occur. But the critical test of whether learning did occur was left up to the child as s/he interacted with the materials.

Children practiced applying skills: If they learned them, fine; we always had more skills for them to practice; if they did not, fine; we always had more worksheets and duplicating sheets for the same skill. And the most important rule in such a mastery role was that practice makes perfect, leading of course, to the ironic condition that children spent most of their time working on precisely that subset of skills they performed least well.

Why did we embrace such a model? There were several forces at work. First, the press for accountability and minimal competencies forced us to be accountable for something. And we opted for all the bits and pieces rather than the entire reading process. Second, the notion of mastery learning, presented so elegantly by Bloom (1968) and Carroll (1963), made such a system seem reasonable. Third, our friends in publishing unwittingly aided and abetted the movement by providing seductively attractive materials and management schemes. The fascination with materials became so prevalent that, in a recent survey, Shannon (1983) found that virtually all the administrators and a high proportion of American teachers believe that materials *are* the reading program.

I would like to propose a new model for the late 1980s—a model in which the teacher assumes a more central and active role in providing instruction, a model in which practice is augmented by teacher modeling, guided practice and substantive feedback, a model in which the teacher and the child move along that continuum of task responsibility (the Figure), a model that says just because we want students to end up taking total responsibility for task completion does not mean that we should begin by giving them total responsibility.

In this model, teachers assume new and different roles: They become sharers of secrets, coconspirators, coaches, and cheerleaders. Because they realize that they are readers and writers who share an interpretive community with their students, they become willing to share the secrets of their own cognitive successes (and failures!) with students.

They often coconspire with their students to see if they can "get to the author" or try to "trick the reader." They act sometimes the way good coaches do; they are there at just the right moment with just the right piece of information or just the right pat on the back. And they act as cheerleaders for their students, encouraging them to take new steps toward independence and focusing on their remarkable strengths rather than their weaknesses.

If we adopt this new view of the teacher, we will be taking the mastery notion of Bloom and Carroll more seriously than ever, because we will be recognizing an often forgotten feature of mastery learning —that additional teacher assistance was, along with additional time on task, a basic component in the models. We will also be recognizing that true individualization has never meant that instruction is *delivered* individually, only that progress is *monitored* individually, and that what may be best for a given individual is not another worksheet but maybe a live body present to provide the guidance and feedback it will take to bring him or her to an independent level of performance.

As a metaphor for this new model, I would like to replace the metaphor of *teacher as manager* with a metaphor of the *teacher as teacher*. I know the idea is not startlingly fresh, but it does have a nice ring to it.

REFERENCES

Beck, Isabel. "Developing Comprehension: The Impact of the Directed Reading Lesson." In *Learning to Read in American Schools: Basal Readers and Content Texts*, edited by Richard C. Anderson, Jean Osborn, and Robert J. Tierney. Hillsdale, N.J.: Lawrence Erlbaum, 1984.

Beck, Isabel L., Margaret G. McKeown, Ellen S. McCaslin, and Ann M. Burkes. *Instructional Dimensions That May Affect Reading Comprehension: Examples from Two Commercial Reading Programs*. Pittsburgh, Pa.: University of Pittsburgh, Learning Research and Development Center, 1979.

Beck, Isabel L., Richard C. Omanson, and Margaret G. McKeown. "An Instructional Redesign of Reading Lessons: Effects on Comprehension." *Reading Research Quarterly*, vol. 17, no. 4 (1982), pp. 462–81.

Beck, Isabel L., Charles A. Perfetti, and Margaret G. McKeown. "The Effects of Long-Term Vocabulary Instruction on Lexical Access and Reading Comprehension." *Journal of Educational Psychology*, vol. 74, no. 4 (1982), pp. 506–21.

Bloom, Benjamin S. "Learning for Mastery." *Evaluation Comment*, vol. 1, no. 2 (1968), pp. 1–12.

Campione, Joseph. "Learning, Academic Achievement, and Instruction." Paper delivered at the second annual conference on Reading Research of the Center for the Study of Reading, New Orleans, La., April 1981.

Carroll, John. "A Model of School Learning." *Teacher's College Record*, vol. 64 (May 1963), pp. 723–33.

Collins, Allan, John S. Brown, and Kathy M. Larkin. "Inferences in Text Understanding." In *Theoretical Issues in Reading Comprehension*, edited by Rand J. Spiro, Bertram C. Bruce, and William F. Brewer. Hillsdale, N.J.: Lawrence Erlbaum, 1980.

Durkin, Dolores. "Reading Comprehension Instruction in Five Basal Reading Series." *Reading Research Quarterly*, vol. 16, no. 4 (1981), pp. 515–44.

Durkin, Dolores. "What Classroom Observations Reveal about Reading Comprehension Instruction." *Reading Research Quarterly*, vol. 14, no. 4 (1978–79), pp. 481–533.

Gordon, Christine J. "Modeling Inference Awareness across the Curriculum." *Journal of Reading*, vol. 28 (February 1985), pp. 444–47.

Gordon, Christine, and P. David Pearson. *Effects of Instruction in Metacomprehension and Inferencing on Students' Comprehension Abilities.* Technical Report No. 269. Urbana, Ill.: University of Illinois, 1983.

Hansen, Jane. "The Effects of Inference Training and Practice on Young Children's Comprehension." *Reading Research Quarterly*, vol. 16, no. 3 (1981), pp. 391–417.

Hansen, Jane, and Ruth Hubbard. "Poor Readers Can Draw Inferences." *The Reading Teacher*, vol. 37 (March 1984), pp. 586–89.

Hansen, Jane, and P. David Pearson. *The Effects of Inference Training and Practice on Young Children's Comprehension.* ED 186 839. Arlington, Va.: ERIC Document Reproduction Service, 1980.

Hansen, Jane, and P. David Pearson. "An Instructional Study: Improving the Inferential Comprehension of Fourth Grade Good and Poor Readers." *Journal of Educational Psychology*, vol. 75, no. 6 (1983), pp. 821–29.

Indrisano, Roselmina. *Reading and Writing Revisited.* Occasional Paper No. 18. Columbus, Ohio: Ginn and Company, 1984.

Johnson, Dale D. *Three Sound Strategies for Vocabulary Development.* Occasional Paper No. 3. Columbus, Ohio: Ginn and Company, 1983.

Johnson, Dale D., and P. David Pearson. *Teaching Reading Vocabulary.* New York, N.Y.: Holt, Rinehart, and Winston, 1978.

Johnson, Dale D., and P. David Pearson. *Teaching Reading Vocabulary*, 2nd ed. New York, N.Y.: Holt, Rinehart, and Winston, 1984.

Johnson, Dale D., Susan Toms-Bronowski, and Susan D. Pittleman. "Vocabulary Development." *Volta Review*, vol. 84, no. 5 (1982), pp. 11–24.

Johnston, Peter. "Background Knowledge and Reading Comprehension Test Bias." *Reading Research Quarterly*, vol. 19, no. 2 (1984), pp. 219–39.

Johnston, Peter, and P. David Pearson. *Prior Knowledge, Connectivity, and the Assessment of Reading Comprehension.* Technical Report No. 245. Urbana, Ill.: University of Illinois, 1982.

Kameenui, Edward J., Douglas W. Carnine, and Roger Freschi. "Effects of Text Construction and Instructional Procedures for Teaching Word Meanings on Comprehension and Recall." *Reading Research Quarterly*, vol. 17, no. 3 (1982), pp. 367–88.

National Assessment of Educational Progress. *Three National Assessments of Reading: Changes in Performance, 1970–80.* Report No. 11-R-01. Denver, Colo.: Education Commission of the States, 1981.

Palincsar, Annemarie S., and Ann L. Brown. "Reciprocal Teaching of Comprehension-Fostering and Comprehension-Monitoring Activities." *Cognition and Instruction*, vol. 1, no. 1 (1984), pp. 117–75.

Pearson, P. David. *Asking Questions about Stories.* Occasional Paper No. 15. Columbus, Ohio: Ginn and Company, 1982.

Pearson, P. David, and Margaret C. Gallagher. "The Instruction of Reading Comprehension." *Contemporary Educational Psychology*, vol. 8, no. 3 (1983), pp. 317–44.

Pearson, P. David, and Dale D. Johnson. *Teaching Reading Comprehension.* New York, N.Y.: Holt, Rinehart, and Winston, 1978.

Pearson, P. David, and Margie Leys. "Teaching Comprehension." In *Resource Manual for Comprehension Instruction*, edited by Eric Cooper. New York, N.Y.: The College Board, in press.

Raphael, Taffy E. "Question-Answering Strategies for Children." *The Reading Teacher*, vol. 36 (November 1982), pp. 186–91.

Raphael, Taffy E. "Teaching Learners about Sources of Information for Answering Questions." *Journal of Reading*, vol. 27 (January 1984), pp. 303–11.

Raphael, Taffy E., and P. David Pearson. "Increasing Students' Awareness of Sources of Information for Answering Questions." *American Educational Research Journal*, in press.

Raphael, Taffy E., and Clydie A. Wonnacut. "Heightening Fourth-Grade Students' Sensitivity to Sources of Information for Answering Questions." *Reading Research Quarterly*, in press.

Shannon, Patrick. "The Use of Commercial Reading Materials in American Elementary Schools." *Reading Research Quarterly*, vol. 19, no. 4 (1983), pp. 68–87.

Singer, Harry, and Dan Donlan. "Active Comprehension: Problem Solving Schema with Question Generation for Comprehension of Complex Short Stories." *Reading Research Quarterly*, vol. 17, no. 2 (1982), pp. 166–86.

Tierney, Robert J., and P. David Pearson. "Toward a Composing Model of Reading." *Language Arts*, vol. 60, no. 5 (1983), pp. 568–80.

What Every Teacher Needs to Know About Comprehension

Laura S. Pardo

Comprehension is a complex process that has been understood and explained in a number of ways. The RAND Reading Study Group (2002) stated that comprehension is "the process of simultaneously extracting and constructing meaning through interaction and involvement with written language" (p. 11). Duke (2003) added "navigation" and "critique" to her definition because she believed that readers actually move through the text, finding their way, evaluating the accuracy of the text to see if it fits their personal agenda, and finally arriving at a self-selected location. A common definition for teachers might be that comprehension is a process in which readers construct meaning by interacting with text through the combination of prior knowledge and previous experience, information in the text, and the stance the reader takes in relationship to the text. As these different definitions demonstrate, there are many interpretations of what it means to comprehend text. This article synthesizes the research on comprehension and makes connections to classroom practice. I begin by introducing a visual model of comprehension.

How Comprehension Works

Comprehension occurs in the transaction between the reader and the text (Kucer, 2001; Rosenblatt, 1978). The reader brings many things to the literacy event, the text has certain features, and yet meaning emerges only from the engagement of that reader with that text at that particular moment in time.

Figure 1 below presents a visual model of this process. Each of the elements in the model (reader, text, context, and transaction) is described in more detail later in this article, along with specific suggestions for how teachers can interact with the model to help children become strong comprehenders, beginning in kindergarten.

The Reader

Any literacy event is made up of a reader engaging with some form of text. Each reader is unique in that

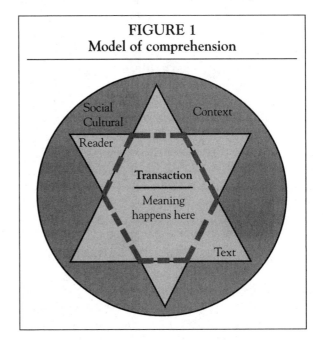

FIGURE 1
Model of comprehension

Reprinted from *The Reading Teacher*, 58(3), pp. 272–280. © 2004 by the International Reading Association.

he or she possesses certain traits or characteristics that are distinctly applied with each text and situation (Butcher & Kintsch, 2003; Fletcher, 1994; Narvaez, 2002). The most important of these characteristics is likely the reader's world knowledge (Fletcher, 1994). The more background knowledge a reader has that connects with the text being read, the more likely the reader will be able to make sense of what is being read (Butcher & Kintsch, 2003; Schallert & Martin, 2003). The process of connecting known information to new information takes place through a series of networkable connections known as schema (Anderson & Pearson, 1984; Narvaez, 2002). In schema theory, individuals organize their world knowledge into categories and systems that make retrieval easier. When a key word or concept is encountered, readers are able to access this information system, pulling forth the ideas that will help them make connections with the text so they can create meaning. Schema theory involves the storage of various kinds of information in long-term memory. Because long-term memory appears to have infinite capacity (Pressley, 2003), it is likely that readers have many ideas stored in long-term memory. When a key word or concept is presented to the reader (through a title, heading, or someone who has recommended the text), some of this stored information is brought forward and temporarily placed into short-term memory so that the reader can return to it quickly as he or she reads. Short-term memory has limited capacity, and often the information pulled from long-term memory prior to or during reading is only available for a short time and then is placed back in long-term memory. Short-term memory shifts and juggles information, using what is immediately pertinent and allowing less pertinent information to slip back into long-term memory (Schallert & Martin, 2003).

The amount and depth of a reader's world knowledge vary as do other individual characteristics. Readers vary in the skills, knowledge, cognitive development, culture, and purpose they bring to a text (Narvaez, 2002). Skills include such things as basic language ability, decoding skills, and higher level thinking skills. Knowledge includes background knowledge about content and text and relates to the available schema a reader has for a particular text. A reader's cognitive development causes that reader to evaluate text in different ways—for example, to make moral judgments. Comprehension is affected by a reader's culture, based on the degree to which it matches with the writer's culture or the culture espoused in the text. Readers also read in particular ways depending on the purpose for reading. Another individual difference that exists in readers is motivation. Motivation can influence the interest, purpose, emotion, or persistence with which a reader engages with text (Butcher & Kintsch, 2003; Schallert & Martin, 2003). More motivated readers are likely to apply more strategies and work harder at building meaning. Less motivated readers are not as likely to work as hard, and the meaning they create will not be as powerful as if they were highly motivated.

Teachers Support Readers

If readers have all these individual differences, how do teachers best support elementary-age readers to become competent comprehenders? They teach decoding skills, help students build fluency, build and activate background knowledge, teach vocabulary words, motivate students, and engage them in personal responses to text.

Teach decoding skills. In order to comprehend, readers must be able to read the words. Some level of automatic decoding must be present so that short-term memory can work on comprehending, not on decoding, words. Teachers help students get to this level of automatic decoding by providing instruction in phonemic awareness and phonics at all grade levels. If students put too much mental energy into sounding out the words, they will have less mental energy left to think about the meaning. While teachers in the primary grades work with phonemic awareness and phonics, teachers in the intermediate grades support students' continued development of automatic decoding through spelling, vocabulary, and high-frequency word activities.

Help students build fluency. As word reading becomes automatic, students become fluent and can focus on comprehension (Rasinski, 2003). Teachers help students become more fluent by engaging them in repeated readings for real purposes (like performances and Readers Theatre). Teachers also model fluent reading by reading aloud to students daily so that they realize what fluent reading sounds like. Some research indicates that reading aloud to students is the single most effective way to increase comprehension (see Morrow & Gambrell, 2000, for a review of this literature).

Build and activate prior knowledge. Background knowledge is an important factor for creating meaning, and teachers should help students activate prior knowledge before reading so that information connected with concepts or topics in the text is more easily accessible during reading (Keene & Zimmermann, 1997; Miller, 2002). If students do not have adequate background knowledge, teachers can help students build the appropriate knowledge. Duke (2003) suggested that one way to add to world knowledge is to use informational books with all students, particularly very young students. By using information books, students build world knowledge so that they will have the appropriate information to activate at a later time. Teachers also support students' acquisition of world knowledge by establishing and maintaining a rich, literate environment, full of texts that provide students with numerous opportunities to learn content in a wide variety of topics.

Another way teachers help students build background knowledge is to create visual or graphic organizers that help students to see not only new concepts but also how previously known concepts are related and connected to the new ones (Keene & Zimmermann, 1997; Miller, 2002). Teachers teach students how to make text-to-text, text-to-self, and text-to-world connections so that readers can more easily comprehend the texts they read.

Reading aloud and teacher modeling show students how to activate schema and make connections. For example, a first-grade teacher read aloud from *Ira Says Goodbye* (Waber, 1991). She began the lesson by thinking aloud about the title and cover of the book. "Oh I see that the author is Bernard Waber and the title is *Ira Says Goodbye*. I think this book is about the same Ira as in *Ira Sleeps Over* (Waber, 1973). I can activate my schema from that book. I am making a text-to-text connection. I remember that...." She continued modeling for her students how to activate schema and make connections that helped her make meaning from this text. As she read the book to her students, she stopped occasionally to model and think aloud how she activated her own schema to make connections.

Teach vocabulary words. If there are too many words that a reader does not know, he or she will have to spend too much mental energy figuring out the unknown word(s) and will not be able to understand the passage as a whole. Teachers help students learn important vocabulary words prior to reading difficult or unfamiliar texts. When teaching vocabulary words, teachers make sure that the selected words are necessary for making meaning with the text students will be reading and that they help students connect the new words to something they already know. Simply using the word lists supplied in textbooks does not necessarily accomplish this task (Blachowicz & Fisher, 2000). Many teachers consider the backgrounds and knowledge levels of their students and the text the students will be engaging in and then select a small number of words or ideas that are important for understanding the text. Once teachers have decided on the appropriate vocabulary words to use, students must actively engage with the words—use them in written and spoken language—in order for the words to become a part of the students' reading and writing vocabularies. For example, asking students to create graphic organizers that show relationships among new words and common and known words helps them assimilate new vocabulary. Asking students to look up long lists of unrelated, unknown words is unlikely to help students access the text more appropriately or to increase personal vocabularies.

Motivate students. Many individual reader factors (e.g., cognitive development, culture) are not within a teacher's control. However, teachers can motivate students by providing them with interesting texts, allowing them choices in reading and writing, and helping students set authentic purposes for reading (e.g., generating reports, writing letters, demonstrating some new ability or skill; Pressley & Hilden, 2002). Many teachers actively seek out students' interests so that they can select texts, topics, themes, and units that will more likely engage students. Teachers also provide and promote authentic purposes for engaging in reading and writing. Authentic literacy events are those that replicate or reflect reading and writing purposes and texts that occur in the world outside of schools. Some teachers do this by providing pen pals, using students' authentic questions for in-depth study, responding to community needs, or having students solve problems.

Engage students in personal responses to text. Teachers encourage students to read both efferently and aesthetically (Rosenblatt, 1978). Researchers (McMahon, Raphael, Goatley, & Pardo, 1997) building on the ideas of Rosenblatt developed a literature-based approach to teaching reading comprehension through the Book Club program. In this instructional approach students read authentic literature; write personal, critical, and creative responses; and talk about books with their classmates (Pardo, 2002). Teachers help students learn and apply comprehension strategies while reading, through writing, and during student-led discussion groups called Book Clubs, where students explore the individual meanings that have emerged as they engage with the text over a period of time. While this program initially focused on the intermediate grades, many teachers have found that students in first and second grades are successful comprehenders when they read and engage in Book Clubs (Grattan, 1997; Raphael, Florio-Ruane, & George, 2001; Salna, 2001).

The Text

Understanding the reader is one important piece of the comprehension puzzle, but features of the text also influence the transaction where comprehension hap-

pens. The structure of the text—its genre, vocabulary, language, even the specific word choices—works to make each text unique. Some would even argue that it is at the word or microstructure level that meaning begins (Butcher & Kintsch, 2003). How well the text is written, whether it follows the conventions of its genre or structure, and the language or dialect it is written in are all factors of the text. The content of a specific text, the difficulty or readability of it, and even the type font and size are factors of a text that can influence a reader's interaction. These features collectively are referred to as "surface features," and studies have shown that the quality of the text at the surface level is important for readers to be able to make meaning effectively (Tracey & Morrow, 2002).

The author's intent in writing the text can influence how a reader interacts with that text, particularly if this intent is made known through a foreword, back-cover biography, or knowledgeable other (as in the case of teachers in schools). Some texts are promoted as carrying a certain message or theme by those who have encountered the book previously (Rosenblatt, 1978). The inherent message that some texts carry with them, often related to the author's intent, is referred to as gist and has been defined as "what people remember...the main ideas in the text" (Pressley, 1998, p. 46). Gist is frequently assessed through basal workbooks and standardized reading tests; therefore, the author's intent is a key feature of text.

Teachers Support Texts

Because certain features make some texts more easily comprehensible, teachers help young readers understand those features so they can comprehend effectively. Teachers teach text structures, model appropriate text selection, and provide regular independent reading time.

Teach text structures. Because features of the text are beyond a teacher's control, teachers select texts that have an obvious structure. They teach a variety of narrative genres and some expository text structures. With narrative works teachers help students understand basic story grammar, including the literary elements that are common across narrative pieces, such as plot, characters, and setting. They teach specific elements that make each genre unique (e.g., talking animals in folk tales). By doing this, students will be able to access a schema for a certain narrative genre when they begin to read a new text and can begin to make text-to-text connections for a particular story genre, which will help them more easily make meaning. Likewise, teachers share some common expository text structures with students, such as sequence, description, comparison, and cause and effect. Teachers discuss the idea of "inconsiderate texts" (Armbruster, 1984) with students and show them how to use cues when reading nonfiction (such as reading tables, charts, graphs, and the captions under pictures; using bold print and italics to determine big or important ideas). Inconsiderate texts do not adhere strictly to one structure, but might be a combination of several structures. Many textbooks have a varied and mixed set of structures, and teachers can address specific features and demands of informational text so that students are more likely to engage in informational text with a repertoire of strategies and schema to help them construct meaning (Duke, 2003).

Model appropriate text selection. Teachers teach students how to select appropriate texts by showing them what features to consider. Some teachers use the Goldilocks approach (Tompkins, 2003), while others suggest that teachers level books and tell students which level books they may select (Fountas & Pinnell, 1996). In the Goldilocks approach, readers look for books that are not too hard or too easy, but just right. Just-right books are those that look interesting, have mostly decodable words, have been read aloud previously, are written by a familiar author, or will be read with a support person nearby (Tompkins, 2003). Teachers have a wide variety of genres and levels of books available for students to select for independent reading, and they support students throughout the year with appropriate book selection.

Provide regular independent reading time. Teachers can make sure they provide students with time to read independently every day. Reading becomes better with practice, and comprehending becomes better with more reading practice (Pressley, 2003). Many teachers use programs such as DEAR (Drop Everything And Read) or SSR (Sustained Silent Reading) to ensure that students read independently every day.

Teachers Create and Support a Sociocultural Context

Reading takes place somewhere between a specific reader and a specific text. A sociocultural influence likely permeates any reading activity (Kucer, 2001; Schallert & Martin, 2003). Depending on the place, the situation, and the purpose for reading, the reader and the text interact in ways that are unique for that specific context. The same reading at another time or in a different place might result in a different meaning. The context also involves the activity that occurs around the transaction. If a teacher assigns his or her students to read a certain text for a specific reason, the transaction that occurs will be based on this context. If students are asked to discuss a text, generate questions from it, or come up with a big idea, these kinds of activities form a context within which the reader and text interact for a specific reason, one that is unlikely to occur in exactly the same manner ever again. Teachers create contexts and learning opportunities that will support the construction of meaning. Environments that value reading and writing, that contain a wide variety of texts, that allow students to take risks, and that find time for reading aloud and reading independently are contexts that effectively promote the construction of meaning (Keene & Zimmermann, 1997; Miller, 2002; Pardo, 2002).

The Transaction

As we consider the reader's individual and unique differences, the characteristics of the context, and the features of the text, we are left to wonder exactly what happens when these three come together.

At the most basic level microstructures (words, propositions) are being decoded and represented by mental images (Butcher & Kintsch, 2003). This is most likely happening quickly, automatically, and in short-term memory. These mental images are calling forth ideas and information stored in long-term memory to assist the reader in building a series of connections between representations (van den Broek, 1994). These connections occur between the reader and the text and between different parts of the text. This representation is fine-tuned by the reader as more information is encountered in the text and more connections are made. Readers exit the transaction maintaining a mental representation or gist of the text.

How do these connections lead to mental representations? One way is through making inferences. A reader is quite intentional as he or she engages with the text, asking, "What is it I'm looking at here?" Readers are searching for coherence and for a chain of related events that can lead them to infer or make meaning. As readers continue moving through the text, they continue to build inferences, drawing from long-term memory specific ideas that seem to create coherence and answer the question posed earlier, "What is it I'm looking at here?" As this answer emerges, meaning is realized. Inferencing is most likely done automatically and is one of the most important processes that occur during comprehension (Butcher & Kintsch, 2003; van den Broek, 1994).

The mental representation needs to make sense to the reader as it emerges; therefore, readers monitor the emerging meaning as they read, using metacognitive and fix-up strategies, sometimes discarding ideas in the text if they do not add to the coherence that the reader is trying to build (Pressley & Afflerbach, 1995). If the reader's background knowledge or personal experiences agree with the text, the reader assimilates this new information and creates new meaning. If, however, the reader's background knowledge and personal experiences do not agree with the new information presented in the text, readers either adjust the information to make it fit (accommodation), or they reject that information and maintain their previous understanding (Kucer, 2001). Readers apply a variety of strategies throughout this process to support their construction of meaning such as summarizing, clarifying, questioning, visualizing, predicting, and organizing. It is through the application of these strategies at various moments throughout the interaction that meaning emerges.

Teachers Support Transaction

At this point, it seems fairly obvious that comprehension occurs in the transaction between a reader and a text within a sociocultural context. That makes the transaction crucial to comprehension and the teacher's role within this transaction very important. Teachers provide explicit instruction of useful comprehension strategies, teach students to monitor and repair, use multiple strategy approaches, scaffold support, and make reading and writing connections visible to students.

Provide explicit instruction of useful comprehension strategies. Good readers use strategies to support their understanding of text. Teachers help students become good readers by teaching them how to use the strategies of monitoring, predicting, inferring, questioning, connecting, summarizing, visualizing, and organizing (Keene & Zimmermann, 1997; Miller, 2002; Pardo, 2002). Teachers are explicit and direct in explaining what these strategies are and why good readers use them (Duffy, 2002; Pressley & McCormick, 1995). They model the strategies (often by thinking aloud) for the students and provide them with numerous opportunities to practice and apply the strategies. In order for strategies to transfer so that students use them on their own or in assessment situations, contexts need to remain similar. Therefore, teachers use texts and classroom structures that are easily maintained for teaching, practicing and applying independently, and assessing. Teachers help students think metacognitively about strategies, considering when and where to apply each strategy, how to use it, and the impact it can have. In addition, teachers occasionally provide students with difficult text. If students encounter only texts that they can read easily, there will be no reason to practice and apply strategies. It is when readers encounter challenging texts that they put strategies to use (Kucer, 2001).

Teach students to monitor and repair. Knowing what is understood and not understood while reading and then applying the appropriate strategy to repair meaning are vital for comprehension to occur. Good readers monitor while reading to see if things make sense, and they use strategies to repair the meaning when things stop making sense (Duke, 2003; Pressley & Hilden, 2002). While some studies support that monitoring is important (Baker, 2002; Pressley & Afflerbach, 1995), other studies indicate that readers often mismonitor (Baker, 1989; Baker & Brown, 1984; Kinnunen, Vauras, & Niemi, 1998). Readers have been found to both over- and underestimate their comprehension of text. So, while monitoring is important and good readers seem to monitor successfully, effective teachers realize that mismonitoring can affect meaning for less able students, and they provide additional support as needed so that all readers comprehend text successfully.

Use multiple strategy approaches. Researchers have found that teaching multiple strategies simultaneously may be particularly powerful (Trabasso & Bouchard, 2002; National Institute of Child Health and Human Development, 2000; Pressley, 2000).

> There is very strong empirical, scientific evidence that the instruction of more than one strategy in a natural context leads to the acquisition and use of reading comprehension strategies and transfer to standardized comprehension tests. Multiple strategy instruction facilitates comprehension as evidenced by performance on tasks that involve memory, summarizing, and identification of main ideas. (Trabasso & Bouchard, 2002, p. 184)

Perhaps the most frequently used multiple strategies approach is transactional strategy instruction (TSI), created and studied by Pressley and colleagues (Brown, Pressley, Van Meter, & Schuder, 1996; Gaskins, Anderson, Pressley, Cunicelli, & Satlow, 1993). TSI teachers encourage readers to make sense of text by using strategies that allow them to make connections between text content and prior knowledge. Teachers and students work in small reading groups to collaboratively make meaning using several teacher-identified strategies. Teachers model and explain the strategies, coach students in their use, and help students use them flexibly. Throughout the instruction, students are taught to think about the usefulness of each strategy and to become metacognitive about their own reading processes.

Scaffold support. When teaching strategies to elementary-age students, teachers gradually release responsibility for comprehending to students. An effective model that has been used by some teachers is the Gradual Release of Responsibility model (Pearson & Gallagher, 1983). In this model, teachers take all the responsibility for applying a newly introduced strategy by modeling, thinking aloud, demonstrating, and creating meaning. As time passes and students have more exposure to and practice with using the strategy, teachers scaffold students by creating activities within students' Zone of Proximal Development (Vygotsky, 1978) and slowly withdrawing more and more responsibility. Teachers work collaboratively with the students and the strategy, giving and taking as much as necessary to create meaning. Eventually, students take on more and more responsibility as they become more confident, knowledgeable, and capable. Finally, students are able to work independently. Teachers and students do not always progress in a linear way, but often slip back and forth between more and less responsibility depending on the task, the text, and the strategy. While adaptations may be made with students of different ages, teachers use this model with students in all elementary grades.

Make reading/writing connections visible. Teachers help students see that reading and writing are parallel processes and that becoming good writers can help them become good readers (Kucer, 2001). Composing a text can be thought of as writing something that people will understand. Writing can bring understanding about a certain topic to the writer, who will have to be clear about the topic he or she is writing about. Meaning matters in comprehending, and becoming a clear writer is all about how the reader will make meaning of the text that is being created. Recalling the earlier discussion of authentic purposes is important here as well; students will likely become engaged with the task of writing if asked to write for authentic and important purposes.

Closing Comments

Comprehending is a complicated process, as we have discovered and explored in this article. Yet it is one of the most important skills for students to develop if they are to become successful and productive adults. Comprehension instruction in schools, beginning in kindergarten, is therefore crucial. Teachers use their knowledge and understandings of how one learns to comprehend to inform classroom practices so they can most effectively help readers develop the abilities to comprehend text. It is hoped that the discussion in this article can open a dialogue with teachers and teacher educators toward this end.

REFERENCES

Anderson, R.C., & Pearson, P.D. (1984). A schema-thematic view of basic processes in reading comprehension. In P.D. Pearson, R. Barr, M.L. Kamil, & P. Mosenthal (Eds.), *Handbook of reading research* (pp. 255–291). New York: Longman.

Armbruster, B.B. (1984). The problem of "inconsiderate texts." In G.G. Duffy, L.R. Roehler, & J. Mason (Eds.), *Theoretical issues in reading comprehension* (pp. 202–217). New York: Longman.

Baker, L. (1989). Metacognition, comprehension monitoring, and the adult reader. *Educational Psychology Review, 1,* 3–38.

Baker, L. (2002). Metacognition in comprehension instruction. In C.C. Block & M. Pressley (Eds.), *Comprehension instruction: Research-based best practices* (pp. 77–95). New York: Guilford.

Baker, L., & Brown, A.L. (1984). Metacognitive skills and reading. In P.D. Pearson, R. Barr, M. Kamil, & P. Mosenthal (Eds.), *Handbook of reading research* (pp. 353–394). New York: Longman.

Blachowicz, C.L.Z., & Fisher, P. (2000). Vocabulary instruction. In M.L. Kamil, P.B. Mosenthal, P.D. Pearson, & R. Barr (Eds.), *Handbook of reading research* (Vol. 3, pp. 503–523). Mahwah, NJ: Erlbaum.

Brown, R., Pressley, M., Van Meter, P., & Schuder, T. (1996). A quasi-experimental validation of transactional strategies instruction with low-achieving second-grade students. *Journal of Educational Psychology, 88*(1), 18–37.

Butcher, K.R., & Kintsch, W. (2003). Text comprehension and discourse processing. In A.F. Healy & R.W. Proctor (Vol. Eds.) & I.B. Weiner (Ed.-in-Chief), *Handbook of psychology, Volume 4, Experimental psychology* (pp. 575–595). New York: Wiley.

Duffy, G.G. (2002). The case for direct explanation of strategies. In C.C. Block & M. Pressley (Eds.), *Comprehension instruction: Research-based best practices* (pp. 28–41). New York: Guilford.

Duke, N. (2003, March 7). *Comprehension instruction for informational text.* Presentation at the annual meeting of the Michigan Reading Association, Grand Rapids, MI.

Fletcher, C.R. (1994). Levels of representation in memory for discourse. In M.A. Gernsbacher (Ed.), *Handbook of psycholinguistics* (pp. 589–607). San Diego: Academic Press.

Fountas, I.C., & Pinnell, G.S. (1996). *Guided reading: Good first teaching for all children.* Portsmouth, NH: Heinemann.

Gaskins, I.W., Anderson, R.C., Pressley, M., Cunicelli, E.A., & Satlow, E. (1993). Six teachers' dialogue during cognitive process instruction. *The Elementary School Journal, 93,* 277–304.

Grattan, K.W. (1997). They can do it too! Book Club with first and second graders. In S.I. McMahon, T.E. Raphael, V.J. Goatley, & L.S. Pardo (Eds.), *The Book Club connection: Literacy learning and classroom talk* (pp. 267–283). New York: Teachers College Press.

Keene, E.O., & Zimmermann, S. (1997). *Mosaic of thought: Teaching comprehension in a reader's workshop.* Portsmouth, NH: Heinemann.

Kinnunen, R., Vauras, M., & Niemi, P. (1998). Comprehension monitoring in beginning readers. *Scientific Studies of Reading, 2,* 353–375.

Kucer, S.B. (2001). *Dimensions of literacy: A conceptual base of teaching reading and writing in school settings.* Mahwah, NJ: Erlbaum.

McMahon, S.I., Raphael, T.E., Goatley, V.J., & Pardo, L.S. (1997). *The Book Club connection: Literacy learning and classroom talk.* New York: Teachers College Press.

Miller, D. (2002). *Reading with meaning: Teaching comprehension in the primary grades.* Portland, ME: Stenhouse.

Morrow, L.M., & Gambrell, L.B. (2000). Literature-based reading instruction. In M.L. Kamil, P.B. Mosenthal, P.D. Pearson, & R. Barr (Eds.), *Handbook of reading research* (Vol. 3, pp. 563–586). Mahwah, NJ: Erlbaum.

Narvaez, D. (2002). Individual differences that influence reading comprehension. In C.C. Block & M. Pressley (Eds.), *Comprehension instruction: Research-based best practices* (pp. 158–175). New York: Guilford.

National Institute of Child Health and Human Development. (2000). *Report of the National Reading Panel: Teaching children to read: An evidence-based assessment of the scientific research literature on reading and its implications for reading instruction* (NIH Publication No. 00-4769). Washington, DC: U.S. Government Printing Office.

Pardo, L.S. (2002). Book Club for the twenty-first century. *Illinois Reading Council Journal, 30*(4), 14–23.

Pearson, P.D., & Gallagher, M. (1983). The instruction of reading comprehension. *Contemporary Education Psychology, 8,* 317–344.

Pressley, M. (1998). *Reading instruction that works: The case for balanced teaching.* New York: Guilford.

Pressley, M. (2000). What should comprehension instruction be the instruction of? In M.L. Kamil, P.B. Mosenthal, P.D. Pearson, & R. Barr (Eds.), *Handbook of reading research* (Vol. 3, pp. 545–561). Mahwah, NJ: Erlbaum.

Pressley, M. (2003, March 7). *Time to revolt against reading instruction as usual: What comprehension instruction could and should be.* Presentation at the annual meeting of the Michigan Reading Association, Grand Rapids, MI.

Pressley, M., & Afflerbach, P. (1995). *Verbal protocols of reading: The nature of constructively responsive reading.* Hillsdale, NJ: Erlbaum.

Pressley, M., & Hilden, K. (2002). How can children be taught to comprehend text better? In M.L. Kamil, J.B. Manning, & H.J. Walberg (Eds.), *Successful reading instruction: Research in educational productivity* (pp. 33–51). Greenwich, CT: Information Age.

Pressley, M., & McCormick, C. (1995). *Advanced educational psychology for researchers, educators, and policymakers.* New York: HarperCollins.

RAND Reading Study Group. (2002). *Reading for understanding: Toward a research and development program in reading comprehension.* Santa Monica, CA: Office of Education Research and Improvement.

Raphael, T.E., Florio-Ruane, S., & George, M. (2001). Book Club Plus: A conceptual framework to organize literacy instruction. *Language Arts, 79,* 159–168.

Rasinski, T. (2003, March 7). *Fluency: Chasing the illusive reading goal.* Presentation at the annual meeting of the Michigan Reading Association, Grand Rapids, MI.

Rosenblatt, L.R. (1978). *The reader, the text, the poem: The transactional theory of the literary work.* Carbondale: Southern Illinois University Press.

Salna, K. (2001). Book Clubs as part of a balanced curriculum. *Illinois Reading Council Journal, 29*(4), 40–47.

Schallert, D.L., & Martin, D.B. (2003). A psychological analysis of what teachers and students do in the language arts classroom. In J. Flood, D. Lapp, J.R. Squire, & J.M. Jensen (Eds.), *Handbook of research on teaching the English language arts* (pp. 31–45). Mahwah, NJ: Erlbaum.

Tompkins, G.E. (2003). *Literacy for the 21st century: Teaching reading and writing in pre-kindergarten through grade 4.* Upper Saddle River, NJ: Merrill Prentice Hall.

Trabasso, T., & Bouchard, E. (2002). Teaching readers how to comprehend text strategically. In C.C. Block & M. Pressley (Eds.), *Comprehension instruction: Research-based best practices* (pp. 176–200). New York: Guilford.

Tracey, D.H., & Morrow, L.M. (2002). Preparing young learners for successful reading comprehension. In C.C. Block & M. Pressley (Eds.), *Comprehension instruction: Research-based best practices* (pp. 319–333). New York: Guilford.

van den Broek, P. (1994). Comprehension and memory of narrative texts: Inferences and coherences. In M.A. Gernsbacher (Ed.), *Handbook of psycholinguistics* (pp. 539–588). San Diego, CA: Academic Press.

Vygotsky, L.S. (1978). *Mind in society.* Cambridge, MA: Harvard University Press.

Waber, B. (1973). *Ira sleeps over.* Boston: Houghton Mifflin.

Waber, B. (1991). *Ira says goodbye.* Boston: Houghton Mifflin.

SECTION FOUR

Literacy Assessment

When we are concerned with appraisal of a person's ability to read insightfully and meaningfully, we almost assume that there will be many different but equally acceptable responses.... Under these circumstances it looms as a very difficult task to conceive a completely objective test that will permit us to assess the quality or richness or correctness of each person's interpretation of a given selection.

—ROGER T. LENNON (1962, p. 336)

The process through which we examine and keep track of children's literacy development is currently dominated by multiple choice, product oriented, group administered, norm referenced reading tests. These tests have been developed in the names of science and efficiency by "experts" so that the teacher need only be a technician who administers a test and later receives scores.

—PETER JOHNSTON (1987, p. 744)

But there may be a disconnect between what is required to meet external demands for scientifically based reading assessment and the type of assessment information teachers need on a day-to-day basis to provide appropriately designed and targeted reading instruction for all students.

—MARCIA A. INVERNIZZI, TIMOTHY J. LANDRUM, JENNIFER L. HOWELL, & HEATHER P. WARLEY (2005, p. 610)

Issues and Innovations in Literacy Education: Readings From The Reading Teacher, edited by Richard D. Robinson. © 2006 by the International Reading Association.

Teachers have always sought effective ways to better understand their students' reading abilities. This need to accurately assess literacy skills is critically important if effective instruction is to take place. Because reading is such a complex and often subtle activity, literacy testing historically has followed a variety of approaches and methods, including standardized tests, various informal assessment procedures, as well as classroom observations. Although the results of these testing measures have had a wide range of usefulness for teachers, research and investigation related to various aspects of literacy assessment continue today. From its inception, *The Reading Teacher* has been in the forefront in helping classroom teachers stay informed on the latest developments in this area.

In today's world, literacy assessment is an educational as well as political activity. Whereas, at one time, testing was considered to be primarily a way to understand individual student achievement, it is today a much broader issue. Results from tests are used regularly at the national and state levels to support wide-ranging political agendas, especially through various types of funding programs. Today these literacy initiatives frequently set curriculum standards and goals, determine the specific literacy materials to be used for instruction, and often set criteria for the evaluation of teacher performance. Viewed from the public perspective, literacy assessment in this context becomes a primary measure for determining the effectiveness of the public school system.

Because of this political pressure placed on literacy educators relating to test results, there is increased emphasis to dictate curriculum changes based solely on assessment scores. It is unfortunate that what is tested and assessed often determines what teachers teach and what learners learn in many literacy classrooms today.

The articles in this chapter clearly recognize many of these problems related to literacy assessment and provide in many cases clear and effective avenues of choice on how classroom teachers can address these difficulties.

Section Readings

Although the first article in this section by George A. Prescott is now more than 50 years old, it addresses many issues and concerns about testing that are still being discussed today. Note the sections on the misuses and misunderstandings that are often associated with literacy assessment. Finally, the last sentence in this article could easily be applied to the current situation in reading testing today.

In the second article, Shelton L. Root, Jr., presents an interesting and encouraging approach to evaluating children's knowledge and experiences of the literature they read. As noted by the author, many teachers use traditional approaches to their understanding of students' book knowledge such as book reports, lists of books read, and various forms of standardized literacy tests. Instead of these more established approaches, Root suggests that teachers consider a broader concept of assessment that is based primarily on students' awareness of their own knowledge of literature. The emphasis is placed on critical evaluation by the individual reader, as well as the importance of group interactions.

The often-wide discrepancy between many standardized literacy assessment tests and what is known about fundamental processes related to reading is the subject of the next article, by Sheila Valencia and P. David Pearson. Unfortunately, the results of literacy tests often do not accurately reflect either actual student ability in reading or the attributes of a school's reading program. Suggestions to remedy this situation are as appropriate today as when they were written in 1956.

It has been evident for a number of years that assessment in general and literacy testing specifically influence much more than just educational decisions. What is now called "high-stakes testing" has come to influence decision makers far beyond local schools and individual classroom teachers. Agencies at the federal, state, and local levels now regularly use assessment results to make critical decisions about allocating funds for education, approving appropriated literacy curriculum choices, and determining teacher instructional methods in the classroom. The next article in this section, a position statement of the International Reading Association, addresses the role of high-stakes assessment and its implications for the teaching of literacy skills.

Finally, the article by Peter Johnston reflects the various latest thinking on what the author believes should be the primary roles of reading testing today. Perhaps the most sobering thought is the conclusion, which supports the view that what is being assessed in literacy is what is being taught in the classroom.

REFERENCES

Invernizzi, M.A., Landrum, T.J., Howell, J.L., & Warley, H.P. (2005). Toward the peaceful coexistence of test developers, policymakers, and teachers in an era of accountability. *The Reading Teacher, 58*(7), 610–618.

Johnston, P. (1987). Teachers as evaluation experts. *The Reading Teacher, 40*(8), 744–748.

Lennon, R.T. (1962). What can be measured? *The Reading Teacher, 15*(5), 336–337.

For Further Reading on Literacy Assessment

The following articles reflect a historical view of literacy assessment as described in past issues of *The Reading Teacher*. They have been selected because of their importance in the development of many of the current views of reading assessment present today.

Gates, A.I. (1952). Standardized reading tests—Their uses and abuses. *The Reading Teacher, 5*(5), 1–2, 14.
    Describes the effective use of the results of standardized reading assessments of different types, and how the results can be misused in determining classroom practices in literacy education.

Tinker, M.A. (1954). Appraisal of growth in reading. *The Reading Teacher, 8*(1), 35–38.
    Summarizes the advantages and disadvantages of the use by classroom teachers of reading survey tests, informal approaches to literacy assessment, and anecdotal records.

Johnson, M.S. (1960). Reading inventories for classroom use. *The Reading Teacher, 14*(1), 9–13.
    Discusses the classroom use of various types of informal literacy assessment as a basis for making instructional decisions in reading instruction.

Calfee, R.C. (1987). The school as a context for assessment of literacy. *The Reading Teacher, 40*(8), 738–743.
    Comments on the influence of externally mandated literacy assessments as opposed to those developed by competent classroom faculty members of a school.

Johnston, P. (1987). Teachers as evaluation experts. *The Reading Teacher, 40*(8), 744–748.
  Supports the fundamental concept that process-oriented evaluations of students' literacy activities are much more valid than externally developed tests of various types.

Davey, B. (1989). Assessing comprehension: Selected interactions of task and reader. *The Reading Teacher, 42*(9), 694–697.
  Notes the external influences of test format, testing conditions, and question type on developing false results on formal literacy comprehension tests.

Invernizzi, M.A., Landrum, T.J., Howell, J.L., & Warley, H.P. (2005). Toward the peaceful co-existence of test developers, policymakers, and teachers in an era of accountability. *The Reading Teacher, 58*(7), 610–618.
  Reviews the current situation in literacy assessment, suggesting ways in which educators and test developers can work together for the common good.

Use Reading Tests Carefully—
They Can Be Dangerous Tools

George A. Prescott

Reading is a highly complex process. There are numerous skills that need to be developed during the elementary school period. Desirable growth in the important reading skills will result only through a carefully planned program of instruction—a program adapted to different levels of ability and different rates of learning. Consequently, if reading instruction is, in any realistic sense, to meet the needs of individual pupils or groups of pupils, continuing and accurate information concerning their abilities and achievements is required.

The more information the school staff—administrators, supervisors, guidance personnel, and classroom teachers—have concerning the proficiency of their pupils with respect to these reading abilities, and the more they are guided by this information in selecting instructional materials, the greater is the likelihood that real progress will be made toward the attainment of their reading goals. Thus, continuous evaluation becomes an integral part of the teaching-learning process.

Uses of Standardized Reading Tests

There are many kinds of information which the various members of the school staff should have if they are to be in a position to deal adequately with pupils. There are also many sources of information—a wide variety of techniques of evaluation, both "test" and "non-test."

Standardized reading tests represent one important source of information which serve administrative, supervisory, guidance, and classroom purposes. For example, the principal or superintendent may be concerned primarily with comparing the general reading status of the pupils in his school or system with the national norm. The supervisor may be concerned, at the moment, with an evaluation of instructional methods or materials. The guidance counselor may need accurate information concerning the reading achievement levels of the pupils whom he is counseling. The classroom teacher may need information to aid her in grouping pupils within a class for reading instruction; she may desire to determine what growth has taken place during a school year; she may wish to identify those pupils who, for any number of reasons, are achieving significantly below their capacity to achieve.

These specific instances in no way represent a complete listing of the ways in which standardized test data may be used; they *do* point to the many ways in which test data serve all members of the school staff.

The most important uses of test data are made by the classroom teacher for pupil guidance and for the improvement of instruction. Her main reason for testing should be to obtain a better understanding of her pupils, individually and as a group, to the end that she may do a better job of teaching them. The real value in testing, then, lies in obtaining information which enables one to adopt a strategy that will provide better guidance and better teaching.

Reprinted from *The Reading Teacher*, 5(5), pp. 3–5. © 1952 by the International Reading Association.

Misuses of Standardized Tests

Used properly and interpreted wisely, standardized reading tests of one type or another can provide valuable information for pupil guidance. Misused, they can be a source of inestimable harm, not only to the pupil whom they should benefit primarily, but to teachers and entire schools as well. Misuses of tests can usually be traced to lack of understanding of the nature and purposes of standardized tests and failure to consider their limitations. Scissors may be employed with excellent results in cutting paper and cloth, but with little success as a screw driver in the repair of a watch, a purpose for which they were not intended.

A complete listing of the misuses of tests would indeed be lengthy. Only three will be cited here: the rating or evaluation of teacher efficiency solely on the basis of standardized test results; the use of achievement test results as the sole basis for promotion of pupils; and the making of major decisions about pupils on the basis of a single test score. All such practices reflect a host of misunderstandings, several of which are discussed below.

Areas of Misunderstanding

The necessity for adhering to the prescribed conditions is regarded lightly by many. One of the outstanding features of a standardized reading test is that it provides "comparative" information; that is, it provides information for comparing the performance of pupils with that of certain reference populations. One of the basic assumptions made when we compare the test scores of pupils with the scores made by the reference population, i.e. with norms, is that the test was administered in exactly the same way that it was to the norm group—with the same directions, time limits, scoring rules, etc. The teacher who fails to follow the instructions for administering and provides extra practice material, gives extra time to the slower pupils in her class, or scores the tests incorrectly cannot meaningfully compare the results made by her pupils with the norms for the test.

There is also considerable misunderstanding concerning the way norms are developed, and their relations to standards. Frequently, norms and standards are used synonymously. Norms are based on the *average* scores made by the pupils constituting the norm population. If the average score of a class on a reading test is at the norm, it is just an average class. Standards, on the other hand, are levels of proficiency set up locally as goals for pupils to attain. To consider attainment of the norm as evidence of satisfactory achievement or the goal to be attained by all pupils is, in most instances, unjustified.

Many teachers fail to recognize that a wide variety of factors, aside from specific in-school instruction, affect achievement test scores. This is particularly true in the case of reading to which out-of-school learnings contribute markedly. In other words, the score obtained by a pupil on a reading test reflects not only the effects of specific instruction, but his mental level, interest in and opportunities for reading, motivation, physical condition, previous schooling, and many other less discernible factors as well. Such factors need to be considered when interpreting reading test results.

One of the most potent of the factors affecting reading achievement is mental ability. An accurate estimate of each pupil's "potentialities for learning" is necessary for accurate identification of those needing special consideration. The teacher must be able to differentiate the poor readers with limited potentialities from poor readers who have average or superior mental ability because the corrective instruction will not be the same for both groups.

Moreover, the teacher should be cognizant of the fact that the pupil who is rather severely handicapped in reading ability will almost surely be penalized if the mental ability test used presupposes normal reading ability for his age, and should be wary of accepting the score obtained from such a test as an accurate indication of the pupil's true mental ability level. Any pupil whose intelligence or reading test results seem greatly out of line in light of his past achievement record and/or the teacher's own estimates should most certainly be subjected to closer scrutiny.

That "a test is a test is a test" is a highly dangerous, though often made, assumption. Many teachers assume automatically that the test title accurately describes the test, and therefore, further inspection is unnecessary. It is safe to say that, of the hundreds of reading tests available to users, no two are identical with respect to purpose, skills measured, and results obtained. This fact is overlooked by the teacher who becomes disturbed and confused because her pupils do not receive identical grade or age equivalents on two or more "reading" tests. It is also overlooked by the teacher who assumes that the obtained reading test score is the properly weighted summation of *all* the important reading skills she is attempting to develop at the moment.

There is, undoubtedly, a wide variety of reading skills which ought to be developed systematically; however, so far as the writer is aware, agreement among reading authorities is far from unanimous as to the important specific skills to be developed, the varying degrees of complexity of each skill, or the exact grade levels at which each should be introduced or developed. Research has not yet given us exact information as to the interrelationships among the various skills, or the extent to which improvement in one skill results in improvement in another. As we find answers to such questions, better and different tests will be forthcoming.

Factors to Be Considered in the Selection of Standardized Reading Tests

The purposes to be served by the testing should be the main criterion in the selection of tests. Reading tests are designed to serve, primarily, a single function; it may be a survey, or a diagnostic or analytic function. A survey reading test is designed to measure *general* achievement in, usually, a limited number of reading skills, whereas the function of a diagnostic test is to provide more *specific* information concerning the nature of a pupil's reading difficulties. Needless to say, each type plays an important and unique role in the appraisal of reading ability.

Because of the differences in function, no single reading test can be "all things to all people." In earlier days, a single remedy was advertised as a cure for a wide variety of ailments; by the same token, many test users, today, are searching for a single test which will serve, equally well, both survey and diagnostic functions.

The standardized silent reading tests available fall into three general categories: (1) tests of general reading comprehension and/or word meaning, and word recognition; (2) tests which measure a single reading skill; and (3) tests which provide separate measures of several reading skills. Tests of the first type usually provide an average reading score which is obtained by combining scores on the parts. Typical of these are the Nelson Silent Reading[1], Metropolitan[2], and Stanford Reading Tests[2]. Measures of single skills are confined almost entirely to word recognition tests such as the Manwiller Word Recognition Test[2], and vocabulary tests. Among tests of the third type are the Iowa Silent Reading Tests[2], Diagnostic Examination of Silent Reading Abilities[3], and the SRA Reading Record[4].

The best known of the few standardized oral reading tests available are the Standardized Oral Reading Paragraphs[5] and Standardized Oral Reading Check Tests[5] by William S. Gray. The former yields a composite score based on rate of reading and errors; the latter, scores for both rate and accuracy. The Gilmore Oral Reading Test[2], soon to be published, provides measures of accuracy, rate, and comprehension. Aside from the comparative information obtained, such tests can be of value in determining the specific nature of a pupil's reading difficulties.

Too often the matter of test selection is not given the attention it deserves, with the result that important considerations are overlooked. Several of these in the form of questions are given below.

---

[1] Published by Houghton Mifflin Company
[2] Published by World Book Company
[3] Published by Educational Test Bureau
[4] Published by Science Research Associates
[5] Published by Public School Publishing Company

(1) Will the test yield the information I need? This is merely another way of saying, "Will the test serve my particular purposes?" As has been pointed out in an earlier section, this question cannot be answered merely by reference to the test title.

(2) Will the test yield information that is sufficiently dependable for my purpose? This refers to the reliability, or consistency, of the test. The phrase, "for my particular purposes" in this question is significant. For example, if the test information is to be used for individual pupil guidance, a more reliable test is needed than if the data are to be used in studying the achievement of class groups.

If a test provides separate measures of several reading skills, it is necessary to study the reliability data given for each skill. Profiles are often misleading due to the unreliability of measures of the separate skills or abilities profiled. One of the greatest errors committed by inexperienced test users is the reluctance to consider a pupil's "obtained" test score as an approximation of his "true" score, thereby failing to make allowances for "errors of measurement."

(3) Are the norms adequate? Norms may be inadequate both with respect to representativeness and to type. If the test provides "national" norms, one should have evidence that they are truly representative of our nation's schools.

The test user should have knowledge of the types of norms—grade or age equivalents, percentiles, etc.—provided, since unavailability of norms of a particular type will limit the types of comparisons that can be made and the ways in which the data can be analyzed.

(4) How many forms of the test are there? If frequent testing with the same instrument is planned, it is normally desirable that more than one form be available.

(5) Will the results be comparable from subtest to subtest, battery to battery, and form to form? This is one of the most important requirements of a test if accurate comparisons between testings, among different groups, or among various subtest scores on the same test are to be made.

(6) Does the test provide suggestions for the proper use and interpretation of the results? Other factors which must be considered are the training required to properly administer and interpret the tests, the cost, and ease of scoring.

In Summary

The data from standardized reading tests represent *one* important source of information required by members of the school staff. With clear recognition of the particular uses and limitations of such tests, they provide valuable and unique information. Used indiscriminately and uncritically, they are not only ineffective, but dangerous tools.

Evaluating Children's Awareness of Literature

Shelton L. Root, Jr.

All of us who work with children and books wish, at one time or another, that we had better methods of discovering whether or not young people are growing in their awareness of the untold riches which lie between the covers of children's books.

Most of us do something about this problem. Some keep lists of books read. Some require oral or written book reports—or both. Others give standardized tests, tests which devote a part of their limited space to measuring children's knowledge of particular books. Still others combine one or more of the aforementioned techniques with some more original plan of their own. But few of us are satisfied that we have really done enough to evaluate the quality of children's experiences in reading.

Perhaps, if we consider the implications of three questions before we next undertake to evaluate children's growth in literature, we might find that we could do a more satisfactory job.

First, What Do We Really Set Out to Do When We Evaluate?

Let's examine this term, *evaluation*. Evaluation means a great deal more than simple measurement. To really evaluate anything we must do more than merely lay it alongside a single, preconceived, and generally agreed upon measuring device. True, a part of evaluation is measurement. But undoubtedly a larger part of our evaluation cannot be made with precise, objective measuring devices.

Evaluation means more than measurement! It means: "The process of determining the extent to which values are achieved, purposes carried out, and goals reached.... Evaluation includes analysis of the purposes themselves and consideration of the techniques by which goals are attained, as well as the degree of achievement."[1] If these are the things with which we are really concerned when we evaluate children's experiences with literature, we had better consider just what kinds of values, purposes, and goals can intelligently be expected when children familiarize themselves with books. And, this leads us into a consideration of our next question.

Second, What Aspects of Children's Experiences With Literature Should Be Evaluated?

One method of determining this is to answer the question: What should experiences with literature do for children? Some of the more obvious answers are:

- It should help children better understand the world in which they live.
- It should help children better to understand themselves.
- It should help children better to understand others.

---

[1] James B. Burr, Lowry W. Harding, and Leland B. Jacobs, *Student Teaching in the Elementary School* (New York: Appleton-Century-Crofts, Inc., 1950), p. 183.

Reprinted from *The Reading Teacher*, 9(3), pp. 149–154. © 1956 by the International Reading Association.

- It should help children to increase the effectiveness of their interpersonal relationships.
- It should help children to recognize the inherent worth and dignity of all peoples.
- It should help provide children with a healthy means of temporarily disassociating themselves from the almost incessant demands of modern, day-to-day living.
- It should help children gain a better understanding of how "things" came to be.
- It should help children establish a sense of direction toward the promise of a better world. (A promise whose fulfillment is dependent upon the sense of direction which young readers gain as they reach maturity.)
- It should help children become increasingly discriminating in the selection of their reading materials.

Of course, there are other objectives which should be added. But this listing provides us with some fairly satisfactory leads.

Third, How Satisfactory Are Our Present Techniques of Evaluation, and What, if Anything, Can We Do to Improve Them?

Most of us have been giving standardized tests for a great many years, and they have been of some help to us in some areas. But of how much actual help can they be in the area of literature. What do they really test?

An examination of the literature part of one such test, which we often administer, and which is accepted by nearly all authorities in the field of testing to be as good as, if not better than, any other instrument available, reveals that it measures children's memory. Memory of (and this test is designed for children in grades five through eight) nursery rhymes, fairy tales, adult poetry, patriotic songs, children's classics (most of which were origi-

nally written for adult consumption), *Bible* stories, an opera, American folk lore, and a knowledge of early American and European history.

These tests demand nothing more of the testee than a good memory—which is all they are designed to measure. To score high on such a test a child is really wasting his time to read anything with a publication date much later than 1920. Actually, other than Joyce Kilmer's, *Trees*, the latest date of publication for information demanded by this particular test is that of *Mrs. Wiggs of the Cabbage Patch*, which was published at the turn of the twentieth century!

More careful scrutiny of standardized tests of this type would lead only to the already obvious conclusion that, insofar as children's literature is concerned, these tests are of minute and questionable value. We might deduce that if a child scores unusually high on such a test he may not have been employing his reading time to the most rewarding advantage.

If, in the light of critical examination, the time hallowed practice of evaluating children's literacy experiences by standardized tests is to be abandoned, what kinds of evaluative practices might replace them?

From some quarters comes the immediate answer, "None! Give children plenty of time to read and don't worry about evaluation." This ready solution is built upon what appears to be, at very least, some misguided, if well intentioned, concepts of what the early leaders of the progressive education movement were aiming at when they leveled their philosophic cannons at the highly formalized, impersonal, and unsatisfactory evaluative techniques of the past. Nowhere, among the responsible leaders of the progressive education movement, can we find one who advocates the elimination of evaluation. In fact, they were advocates of more evaluation, not less! Their concern lay with the quality of evaluation and with the problem of what was to be evaluated.

A Broad Concept of Evaluation

Most of us agree, at least in principle, that education without evaluation is neither practical, desirable, nor possible. And we also agree that an important part of children's educative experience is an increasing awareness of the rapidly growing potentiality of literature. So, the answer is not to be found in the abandonment of evaluation. The answer is to be found in the acceptance of a broader concept of the term *evaluation*, and in the implementation of better evaluative techniques.

We must first determine the variety of reading experiences which children are having. Is there a balance between classic and contemporary, between factual and fictional, between national and international, between cultural and intercultural, and between prose and poetry? This determination is simply a matter of record keeping. The children, themselves, can do much of it with the help of their teacher or librarian.

Using these records, once we have them, to their best advantage is somewhat more difficult. Prerequisite to satisfactory use is, as with other aspects of the literature program, the provision of ample time. Then, under the guidance of teachers, there should be developed an increasing understanding of the advantages of becoming a well-balanced reader. This kind of balance is determined on an individual basis, however, and not on any such basis as an assigned ratio, such as two fictional to one factual, and three national to two international, etc., for all members of the group. An evaluation, such as this, of what has been read should help each reader to discover the gaps in his own reading, and, under the expert guidance of his teacher and librarian, should help him close such gaps.

Criteria of Evaluation Should Be Evolved Also by the Group

This very consideration is in itself, perhaps, the keystone of all effective programs of evaluation. During such considerations teachers not only help children to determine the types of books which they have been reading, but, with a slight shift in emphasis, help children to establish criteria by which to judge the quality of their literature. For, as in the evaluation of other aspects of school experience, children profit most when the criteria for evaluation are evolved by the group. Little insightful evaluation results from the utilization of autocratically imposed standards to democratically appraise one's own growth.

From group establishment of criteria very naturally grows the establishment by individuals of their own criteria. These criteria take into account individual differences in interest, reading background, and reading ability. They do not negate the criteria previously established by the group. They are outgrowths of them, tailored to fit the uniqueness of each individual reader.

Once established, these criteria, both individual and group, must be given a chance to operate and be modified in the light of experience. Time must be provided for periodic assessments by children of the quality of their reading experience and the effectiveness of their criteria. Here, again, records should be kept, both by the teacher and by the children. By keeping simple records of the modifications through which their criteria go, children will be able to more completely evaluate their own growth. And teachers at year's end will be helped in visualizing the effects of their own patient guidance.

Group Discussions Are Helpful

Group discussion of particular books or specific types of books is another invaluable aid to effective evaluation. Here, discussion goes below plot level whenever appropriate. Questions are asked such as: What was the author really trying to say? Are the people described by the author true to life, or do they lack blood and sinew? How can we reconcile the different points of view expressed by these two authors? These questions are answered as well as possible by further reading, by other members of the class, by the school librarian, and by the teacher. Questions whose answers lie not in fact but in point of view are examined and plainly labelled as being outside the realm of empirical testing. Children are not browbeaten into the acceptance of popular answers to such questions. In matters of this nature, deviation is encouraged.

Evaluation also comes from observation—observation by the teacher of the way children interpret, through dramatic media, what they have read.

Children frequently draw upon their literary ventures to provide plots and characters for dramatic play and informal dramatics. Though the teacher cannot and should not attempt to guide dramatic play, she can and should learn much from its observation. Here children re-create the scenes and characters they have read about, or been read to about. And it is here, by observation, that teachers can determine what children "make" of their reading.

Among older children, informal dramatics serve much the same purpose. But, in addition to being an observer, the teacher can be one of the interpreters. For, as children and teacher work together to re-enact a situation or scene taken from their reading, some communality of understanding is required. In reaching such communality of understanding, it is the teacher's responsibility to help children see deeper and deeper beneath the surface of plot.

Children of upper elementary school age and beyond have much to gain through written and oral evaluations of the books which they have read. Evaluations, such as these, are not to be confused with the dull, uninspired, halting retelling of plot. This procedure of retelling the plot invariably results in the listening audience being bored beyond the point of discomfort, or the reading audience (most often of one—the teacher) making a note that here is another assignment completed. It takes greater artistry than most children have, or most adults for that matter, to narrate an improved version of an author's original.

Critical Analysis Should Be Used

There is however, a definite place for critical evaluations in which children, either orally or in writing, analyze the method of presentation, the effectiveness of presentation, the point of view of the presentation, and the intentions which the author had when he wrote. It is this type of critical analysis which encourages young readers to compare and contrast their own assumptions about life with those of many authors from many places and out of many times. From such comparisons and contrastings comes an ever increasing ability to evaluate one's own experiences with literature. And out of such endeavors come readers with an ever increasing sense of discrimination. Evaluations of this nature, also demand the help of a teacher.

Certainly, a critical evaluation should not be required for every book read, probably not even for every second or third book read. But when they are made they should be made with the help of the teacher whose responsibility it is to encourage the evaluator to keep before him the criteria by which he is evaluating. It is, too, the teacher's job to see that such evaluations find the audience which they deserve. This can be done by posting the evaluations as they are made, or by keeping them in a card file in the library corner to be used by others as they select books, or by keeping them in a loose-leaf folder for the same purpose. If the school is a large one, many of these evaluations can be posted in the library. It takes an audience to encourage most writers. Oral evaluations should be informal and infrequent enough to help make of the occasion one which is looked forward to with eager enthusiasm rather than with sickening fear. With evaluation, as with reading, the greatest growth comes when a sense of excitement prevails.

To these evaluative techniques, others can and should be added by teachers who know intimately their own classroom situations. If it appears that more space has been devoted to the problem of helping children evaluate their own growth in reading than to the problem of helping teachers evaluate the growth of children in reading, this is probably as it should be. For our task of evaluating becomes many times easier and more effective as our children become more astute in the art of evaluating their own progress.

Reading Assessment: Time for a Change

Sheila Valencia and P. David Pearson

Reading assessment has not kept pace with advances in reading theory, research, or practice. On the one hand, we argue vehemently for richer and more liberating instructional materials and practices—practices that help students become sophisticated readers, readers who have a sense of ownership and awareness of their reading habits and strategies.

On the other hand, we stand idly by and observe yet another round of standardized or end-of-unit basal tests. Even those of us who argue that the current tests do not measure what we mean by reading take secret pride that our pet instructional technique produces greater gains than another technique on one of those very tests.

In this article, we explain the nature, contributing factors, and consequences of this frightening dilemma in order to set the stage for some possible solutions.

The accountability movement of the 1970s, the wave of recent national reports (Education Commission of the States, 1983) and the focus of the effective schools research (Fisher et al., 1978) have set the stage for major educational reforms in the U.S. In most instances, these reports have had reading achievement as one major focus, and in many cases they have relied on students' standardized test scores as measures of educational effectiveness. Such reliance has led to an increased focus on minimal competency, norm referenced, and criterion referenced testing.

As evidence of the increasing use of tests, one need only note that there are at least 40 statewide competency testing programs in place. Add to this the thousands of locally regulated programs, the criterion referenced tests accompanying every basal reading program, and the countless school and teacher made tests, and the picture of a nation of schools, teachers, and students engulfed by tests is complete. No matter the perspective one takes, the conclusion is inescapable: The influence of testing is greater now than at any time in our history.

The time has come to change the way we assess reading. The advances of the last 15–20 years in our knowledge of the basic reading processes have begun to impact instructional research (Pearson, 1985) and are beginning to find a home in instructional materials and classroom practice (Pearson, 1986). Yet the tests used to monitor the abilities of individual students and to make policy decisions have remained remarkably impervious to advances in reading research (Farr and Carey, 1986; Johnston, in press; Pearson and Dunning, 1985).

New Views of the Process

A major contribution of recent research has been to articulate a strategic view of the process of reading (e.g., Collins, Brown, and Larkin, 1980; Pearson and Spiro, 1980). This view emphasizes the active role of readers as the use print clues to "construct" a model of the text's meaning. It deemphasizes the notion that progress toward expert reading is the aggregation of component skills. Instead, it suggests that at

Reprinted from *The Reading Teacher*, 40(8), pp. 726–732. © 1987 by the International Reading Association.

all levels of sophistication, from kindergartener to research scientist, readers use available resources (e.g., text, prior knowledge, environmental clues, and potential helpers) to make sense of the text.

Progress toward expert reading is guided by the increasing sensitivity of readers to issues of *how*, *when*, and *why* those resources can best be used. This strategic view also suggests that skilled, but not unskilled, readers can use knowledge flexibly—they can apply what they have learned from reading to new situations (e.g., Campione and Brown, 1985; Spiro and Meyers, 1984); in fact, the ability to use knowledge flexibly predicts how well students will acquire future knowledge.

Assessment has not been touched by this strategic view of reading. The Figure describes the litany of conflicts we see between what is known about reading and what is done to assess it.

The point is simple but insidious: As long as reading research and instructional innovations are based upon one view of the reading process while reading assessment instruments are based upon a contradictory point of view, we will nurture tension and confusion among those charged with the dual responsibility of instructional improvement and monitoring student achievement.

Instruction and Assessment

During the last 20 years, the relationship between assessment and instruction in reading curriculum has been framed by the logic of mastery learning, introduced in the early 1960s and developed fully by the end of the decade. The goal in mastery learning is to assure a given achievement across students by varying input such as the amount and kind of instruction and practice, or the attention paid to presumably prerequisite skills or to aptitudes of individual learners (matching the method to the child).

What has happened, of course, is that with reading conceptualized as the mastery of small, separate enabling skills, there has been a great temptation to operationalize "skilled reading" as an aggregation—not even an integration—of all these skills; "instruction" becomes operationalized as opportunities for students to practice these discrete skills on worksheets, workbook pages, and Ditto sheets.

The essence of the relationship is this: Mastery learning encourages us to think of instruction in reading as a matter of making certain that students master a "scope and sequence" of enabling skills. The "reader" moves along an assembly line, picking up a new part (new skill) at each station. When all the parts are in place, we have a reader ready to tackle real reading. Or do we?

Hidden Dangers. There are serious consequences of using one model to define skilled reading and the assessment-instruction link and another to define reading assessment. One danger lies in a false sense of security if we equate skilled reading with high scores on our current reading tests. A close inspection of the tasks involved in these tests would cast doubt upon any such conclusion.

A second danger stems from the potential insensitivity of current tests to changes in instruction motivated by strategic views of reading. Educators bold enough to establish new programs might abandon it as ineffective on the basis of no (or only a small) measurable advantage over a conventional program; they might never consider the alternative interpretation that the tests they are using are insensitive to effective instruction.

A third danger is that given the strong influence of assessment on curriculum, we are likely to see little change in instruction without an overhaul in tests. Conscientious teachers want their students to succeed on reading tests; not surprisingly, they look to tests as guides for instruction. In the best tradition of schooling, they teach to the test, directly or indirectly. Tests that model an inappropriate concept of skilled reading will foster inappropriate instruction.

A fourth danger stems from the aura of objectivity associated with published tests and the corollary taint of subjectivity associated with informal assessment. For whatever reasons, teachers are taught that the data from either standardized or basal tests are somehow more trustworthy than the data that they collect each day as a part of teaching. The price we pay for such a lesson is high; it reduces the

A set of contrasts between new views of reading and current practices in assessing reading

New views of the reading process tell us that....	Yet when we assess reading comprehension, we....
Prior knowledge is an important determinant of reading comprehension.	Mask any relationship between prior knowledge and reading comprehension by using lots of short passages on lots of topics.
A complete story or text has structural and topical integrity.	Use short texts that seldom approximate the structural and topical integrity of an authentic text.
Inference is an essential part of the process of comprehending units as small as sentences.	Rely on literal comprehension test items.
The diversity in prior knowledge across individuals as well as the varied causal relations in human experiences invite many possible inferences to fit a text or question.	Use multiple choice items with only one correct answer, even when many of the responses might, under certain conditions, be plausible.
The ability to vary reading strategies to fit the text and the situation is one hallmark of an expert reader.	Seldom assess how and when students vary the strategies they use during normal reading, studying, or when the going gets tough.
The ability to synthesize information from various parts of the text and different texts is hallmark of an expert reader.	Rarely go beyond finding the main idea of a paragraph or passage.
The ability to ask good questions of text, as well as to answer them, is hallmark of a expert reader.	Seldom ask students to create or select questions about a selection they may have just read.
All aspects of a reader's experience, including habits that arise from school and home, influence reading comprehension.	Rarely view information on reading habits and attitudes as being as important information about performance.
Reading involves the orchestration of many skills that complement one another in a variety of ways.	Use tests that fragment reading into isolated skills and report performance on each.
Skilled readers are fluent; their word identification is sufficiently automatic to allow most cognitive resources to be used for comprehension.	Rarely consider fluency as an index of skilled reading.
Learning from text involves the restructuring, application, and flexible use of knowledge in new situations.	Often ask readers to respond to the text's declarative knowledge rather than apply it to near and far transfer tasks.

likelihood that teachers will use their own data for decision making.

An alternative relationship. Consider a completely different relationship between instruction and assessment, based upon a strategic view of the reading process: Every act of reading requires the orchestration of many resources, including the text, the reader's prior knowledge, other learners, and the constraints of the situation. The goal of every act of reading, and therefore every act of assessment, is identical regardless of who is performing it. What varies across readers, situations, and levels of sophistication is exactly how readers orchestrate available resources.

Given such a view, the best possible assessment of reading would seem to occur when teachers observe and interact with students as they read authentic texts for genuine purposes. As teachers interact with students, they evaluate the way in which the students construct meaning, intervening to provide support or suggestions when the students appear to have difficulty. This model, referred to as dynamic assessment (Campione and Brown, 1985), emanates from Vygotsky's notion of the "zone of proximal development," that region of just far enough—but not too far—beyond the students' current level of competence such that sensitive teachers, using scaffolding tools such as modeling, hints, leading questions and cooperative task completion, can assist learners in moving to their next level of learning. In such a model, instruction consists of guiding learning through the interplay of assessment and meaningful application of skills; the "measure" of students' ability is not a score but an index of the type and amount of support required to advance learning.

A scenario in which there is no difference between reading, instruction and assessment is the ideal. While this model may never be fully integrated into large scale testing, it holds enormous promise for classroom and individual student assessment.

The Near Future

What we must do, then, is to help educators and policymakers at all levels begin to think about as-sessment strategies that are consistent with strategic reading and that redefine the instruction/assessment link. What we need are not just new and better tests. We need a new framework for thinking about assessment, one in which educators begin by considering types of decisions needed and the level of impact of those decisions.

We propose a framework for developing a complete assessment system based on known attributes of strategic reading and reading programs, and the decision making levels of our educational system. Imagine a matrix in which the attributes of skilled reading and effective reading programs are listed down the first column—those outcomes which students and teachers agree are desirable. Across the top of this matrix, heading columns 2, 3 and 4, are the levels of decision—state/provincial or district, school or classroom, classroom or individual. The underlying assumption is that different sorts of decisions must be made at each level and that each type of decision may require or lend itself to different types of assessment.

Note 3 critical features of such a matrix:

(1) The attributes listed must reflect a sound model of the reading process.

(2) These attributes are interdependent and cannot be measured discretely, but they may be loosely clustered—prior knowledge, comprehension, metacognition habits and attitudes—and described in terms of their interrelations.

(3) Whatever is worthy of assessment ought to be assessable in different contexts for different purposes using different strategies.

For example, because of the large number of students involved, units as large as national and state education agencies and even most large school districts need some measures that can be administered to large groups to determine trends. However, since these tools sample such a limited range of the achievements of any individual, they are likely to prove invalid and unreliable for making decisions about individuals.

Some decisions made about individuals may simply require interview techniques. In trying to validate our paper and pencil measures of reading (some examples appear later in this article), we have conducted hundreds of interviews with children who have answered novel machine scorable items. We found that there are some things you can learn only by talking to a student one on one. And student constructed responses of the type generated on daily assignments may even be most useful in making decisions about groups or whole classes.

It should not be inferred that we are advocating machine scorable formats for large scale testing and constructed response formats for individual assessment. There are possibilities for both formats at different levels of impact.

For example, while the constraints of large scale assessment have led to multiple choice, machine scorable tests, there is some indication that this is changing. In fact, the writing assessment done by the National Assessment of Educational Progress, along with those administered by most states, require students to write compositions that are evaluated by human judges. This change in writing assessment reflects the advances in our understanding of the writing process. Those of us in reading can take at least one lesson from the writing field: Those professionals stood firm in demanding large scale assessments that exhibited face, curricular, and instructional validity until they got them.

Conversely, we can see the usefulness of some machine scorable formats at the individual level if items can be constructed to provide opportunities that are usually reserved for student constructed responses.

We suspect there will be machine scorable formats useful at the individual assessment level and open ended formats useful and necessary at the district, state, or national levels. Nonetheless, if something like our proposed "imaginary" matrix ever does come to pass, we predict that, on average, as one move from large scale to school to classroom to individual levels, assessment will become more informal, open ended, and frequent. Dynamic, interactive, daily assessment could become a norm at the reading group level.

A Call for Action

Because standardized, norm referenced tests are still the most prevalent in U.S. schools, one important focus for immediate research should be to develop and evaluate new assessment techniques that are both consistent with our understanding of reading and its instruction *and* amenable to large scale testing. Unless we can influence large scale assessment, we may not be able to refocus assessment at all.

To this end, a group of us in Illinois has begun to reshape statewide assessment of reading. Within the constraints of large scale formats, we are using concepts that encourage strategic reading and redefine the assessment/instruction link. In our pilot work with 15,000 students in grades 3, 6, 8, and 10, we are evaluating many novel formats:

- **Summary writing.** Students read 3 or 4 summaries written by other students in response to the selection they read and pick the one they think best. In one version, they get a list of features of summaries and check off the reasons for their choice.

- **Metacognitive judgments.** Students encounter a scenario about a task they might have to perform in response to the selection they just read, such as retelling it to different audiences (peer, younger child, teacher). They rate the helpfulness of several different retellings for each audience.

- **Question selection.** From 20 questions, students pick the 10 they think will help a peer best understand the important ideas about a selection.

- **Multiple acceptable responses.** In a discussion, a group can consider many alternative acceptable responses to good questions, especially inferential or evaluative questions. In one format, students select all responses they find plausible. In another, students grade responses as "really complete" or "on the right track" or "totally off base" (much as a teacher grades short answer or essay responses).

- **Prior knowledge.** We have two machine scorable formats for assessing prior knowledge.

In one, students predict (yes/no/maybe) whether certain ideas are likely to be included in a selection on a specified topic. In another, they rate the relatedness of vocabulary terms to a central concept of the selection, for example, blood circulation. However, while we begin to explore new large scale formats and techniques, we are committed to developing valid, reliable and usable strategies to be included in all three columns of our "imaginary" matrix—to provide educators and policymakers with a portfolio approach to assessment that can be used to fit the types of decisions they need to make.

While we have argued that there is an urgency about these issues in 1987 not felt in previous eras, we would not want to leave readers with the impression that the battle is new. In fact, we have located a similar concern nearly a century old. In 1892 H.G. Wells bemoaned the influence of the external examiners in determining curricula in England:

> The examiner pipes and the teacher must dance—and the examiner sticks to the old tune. If the educational reformers really wish the dance altered they must turn their attention from the dancers to the musicians. (p. 382)

While some amongst us will argue that musical instruments ought to be outlawed, others will strive to change the tune, perhaps in a way that reflects less concern for melody but greater concern for harmony.

REFERENCES

Campione, Joseph C., and Ann L. Brown. *Dynamic Assessment: One Approach and Some Initial Data.* Technical Report No. 361. Urbana, Ill: Center for the Study of Reading, 1985.

Collins, Allan, John Seely Brown, and Kathy M. Larkin. "Inference in Text Understanding." In *Theoretical Issues in Reading Comprehension*, edited by Rand J. Spiro, Bertram C. Bruce, and William F. Brewer. Hillsdale, N.J.: Erlbaum, 1980.

Education Commission of the States. *Calls for Educational Reform: A Summary of Major Reports.* Denver, Colo.: ECS, 1983.

Farr, Roger, and Robert F. Carey. *Reading: What Can Be Measured?* Newark, Del.: International Reading Association, 1986.

Fisher, Charles, W., David Berliner, Nikola Filby, Richard Marliave, Leonard Cahen, Marilyn Dishaw, and Jeffrey Moore. *Teaching and Learning in Elementary Schools: A Summary of the Beginning Teacher Evaluation Study.* San Francisco, Calif.: Far West Regional Laboratory for Educational Research and Development, 1978.

Johnston, Peter. "Steps Toward a More Naturalistic Approach to the Assessment of the Reading Process." In *Content-Based Educational Assessment*, edited by James Alginn. Norwood, N.J.: Ablex, in press.

Palincsar, Annemarie S., and Ann L. Brown. "Reciprocal Teaching of Comprehension-Fostering and Comprehension-Monitoring Activities." *Cognition and Instruction*, vol. 2 (Spring 1984), pp. 117 75.

Palincsar, Annemarie, S., and Ann L. Brown. "Interactive Teaching to Promote Independent Learning from Text." *The Reading Teacher*, vol. 39 (April 1986), pp. 771–77.

Pearson, P. David, and Rand J. Spiro. "Toward a Theory of Reading Comprehension." *Topics in Language Disorders*, vol. 1 (December 1980), pp. 71–88.

Pearson, P. David. Changing the Face of Reading Comprehension Instruction. *The Reading Teacher*, vol. 38 (April 1985), pp. 724–38.

Pearson, P. David, and David B. Dunning. The Impact of Assessment on Reading Instruction. *Illinois Reading Council Journal*, vol. 3 (Fall 1985), pp. 18–19.

Pearson, P. David. "Twenty Years of Research in Reading Comprehension." In *The Context of School-based Literacy*, edited by Taffy E. Raphael. New York, N.Y.: Random House, 1986.

Spiro, Rand, J., and Ann Meyers. "Individual Differences and Underlying Cognitive Processes." In *Handbook of Reading Research*, edited by P. David Pearson, pp. 471–504. New York, N.Y.: Longman, 1984.

Wells, Herbert G. "On the True Lever of Education." *Educational Review*, vol. 4 (June–December 1892), pp. 380–85.

High-Stakes Assessments in Reading

A Position Statement of the International Reading Association

The Board of Directors of the International Reading Association is opposed to high-stakes testing. High-stakes testing means that one test is used to make important decisions about students, teachers, and schools. In a high-stakes testing situation, if students score high on a single test they could be placed in honors classes or a gifted program. On the other hand, if students score low on a high-stakes test, it could mean that they will be rejected by a particular college, and it could affect their teacher's salary and the rating of the school district as compared with others where the same test was given.

In the United States in recent years there has been an increase in policy makers' and educators' reliance on high-stakes testing in which single test scores are used to make important educational decisions. The International Reading Association is deeply concerned about this trend. The Board of Directors offers this position statement as a call for the evaluation of the impact of current types and levels of testing on teaching quality, student motivation, educational policy making, and the public's perception of the quality of schooling. Our central concern is that testing has become a means of controlling instruction as opposed to a way of gathering information to help students become better readers. To guide educators who must use tests as a key element in the information base used to make decisions about the progress of individual children and the quality of instructional programs, we offer this position in the form of a question and answer dialogue. This format is intended to ensure that important conceptual, practical, and ethical issues are considered by those responsible for designing and implementing testing programs.

What Does the Term *High-Stakes Testing* Mean?

High-stakes testing means that the consequences for good (high) or poor (low) performance on a test are substantial. In other words, some very important decisions, such as promotion or retention, entrance into an educational institution, teacher salary, or a school district's autonomy depend on a single test score.

High-stakes tests have been a part of education for some time. Perhaps the most conspicuous form of high-stakes testing, historically speaking, was in the British educational system. National exams in England and in other countries that adopted the British system separated students into different educational tracks. In the United States, tests such as the Medical College Admission Test and Law School Admission Test, as well as professional

Reprinted from *The Reading Teacher*, 53(3), pp. 257–263. © 1999 by the International Reading Association.

certification examinations (for example, state bar examinations, medical board examinations, state teacher examinations) all represent high-stakes tests.

The meaning of high stakes can be confusing at times. Tests that have no specific decision tied to them can become high stakes to teachers and school administrators when they must face public pressure after scores are made public. In other cases, a low-stakes state test can be transformed into a high-stakes test at a school district level if a local school board decides to make educational or personnel decisions based on the test results.

Why Are We Concerned With High-Stakes Testing?

Although high-stakes testing has been and probably will continue to be part of the educational landscape, there has been an increase in such testing in recent years, particularly at the state level. More children are being tested at younger ages, and states and local school districts are using these tests to make a greater variety of important decisions than ever before. Increased frustration with lack of achievement has led to a greater reliance on testing. In response to these frustrations, many states have adopted educational standards and assessments of those standards. The logic is that tests of standards accompanied by a reward and penalty structure will improve children's achievement. In too many cases the assessment is a single multiple-choice test, which would be considered high stakes and would not yield enough information to make an important instructional decision.

Is Testing an Important Part of Good Educational Design?

Yes, testing students' skills and knowledge is certainly an important part of education, but it is only one type of educational assessment. Assessment involves the systematic and purposeful collection of data to inform actions. From the viewpoint of educators, the primary purpose of assessment is to help students by providing information about how instruction can be improved.

Assessment has an important role to play in decision making beyond the classroom level, however. Administrators, school board members, policy makers, and parents make significant decisions that impact students. The needs of many audiences must be considered in building a quality assessment plan.

Testing is a form of assessment that involves the systematic sampling of behavior under controlled conditions. Testing can provide quick, reliable data on student performance. Single tests might be used to make decisions that do not have major long-term consequences, or used to supplement other forms of assessment such as focused interviews, classroom observations and anecdotal records, analysis of work samples, and work inventories.

Different kinds of assessment produce different kinds of information. If a teacher needs to know whether a student can read a particular textbook, there are many sources of information available to her. She can consult districtwide achievement tests in reading, estimate the level of the textbook, determine what score a student would need to read the textbook effectively, and then make a decision. However, it might be simpler for the teacher to ask the student to read a section of the text and then talk with the student about the text. This would probably be faster and more accurate than looking up test scores and conducting studies to see what kind of a test score is needed to comprehend the textbook. In general, teachers need information specific to the content and strategies they are teaching, and they can best get that information through assessments built around their daily educational tasks.

The public and policy makers have different needs from teachers. In general they need to know whether the school, school district, and state are effectively educating the students in their charge. For this purpose they need to collect information about many students and they need to know how those students stand in relation to other students across the United States or in relation to some specific standards set by the state. For these purposes, standardized norm-referenced or criterion-referenced tests are efficient and can give a broad picture of achievement on certain kinds of tasks. These kinds of tests are used most commonly for high-stakes decisions regarding schools and school districts.

Why Does Using Tests for High-Stakes Decisions Cause Problems?

There are several possible problematic outcomes of high-stakes testing. These include making bad decisions, narrowing the curriculum, focusing exclusively on certain segments of students, losing instructional time, and moving decision making to central authorities and away from local personnel.

Tests are imperfect. Basing important decisions on limited and imperfect information can lead to bad decisions—decisions that can do harm to students and teachers and that sometimes have unfortunate legal and economic consequences for the schools. Decision makers reduce the chance of making a bad decision by seeking information from multiple sources. However, the information from norm-referenced and criterion-referenced tests is inexpensive to collect, easy to aggregate, and usually is highly reliable; for those reasons it is tempting to try to use this information alone to make major decisions.

Another problem is that high-stakes tests have a tendency to narrow the curriculum and inflate the importance of the test. Schools should address a broad range of student learning needs, not just the subjects or parts of subject areas covered on a particular test. As the consequences for low performance are raised, teachers feel pressured to raise scores at all costs. This means they will focus their efforts on activities that they think will improve the single important score. Time spent focusing on those activities will come from other activities in the curriculum and will consequently narrow the curriculum. Most state assessments tend to focus on reading, writing, and mathematics. Too much attention to these basic subjects will marginalize the fine arts, physical education, social studies, and the sciences.

Narrowing of the curriculum is most likely to occur in high-poverty schools that tend to have the lowest test scores. Compared to students in schools in affluent communities, students in high-poverty schools receive teaching with a greater emphasis in lower level skills, and they have limited access to instruction focusing on higher level thinking. A recent survey in one state that uses high-stakes assessments found that 75% of classroom teachers surveyed thought the state assessment had a negative impact on their teaching (Hoffman et al., in press).

Another way that educators sometimes respond to test pressure is to focus their attention on particular students. Sometimes this means that only low-performing readers get the instructional resources they need, and those doing only slightly better are ignored. Sometimes there is an attempt to raise test scores by focusing instructional initiatives on those students scoring just below cut-off points, and ignoring those both above or far below cutoff points. And sometimes schools place children in expensive special education programs they do not need, discourage particular children from attending school on testing days, or encourage low-achieving students to drop out of school altogether, all in the name of getting higher test scores.

The loss of instructional time also is a negative result of high-stakes tests. The time for preparing for and taking tests is time taken away from basic instruction. The consequences of lost instructional time, particularly for low-performing students, are too great for information that can be gathered more efficiently.

Finally, we are concerned that instructional decision making in high-stakes testing situations is diverted from local teachers and is concentrated in a central authority far away from the school. The further decision making is removed from the local level of implementation, the less adaptive the system becomes to individual needs. High-stakes assessment shifts decisions from teachers and principals to bureaucrats and politicians and consequently may diminish the quality of educational services provided to students.

Do Test Scores Improve When High-Stakes Assessment Is Mandated?

Test scores in the states with high-stakes assessment plans have often shown improvement. This could be because high-stakes pressure and competition lead teachers to teach reading more effectively. An alternative interpretation is that gains in test scores are the result of "teaching to the test" even when reading does not improve. Analyses of national reading scores do not show the substantial gains claimed by state reading assessments. Studies of norm-referenced tests in states with sustained patterns of growth in state skill assessments (for example, Texas and Kentucky) show no comparable patterns of gain. Although Texas showed steady improvement on state tests, its National Assessment of Educational Progress (NAEP) reading scores are not among the highest, and the scores did not show significant improvement between 1992 and 1998 (U.S. Department of Education, 1999). This may be the result of high-stakes assessments that tend to narrow the curriculum and emphasize only parts of what students need to learn to become successful readers.

Why Don't We Just End High-Stakes Assessment?

It is unlikely that states using these assessments will abandon them. Indeed, the most likely scenario is for an increasing number of states to develop and adopt similar assessment plans. Tests can be useful for making state-level educational decisions, and they provide the public with at least a partial understanding of how well schools are doing. Less positively, politicians, bureaucrats, and test publishers have discovered that they can influence classroom instruction through the use of high-stakes tests. Tests allow these outside parties to take control away from local educational authorities without assuming the responsibilities of educating the students.

Is There a Way to Help States Monitor Student Success in the Curriculum?

If the intent of state assessments is to measure how well students are learning the outcomes identified in the state curriculum framework, then one way students' success can be monitored is by following the NAEP model with selective sampling across student populations and across content areas on a systematic basis. This model monitors achievement without encouraging high-stakes testing. The tests are directed toward particular grade levels and are not given every year. A sampling procedure is used so very few students actually participate in testing. NAEP is designed to give a report card on general achievement levels in the basic subject areas over time.

Many aspects of the NAEP assessment in reading are commendable. The NAEP sampling strategy has been useful in keeping efficiency high and maintaining a focus on the questions that the national assessment is designed to address. Sampling also has provided NAEP with an opportunity to experiment with a wide variety of testing formats and conditions. Such a strategy would avoid most of the problems associated with teaching to the test. This type of plan would reflect sound principles of instructional design and assessment.

In the book *High Stakes: Testing for Tracking, Promotion, and Graduation* (Heubert & Hauser, 1999), the following basic principles for test use are presented:

- The important thing about a test is not its validity in general, but its validity when used for a specific purpose. Thus, tests that are valid for influencing classroom practice, "leading" the curriculum, or holding schools accountable are not appropriate for making high-stakes decisions about individual student mastery unless the curriculum, the teaching, and the tests are aligned.

- Tests are not perfect. Test questions are a sample of possible questions that could be asked in a given area. Moreover, a test score is not an exact measure of a student's knowledge or skills. A student's score can be expected to vary across different versions of a test—within a margin of error determined by the reliability of the test—as a function of the particular sample of questions asked and/or transitory factors, such as the student's health on the day of the test. Thus, no single test score can be considered a definitive measure of a student's knowledge.

- An educational decision that will have a major impact on a test taker should not be made solely or automatically on the basis of a single test score. Other relevant information about the student's knowledge and skills should also be taken into account.

- Neither a test score nor any other kind of information can justify a bad decision. Research shows that students are typically hurt by a simple retention and repetition of a grade in school without remedial and other instructional support services. In the absence of effective services better tests will not lead to better educational outcomes. (p. 3)

State testing programs should respect these basic principles.

What Are the Recommendations of the International Reading Association Regarding High-Stakes Reading Assessments?

In framing our recommendations the Association would like to stress two points. First, we recognize accountability is a necessary part of education. Concerns over high-stakes tests should not be interpreted as fear of or disregard for professional accountability. Second, the intent in this position statement is not to blame policy makers for the current dilemma with high-stakes testing.

Our recommendations begin with a consideration of teachers and their responsibility to create rich assessment environments in their classrooms and schools. Next, we suggest that researchers must continue to investigate how assessment can better serve our educational goals. Third, we stress the importance of parents and community members in bringing balance to the assessment design. Finally, we offer recommendations to policy makers for developing a plan of action.

Recommendations to teachers:

- Construct more systematic and rigorous assessments for classrooms, so that external audiences will gain confidence in the measures that are being used and their inherent value to inform decisions.

- Take responsibility to educate parents, community members, and policy makers about the forms of classroom-based assessment, used in addition to standardized tests, that can improve instruction and benefit students learning to read.

- Understand the difference between ethical and unethical practices when teaching to the test. It is ethical to familiarize students with the format of the test so they are familiar with the types of questions and responses required. Spending time on this type of instruction is helpful to all and can be supportive of the regular curriculum. It is not ethical to devote substantial instructional time teaching to the test, and it is not ethical to focus instructional time on particular students who are most likely to raise test scores while ignoring groups unlikely to improve.

- Inform parents and the public about tests and their results.

- Resist the temptation to take actions to improve test scores that are not based on the idea of teaching students to read better.

Recommendations to researchers:

- Conduct ongoing evaluations of high-stakes tests. These studies should include but not be limited to teacher use of results, impact on the curriculum focus, time in testing and test preparation, the costs of the test (both direct and hidden), parent and community communication, and effects on teacher and student motivations. There are few data on the impact of tests on instruction. Good baseline data and follow-up studies will help in monitoring the situation. These studies should not be left to those who design, develop, and implement tests; they should be conducted by independent researchers.

- Find ways to link performance assessment alternatives to questions that external audiences must

Suggested readings

1. **What does the term *high-stakes testing* mean?**

   Downing, S., & Haladyna, T. (1996). A model for evaluation of high-stakes testing programs: Why the fox should not guard the chicken coop. *Educational Measurement: Issues and Practice, 5*(1), 5–12.

   Popham, W. (1987). Can high-stakes tests be developed at the local level? *NASSP Bulletin, 71*(496), 77–84.

2. **Why are we concerned with high-stakes testing?**

   Pipho, C., & Hadley, C. (1985). *State activity: Minimum competence testing as of January 1985* (Clearinghouse notes). Denver, CO: Education Commission of the States.

3. **Is testing an important part of good educational design?**

   International Reading Association. (1995). *Reading assessment in practice.* Newark, DE: Author.

4. **Why does using tests for high-stakes decisions cause problems?**

   Allington, R.L., & McGill-Franzen, A. (1992). Unintended effects of educational reform in New York State. *Educational Policy, 6*(4), 396–413.

   Madaus, G.F. (1985). Test scores as administrative mechanisms in educational policy. *Phi Delta Kappan, 66*(9), 611–617.

   Mathison, S. (1989). *The perceived effects of standardized testing on teaching and curriculum.* Paper presented at the annual meeting of the American Educational Research Association, San Francisco, CA.

   McGill-Franzen, A., & Allington, R.L. (1993). Flunk 'em or get them classified: The contamination of primary grade accountability data. *Educational Researcher, 22*(1), 19–22, 34.

   Paris, S.G. (1998). Why learner-centered assessment is better than high-stakes testing. In N.M. Lambert & B.L. McCombs (Eds.), *How students learn: Reforming schools through learner-centered education* (pp. 189–209). Washington, DC: American Psychological Association.

5. **Do test scores improve when high-stakes assessment is mandated?**

   Cornet, H.D., & Wilson, B.L. (1991). *Testing reform and rebellion.* Norwood, NJ: Ablex.

   Resnick, D.P., & Resnick, L.B. (1985). Standards, curriculum, and performance: A historical and comparative perspective. *Educational Researcher, 14*(4), 5–20.

   Wise, A.E. (1990, January 10). A look ahead: Education and the new decade. *Education Week,* p. 30.

6. **Why don't we just end high-stakes assessment?**

   Madaus, G.F. (1985). Test scores as administrative mechanisms in educational policy. *Phi Delta Kappan, 66*(9), 611–617.

7. **Is there a way to help states monitor student success in the curriculum?**

   Linn, R.L. (1993). Educational assessment: Expanded expectations and challenges. *Educational, Evaluation and Policy Analysis, 15*(1), 1–16.

   Messick, S. (1993). Validity. In R.L. Linn (Ed.), *Educational measurement* (3rd ed., pp. 13–103). Washington, DC: American Council on Education.

   Moss, P. (1998). The role of consequences in validity theory. *Educational Measurement: Issues and Practice, 17*(2), 6–12.

address on a regular basis. Researchers must continue to offer demonstrations of ways that data from performance assessments can be aggregated meaningfully. This strategy will allow them to build trustworthy informal assessments.

Recommendations to parents, parent groups, and child advocacy groups:

• Be vigilant regarding the costs of high-stakes tests on students. Parents must ask questions about what tests are doing to their children and their schools. They cannot simply accept the "we're just holding the school accountable" response as satisfactory. They must consider cost, time, alternative methods, and emotional impact on students as a result of these tests.

• Lobby for the development of classroom-based forms of assessment that provide useful, understandable information, improve instruction, and help children become better readers.

Recommendations to policy makers:

- Design an assessment plan that is considerate of the complexity of reading, learning to read, and the teaching of reading. A strong assessment plan is the best ally of teachers and administrators because it supports good instructional decision making and good instructional design. Consider the features of good assessment as outlined in *Standards for the Assessment of Reading and Writing* (International Reading Association & National Council of Teachers of English, 1994) in designing an assessment plan. Be aware of the pressures to use tests to make high-stakes decisions.

- When decisions about students must be made that involve high-stakes outcomes (e.g., graduation, matriculation, awards), rely on multiple measures rather than just performance on a single test. The experiences in England with high-stakes assessment have been instructive. England has moved to an assessment system that values teacher informal assessments, ongoing performance assessments, portfolios, teacher recommendations, and standardized testing. The triangulation of data sources leads to more valid decision making.

- Use sampling strategies when assessments do not involve decisions related to the performance of individual students (e.g., program evaluation). Sampling is less intrusive, less costly, and just as reliable as full-scale assessment plans. Sampling strategies also provide an opportunity to design alternate forms and types of assessments. Such a variety of assessments encourages careful inspection of issues of validity and reliability.

- Do not use incentives, resources, money, or recognition of test scores to reward or punish schools or teachers. Neither the awards (e.g., blue ribbon schools) nor the punishing labels (e.g., low-performing schools) are in the interest of students or teachers. The consequences of achieving or not achieving in schools are real enough. Well-intentioned efforts to recognize achievement often become disincentives to those who need the most help.

- Do not attempt to manipulate instruction through assessments. In other words, do not initiate, design, or implement high-stakes tests when the primary goal is to affect instructional practices. Ask the question, "Is the primary goal of the assessment to collect data that will be used to make better decisions that impact the individual students taking the test?" If the answer is "no," high-stakes tests are inappropriate.

The pattern of testing as the preferred tool to manipulate teaching continues to expand. We call on educators, policy makers, community leaders, and parents to take a common-sense look at the testing in schools today. Visit classrooms. Talk to teachers. Listen to teachers talk about the curriculum and the decisions they are making. Talk to the teachers about the kinds of assessments they use in the classroom and how they use collected data. To be opposed to large-scale, high-stakes testing is not to be opposed to assessment or accountability. It is to affirm the necessity of aligning our purposes and goals with our methods.

REFERENCES

Heubert, J.P., & Hauser, R.M. (1999). *High stakes: Testing for tracking, promotion, and graduation.* Washington, DC: National Academy Press.

Hoffman, J., Paris, S., Patterson, E.U., Pennington, J., & Assaf, L.C. (in press). High-stakes assessment in the language arts: The piper plays, the players dance, but who pays the price? In J. Flood, J.M. Jensen, D. Lapp, & J. Squire (Eds.), *Handbook of research on teaching the English language arts* (2nd ed.).

International Reading Association & National Council of Teachers of English. (1994). *Standards for the assessment of reading and writing.* Newark, DE: International Reading Association; Urbana, IL: National Council of Teachers of English.

U.S. Department of Education. (1999). *The NAEP 1998 reading report card for the nation and the states* (NCES 1999-459). Washington, DC: Author.

Literacy Assessment and the Future

Peter Johnston

I once asked a group of fourth graders, "Are there different kinds of readers in your class?" Sean (all student names are pseudonyms) told me that "There's ones like the people who's not good and the people who are good" and made it clear that he saw himself in the former category. For example, he did not feel sufficiently worthy to contribute to class book conversations (Johnston, 2004, p. 19). To learn about a pen pal as a reader, Sean said he would ask the pal's "level." In another fourth-grade class, Henry used a different scale. He responded, "Steve, he reads longer books than other people. And Dan, when he gets into a book, you're not going to stop him. Jenny, she reads hard books like Steve. But, she finishes books, like, really fast.... Priscilla, she really likes to read mysteries. She reads long stories, like Nancy Drew" (p. 94). Roger, he said, prefers the Bailey School Kids books, just like he does. To learn about a pen pal as a reader, Henry would ask what that pal was reading and about favorite books and authors.

Henry and Sean's assessments of themselves and their peers are important because they tell us about the literacies they are acquiring, something on which their test scores are largely silent. Their comments remind us what it means to acquire literacy—not merely particular knowledge and skills but also identities, values, dispositions, and relationships (Gee, 1996). We have to ask what sort of literacies we want children to acquire so that they will thrive along with the literate society to which they contribute. Children's assessments of themselves and their peers are also important because children are in part socialized by classroom assessment practices (Black & Wiliam, 1998; Crooks, 1988).

What Kind of Literacy Should Assessments Reflect?

The literate demands of the real world are changing rapidly. Indeed, the only certainties are the rapid change, an increasingly multicultural and multilingual environment, and the disappearance of any remaining boundaries between print and other media. How do we prepare students for this future and a lifetime of literate change? They will need literacies that are resilient, flexible, self-directed, open, and collaborative (Kalantzis, Cope, & Harvey, 2003), and acquisition of these literacies begins early. These kinds of literacies are also necessary if students are to help societies evolve into strong democracies—literacies in which it seems natural to consider others' interests and views as strongly as one's own, knowing that engaging them opens possibilities for new meanings, solutions, and actions. Our assessments must reflect and encourage these literacies.

Monitoring and Guiding Literate Learning

Classroom assessment can socialize children into monitoring and guiding their own literacy learning. It requires organizing our assessment interactions so that rather than telling children how they are doing, we help them to self-evaluate and to have a propensity for doing so. Children struggling with literacy constantly turn to the teacher for feedback. This reliance on external monitoring indicates that children have assessed themselves as incapable of

Reprinted from *The Reading Teacher*, 58(7), 684–686. © 2005 by the International Reading Association.

assessing their own learning. Turning this situation around requires teachers to view children as if they can know what they know, how they are doing, and how they can tell. Just starting with "How's it going?" and moving to "How can you tell?" or "How can you check?" will help. Practices like having children rank different pieces of writing (perhaps work in their portfolio, anonymous work from previous students, or even writing from published sources) while articulating their logic builds conversations in which children can internalize productive self-monitoring criteria. Asking questions like "As a writer, what have you learned most recently, how did you learn that, what would you like to learn next, and how will you go about that?" force on the child the identity of a writer with a sense and position of agency and learning trajectory (Johnston, 2004). Developing children's self-assessment gives them control of their own learning with the added bonus that they increase their achievement (McDonald & Boud, 2003).

Resilience

Resilience is the disposition to maintain a focus on learning in the face of difficulty. It's opposite is brittleness and ego-defensive behaviors (Carr & Claxton, 2002). Assessments of this disposition in kindergarten can predict word recognition in grades 1 and 2 better than assessments of phonological awareness (Niemi & Poskiparta, 2002). Resilience is not the same as competence. The most competent students can be brittle learners, making them prone to giving up when the going gets tough.

Resilient learners believe that ability is less relevant than engagement and that engagement and challenge lead to ability. Their assessment experiences have turned their attention toward the learning process more than to the performance and have not led them to believe that ability is permanent or that it has anything to do with their value as a human being. The opposite is true for brittle learners. They believe that experiencing difficulty with a literate task demonstrates either a lack of ability (or a disability), so they systematically avoid challenging

tasks (Dweck, 1999). When brittle learners feel they have been unsuccessful, they indulge in negative talk about themselves and inaccurately recall more occurrences of failure than they have actually experienced. Resilient learners are quite accurate in their recall of successes and failures, though they do not necessarily concede that they failed, only that they aren't yet where they want to be in their learning. Unlike brittle learners, they choose challenging tasks when they feel they will learn something, even when they might risk getting a bad grade. Resilient learners view more competent students as a resource rather than a threat.

Normative testing practices make both teachers and students view learners the way Sean did: They are "good ones" or "not good ones." This view can foster brittleness. Competitive pressure and overly difficult situations (just the sort of context produced for some children by current testing practices) actually magnify the effects of brittle learning dispositions, and our ongoing classroom assessments strongly contribute to these dispositions. The statement, "Good job, you're a good writer," and its implicit possibility of not being a good writer is the kind of assessment that can lead to brittleness. "The dialogue you have used to open this draft really got my attention. How did you learn to do that?" is the kind of assessment that develops a resilient literacy learner, particularly if it is coming from peers as well as the teacher.

Reciprocity

A literate disposition of reciprocity is required of citizens in a democracy—"a willingness to engage in joint learning tasks, to express uncertainties and ask questions, to take a variety of roles in joint learning enterprises and to take others' purposes and perspectives into account" (Carr & Claxton, 2002, p. 16). Standard comprehension assessment practices such as retellings and known-answer questions do not develop this disposition. Collaborative retellings or discussions of controversial or complex issues in books would develop it, as would turning attention to the process or collaborative meaning making as in the following example: "How did your book discussion go today? How might you make it better next time?"

The National Educational Monitoring Project (NEMP), charged with evaluating the qualities of education in New Zealand, takes this kind of literacy seriously. In one of the NEMP's test items, a group of children, within a limited time frame, must act as a class library committee, evaluating a set of books first individually and then together as a group and justify their selections (Flockton & Crooks, 1996). The activity requires the students to generate and negotiate evaluative criteria for the qualities of books, apply the criteria, take a position, argue persuasively, actively listen, and negotiate a group position. This authentic activity reveals independent and interdependent literate practices that foreground reciprocity. A teacher following such an activity with the question "What did you learn from that process?" would encourage children to recognize the significance of engaging others' interests and perspectives and to view diversity not as error or distraction but as a potential learning resource.

What Is Assessed Is What Is Taught

It is true that what is assessed is what is taught—perhaps truer than we have acknowledged. The ways we make assessments contribute to the development or demise of forms of literacy. Our assessment practices must help produce learners who are resilient and view literacy learning, rather than performance or ability, as their priority. They should produce literacy learners with the disposition to articulate their learning processes and perspectives, including their struggles, in ways that sustain strategic flexibility and mutual engagement.

REFERENCES

Black, P., & Wiliam, D. (1998). Assessment and classroom learning. *Assessment in Education: Principles, Policy & Practice, 5*(1), 7–74.

Carr, M., & Claxton, G. (2002). Tracking the development of learning dispositions. *Assessment in Education, 9*(1), 9–37.

Crooks, T.J. (1988). The impact of classroom evaluation practices on students. *Review of Educational Research, 58,* 438–481.

Dweck, C.S. (1999). *Self-theories: Their role in motivation, personality, and development.* Philadelphia: Psychology Press.

Flockton, L., & Crooks, T. (1996). *National education monitoring project: Reading and speaking, assessment results, 1996* (No. 6). Dunedin, New Zealand: Educational Assessment Research Unit.

Gee, J.P. (1996). *Social linguistics and literacies: Ideology in discourses* (2nd ed.). London: Falmer.

Johnston, P.H. (2004). *Choice words: How our language affects children's learning.* York, ME: Stenhouse.

Kalantzis, M., Cope, B., & Harvey, A. (2003). Assessing multiliteracies and the new basics. *Assessment in Education: Principles, Policy & Practice, 10*(1), 15–26.

McDonald, B., & Boud, D. (2003). The Impact of self-assessment on achievement: The effects of self-assessment training on performance in external examinations. *Assessment in Education: Principles, Policy & Practice, 10*(2), 209–220.

Niemi, P., & Poskiparta, E. (2002). Shadows over phonological awareness training: Resistant learners and dissipating gains. In E. Hjelmquist & C.V. Euler (Eds.), *Dyslexia and literacy* (pp. 84–99). London: Whurr.

SECTION FIVE

Content Literacy

The teacher of a content field…should guide his students in the application of the basic skills to the reading materials used in his area, and should also teach the special reading skills required.

—GERTRUDE WHIPPLE
(1955, p. 209)

Learning in the content area classroom usually occurs as a direct result of reading content textbooks. However, many students find reading and remembering content material difficult. One way to improve student comprehension of textbooks is to integrate reading and writing.

—KAREN D'ANGELO BROMLEY
(1985, p. 406)

Whether you refer to it as nonfiction, content area reading, or informational text, the genre it represents is often neglected—or, heaven forbid, thought of in the context of history or science textbooks.

—NANCY LIVINGSTON, CATHERINE KURKJIAN, TERRELL YOUNG, & LAURENCE PRINGLE (2004, p. 582)

Issues and Innovations in Literacy Education: Readings From The Reading Teacher, edited by Richard D. Robinson. © 2006 by the International Reading Association.

An old axiom in reading states, "Students learn to read in the first few years in school and then read to learn for the rest of their school experience." Implied here is the notion that formal training in reading exists for most students only during their early school experiences, and after about third grade they receive little, if any, literacy instruction. Traditionally, they then are involved in various types of content classes that are based to a large extent on reading for information, such as that presented in textbooks. This change from "learning to read" to "reading to learn" often presents many problems for students; for example, textbook reading frequently requires literacy skills not often experienced in other types of reading. Content reading assignments tend to rely on prior knowledge and abilities that are often unique to each subject matter area. For instance, the reading of symbols in mathematics, the effective use of charts and graphs in science, and the understanding of vocabulary in social studies present literacy challenges unique to each content area.

For many classroom teachers, the challenge of teaching reading in the content areas presents many problems (McKenna & Robinson, 2006). Classroom teachers often mention the following issues:

- Teachers do not believe students need specific instruction in subject matter literacy skills.
- Literacy activities would take away from subject matter instructional time.
- Teachers are not aware of the specific literacy skills needed in each subject matter area.
- Students should have learned content reading skills prior to their current class.
- The teaching of literacy skills related to any specific content class are not the responsibility of the teacher.

Armbruster (1992) notes that the relatively few articles related to content reading found in the pages of *The Reading Teacher* are due probably to the creation in 1964 of the *Journal of Reading* (now titled *Journal of Adolescent & Adult Literacy*). This is not to say that there have not been significant articles on various aspects of content reading in past issues of *The Reading Teacher*; however, the content reading materials in this section represent a wide variety of viewpoints and beliefs related to this very important aspect of literacy instruction.

Section Readings

An article by George D. Spache, an early pioneer in literacy education, sets the stage for many of the fundamental issues in content reading. The discussion of the various types of reading skills that must be addressed if students are to be successful in the different academic areas is particularly interesting. As you read this article, note how often many of these basic concerns related to content reading will be addressed in later articles in this section as well.

The emphasis in the article by Larry D. Kennedy is on the effective use of the content textbook. The author provides a variety of specific suggestions on how the classroom teacher can prepare students successfully for the use of the textbook in different content areas. Note especially in this discussion the importance of the teacher in taking an active role in helping students comprehend the often difficult content material typically encountered in textbook reading.

Next, an article written 17 years later by Karen D. Wood continues the discussion on the effective use of content literacy materials. The emphasis here is on the importance of building on students' background knowledge in a particular content field as a basis for the use of a variety of textbook materials. The author presents information on the use of a variety of reading guides that can be developed by the teacher to aid in the better understanding of content text material.

The emphasis in the article by Laura S. Pardo and Taffy E. Raphael is on the importance of using a variety of organizational plans in content instruction. These different grouping practices are suggested as a basis for students' better literacy understanding. These ideas range from whole-class grouping to those that emphasize cooperative small groups for a variety of instructional purposes. Information is provided for individual literacy activities as well.

The concluding article by Rosemary G. Palmer and Roger A. Stewart is an excellent discussion of the extended use of nonfiction as a basis for both literacy skill development as well as an encouragement for wide reading by students outside the classroom setting. A variety of teaching models are suggested including teacher-directed, scaffolded student investigations and independent student activities.

REFERENCES

Armbruster, B.B. (1992). Content reading in *RT*: The last 2 decades. *The Reading Teacher, 46*(2), 166–167.

Bromley, K.D. (1985). Précis writing and outlining enhance content learning. *The Reading Teacher, 38*(4), 406–411.

Livingston, N., Kurkjian, C., Young, T., & Pringle, L. (2004). Nonfiction as literature: An untapped goldmine. *The Reading Teacher, 57*(6), 582–591.

McKenna, M.C., & Robinson, R.D. (2006). *Teaching through text* (4th ed.). Boston: Allyn & Bacon.

Whipple, G. (1955). Controversial issues relating to reading in the curricular areas. *The Reading Teacher, 8*(4), 208–211.

For Further Reading on Content Literacy

The following articles on content reading have been selected from *The Reading Teacher* because they represent the developing nature of literacy education in this area.

Fay, L. (1953). How can we develop reading study skills for the different curriculum areas? *The Reading Teacher, 6*(4), 12–18.

>Discusses the importance of reading as a foundation for all content areas, noting that each subject matter discipline requires a variety of different literacy skills.

Horn, E. (1955). Responsibility for the development of reading skills needed in content areas. *The Reading Teacher, 8*(4), 212–214.

>Emphasizes the importance of the content teacher as being the primary literacy instructor in each academic area.

Glock, M.D. (1958). Developing clear recognition of pupil purposes for reading. *The Reading Teacher, 11*(3), 165–170.

> Stresses the importance of helping students establish significant and realistic purposes for their reading in the various content areas.

Robinson, H.A. (1965). Reading skills employed in solving social studies problems. *The Reading Teacher, 18*(4), 263–269.

> Describes an important study by a leader in the field of content reading on the necessary skills needed by students in the social studies discipline.

Billig, E. (1977). Children's literature as a springboard to content areas. *The Reading Teacher, 30*(8), 855–859.

> Shows how the extensive use of various types of trade books can be effectively used in content area instruction.

Taylor, B.M. (1982). A summarizing strategy to improve middle grade students' reading and writing skills. *The Reading Teacher, 36*(2), 202–205.

> Presents a hierarchical summary plan for helping students better comprehend the organizational plan for various types of content textbook selections.

Armbruster, B.B. (1992). Content reading in *RT*: The last 2 decades. *The Reading Teacher, 46*(2), 166–167.

> Reviews articles from *The Reading Teacher* during the period 1969 to 1991 that deal with the topic of "content reading," noting relevant literacy teaching techniques appropriate to various disciplines.

Guillaume, A.M. (1998). Learning with text in the primary grades. *The Reading Teacher, 51*(6), 476–486.

> Describes a plan for student comprehension of various types of content area text material, including trade books, textbooks, and other print material.

Moss, B. (2004). Teaching expository text structures through information trade book retellings. *The Reading Teacher, 57*(8), 710–718.

> Details how teachers can help their students comprehend various types of expository text structures through a retelling process.

Types and Purposes of Reading in Various Curriculum Fields

George D. Spache

We can define the major types of reading in curricular fields and their respective purposes by surveying the recent literature and the thinking of leading reading authorities.

When we do so, we find widespread agreement upon these types of reading: (1) understanding and interpreting content; (2) grasping the organization of the content; (3) developing special vocabularies, concepts, and symbols; (4) evaluating critically what is read; (5) collecting and collating materials; (6) recalling and applying what is read; and (7) broadening interests, tastes, and experiences.

Factors Influencing Successful Content Reading

It is apparent, however, that no matter how essential these types of reading are, in the minds of reading experts, their acceptance and use by classroom teachers is not universal. For example, contrast the extent of use of these types of reading by the textbook-oriented teacher with the use by the teacher who individualizes her instruction in dealing with broad topics of common interest. Certainly there is wide variation in the classroom situation in the types of reading considered essential.

The curriculum design within which the teacher functions also tends to define the role of reading in the various curriculum fields, as Gordon N. Mackenzie has pointed out (5). In the subject cur-riculum the greatest emphasis is upon reading to understand and interpret content, to grasp organization, and to recall and apply what is read. In the child-centered curriculum reading may receive less direct attention, but make even more contribution to academic success. Here, reading to broaden tastes, interests and experiences, to collect and collate materials, and to evaluate critically what is read are the major reading activities. Reading is considered a major tool for promoting personal growth and social development in the child-centered curriculum.

A third type of curriculum, the core curriculum oriented to social functioning or social problems, is prevalent in our schools. Teachers functioning in this framework commonly stress grasping organization of content, collecting and collating, and the problem-solving aspect of applying what is read. Some also emphasize critical evaluation and understanding and interpreting. A few apparently emphasize the broadening of tastes, interests, and experiences through reading as the major type of reading activity, as a recent report shows (7). The extensive use of small-group work, of reports to the body of the class, of a wide variety of source materials, and of changing units of study tend to limit the role of reading in the core curriculum. The major purposes for reading become its use as a means of communication, as one aspect of the language arts, and as a tool for learning.

The types of reading which may be employed in various curriculum fields are also influenced by

---

Reprinted from *The Reading Teacher*, 11(3), pp. 158–164. © 1958 by the International Reading Association.

pupil readiness to engage in these activities. Intelligence, type of previous schooling, general reading ability, and, to a lesser degree, social-economic background are some of the factors which determine readiness for a variety of reading activities (4). The value systems, prejudices, and attitudes of pupils markedly affect their abilities to interpret, to evaluate, and to react critically despite basically good comprehension skills. Most significant is the early training in diversified reading skills in preparing pupils to read and study effectively in the content fields.

In many school systems the only training in reading received by most pupils is of a basal reading type. This instruction, which emphasizes largely the reading of narrative or simple factual materials, is often concluded at the end of the fourth or sixth grade. Beyond this point, training in how to read is largely optional and dependent upon the individual teacher's recognition of her pupils' needs. Thus, many pupils who enter secondary schools or colleges have received little instruction in the reading skills necessary for effective study in the various curricular fields.

Many secondary and college students are unable to perform efficiently in the seven types of reading listed above. They are lacking not only in intellectual and cultural readiness but also in general reading skills which are essential to mature, efficient reading. Many teachers, themselves, like their pupils, are untrained and unskilled readers. Moreover, teachers who identify themselves as specialists in a content field hesitate to instruct pupils in a group of skills which seem to lie outside their area of specialization.

Basic General Reading Skills

Before secondary and college students can read efficiently in the curriculum fields they must be skillful in a number of fundamental reading practices. These fundamental skills maybe defined and illustrated as follows:

1. **Ability to survey materials to determine general nature, main ideas, appropriate reading approach, and to formulate the purpose of the reading.** Essentially, surveying is an organized, rapid coverage of difficult material, such as a report, bulletin, or chapter of a book. It is intended to answer such questions as: What information may be gained from the material? How is this information organized or presented? Is this information significant? How detailed must comprehension be? How does the style or complexity of the presentation influence the manner in which it should be read?

Surveying is, or should be, the initial step in the study of significant of difficult material. Several research studies show that when surveying is used in this fashion there is more comprehension, and study time is used more economically. Other uses for surveying are found in reviewing large amounts of material for a written examination, in quick brush-ups before oral recitation, and in evaluating materials collected for a written report.

In practice, surveying includes (1) reading the title critically, (2) examining the illustrative and graphic material, (3) reading each heading and subheading, and (4) reading the first sentence or two of each paragraph. If the nature of the material permits, two other steps may be included in surveying: reading the introductory paragraph, and reading the closing or summary paragraph.

2. **Ability to relate knowledge gained by surveying to the choice of an appropriate reading technique.** Mere knowledge of the theory of surveying, or comprehension of the steps involved, is not sufficient. Planning and structuring of the reading purpose, choice of an appropriate reading technique, and skill in relating the information gained from surveying to other materials requires thinking on the part of the reader.

Implementing the information gained from surveying by the reading and study procedures which will facilitate the degree of learning desired is not an integral part of the act of surveying. The student does not necessarily handle material in the most efficient manner simply because he knows how to survey it. He must still be able to modify his rate or technique of reading. He must be able to recognize the relevance of the material to his purpose for reading, and adjust accordingly. In other words, in addition to being able to survey effectively, the student must be able to translate the results of surveying into appropriate next steps.

3. Flexibility in rate of reading sufficient to permit varying speeds or reading techniques such as skimming, moderate rate, careful reading, and scanning for details. The efficient reader must be able to vary his rate according to the nature of the material being read and his purpose in reading it. This flexibility in rate is so widely accepted by reading authorities that the principle has become an axiom.

Flexibility in rate results in higher school grades, in economy of study time, and greater enjoyment of reading. The flexible reader achieves greater total comprehension, completes more work, and finds time available for recreational reading. But these satisfactions are not gained without instruction and practice.

4. Ability to handle graphic and illustrative materials effectively. Some instruction is given in the reading of tabular, graphic, and statistical materials in the elementary schools. Further instruction is usually experienced by those who study high school and college mathematics. Yet the average adult is often embarrassed by his inability to handle or interpret these types of materials.

For adequate functioning in the curricular fields the student should be able to read and interpret pictures, maps, charts, graphs, and cartoons. Most of these involve the expression of relationships and are a sort of condensed mathematical language.

These various ways of representing relationships are not found exclusively in the field of mathematics. They occur regularly in most of the physical and social sciences, in home economics and business courses, in agriculture and architecture. Moreover, these materials are particularly difficult to read. Even the most efficient readers must handle them slowly and analytically. For these reasons all teachers in fields using graphic, tabular, or statistical matter must assume the responsibility of offering instruction in how to read these materials.

5. Skill in use of the library and basic references peculiar to the field. The various skills and knowledges needed for intelligent use of the library are numerous. They are described in detail in many recent publications and need not be repeated here (1). The point we would like to stress is the necessity for teachers in the various curricular fields to assume the responsibility of instructing pupils in the use of the basic references peculiar to their fields. In the teaching of English, for example, we cannot assume that pupils are entirely competent in the use of such tools as the dictionary, indexes to poetry, short stories, plays, fiction, and biography, the thesaurus, periodical indexes, and magazines such as *Literary Cavalcade*, and *Practical English*. Direct instruction and practice in the effective use of these reference materials which are fundamental to successful study are the responsibility of each teacher in the curriculum fields.

6. Skill in general reading abilities such as rate, comprehension, and vocabulary. Reasonably good reading abilities are fundamental to success in almost all curriculum fields. It is true that pupils vary considerably in their reading proficiency in handling materials from the different fields. Two pupils of average general reading ability may achieve quite differently in reading in a particular curriculum content because of such factors as interest, reading background, confidence, and motivation. But it is widely recognized that pupils of very poor general reading ability also tend to perform poorly in most, if not all, reading efforts in the content fields. Good general reading ability forms a sound foundation for the growth of desirable reading skills in the content fields.

These six basic reading skills are not the only essentials for success in the curriculum fields. Systematic study habits of proven values, effective techniques in note-taking, outlining, summarizing, and listening, skill in preparing for and taking examinations, and intelligent planning of a personal schedule are also important in academic studies. Students must be well grounded in all of these habits and skills before they can be expected to read competently in the content fields.

Types of Reading in the Curriculum Fields

Understanding and interpreting content. This is undoubtedly the most common type of reading used in working in any curriculum field. In this type of reading, Gray (3) distinguishes the two major purposes of grasping the literal meaning and recognizing the broader, inherent meanings. In obtaining the literal meaning, the reader is asking, "What does it say?" In recognizing inherent meanings, he is, in effect, reading between the lines for intent and tone, for unexpressed generalizations or inferences, or to interpret rhetorical devices and figurative language.

We cannot leave this most important type of curricular reading without mentioning two dangers inherent in common practices in content classes. There is a false emphasis upon the detailed type of reading such as drill upon selecting main ideas, finding details, and enumerating conclusions. Teachers often assume that repeated practice in answering a stereotyped sequence of questions promotes development of intelligent comprehension. Overemphasis upon this approach may stifle the creative, interpretive reading with which each new reading should be approached.

Another dangerous, common classroom practice is that of reading texts aloud to promote comprehension. This is based on a mistaken assumption of the values of oral reading for the comprehension of the reader. The substitution of easier texts, more general discussion, and training in effective listening habits are much better solutions when the reading skills of a class are weak or the textbook is too difficult (6).

Grasping organization of the content. Training in recognizing organization may progress from practice in outlining or identifying the main idea in a single paragraph, to that in several paragraphs, in a section, in an entire chapter. Fuller outlines may then be introduced which would include details as well as main ideas. Many teachers in social sciences and English will also aid students in recognizing the temporal order of events, in relating events in a cause and effect sequence, in recognizing plot arrangement, and in relating events to the characteristics of the era in which they occurred. In the teaching of science pupils need help in reading deductively from the principle or law to specific applications, and in reading inductively from observations or experiments to the formulation of an hypothesis.

Developing special vocabularies, concepts, and symbols. There are three tasks inherent in learning the terms of a curriculum field. The first is that of learning the technical vocabulary and special concepts implicit in these technical words. Teachers in the content fields must assume the responsibility for direct, concentrated instruction not only in the technical terms peculiar to their subject but also in the broad meanings of those terms that involve special concepts.

The second task present in the special vocabulary of each field is that of the use of specialized meanings for general words. Specialized meanings are used for such general words as mouth, cape, and court in the social sciences, and for scale, charge, conduct in the sciences. While these words are often within the general reading vocabularies of students, their specialized meanings in a particular curricular field must also be taught.

The third task present in the special vocabulary field is that presented by the use of symbols. The problem of learning symbols is most acute in the fields of mathematics and science since these employ literal numbers ($4a$, $5b + 2d$), operational symbols (roots, plus, parentheses), directed numbers ($+4$ -8), methods of showing relationship (graph, equation, formula), as well as a host of other symbols (H_2O, Zn, U-238).

Evaluating critically what is read. DeBoer (2) has pointed out that critical reading involves a search for materials, evaluation of the data, comparison of sources, and synthesis of the findings. He also mentions the need for suspended judgment and interpretation of the author's motive. To these we might add the need for skill in using personal knowledge or other sources in judging accuracy, completeness, and authenticity and in distinguishing opinion from fact.

In addition to all these judgmental reactions, the student should be familiar with the common tricks of the propagandist's trade.

Recalling and applying what is read. This type of reading is secondary in frequency of use only to understanding and interpreting content. Yet, like most of the other types of reading in the curriculum fields, it is seldom taught thoroughly to students. Basically, recalling and applying involves three groups of skills. First, it demands ability to use effectively such aids to retention as outlines, summaries, note-taking, underlining, and selective re-reading.

Secondly, recall and application requires the ability to practice self-evaluation of learning. The student needs effective methods of self-recitation and review.

Finally, recall and application implies skill in re-expressing ideas in one's own words and using facts as a springboard to further learning. In this sense, the student must develop his ability to proceed from simple recall to solving problems, and through applying generalizations to formulating new generalizations. If taught thoroughly, this kind of reading leads the student far beyond the primitive recall of facts, or even recognition of facts, to new uses for the ideas he has thus gathered.

Collecting and collating materials. More than any other type of reading, collecting and collating materials demands flexibility on the part of the reader. Here his library skills, and his ability to skim, to scan, to read thoroughly, to preview or survey must function adequately.

Students may function on several levels in this type of reading. Some can merely find answers to specific questions, and even this is done slowly and laboriously. Others can summarize or condense facts from several sources. A few can show discrimination in organizing materials from a variety of sources into a unified and coherent new whole.

Broadening interests, tastes, and experiences. Reading of this type is undoubtedly most significant in terms of the development of the individual. Every curriculum field can serve as a springboard for the expansion of reading interests when teachers introduce pupils to the variety of materials actually available. Books and magazines which offer nontechnical, semipopularized treatments of the content of each field are available. These may serve to introduce students to kinds of reading they may learn to enjoy. There is great need for emphasis upon these aspects of reading. Extensive studies indicate that schools are failing to establish permanent reading interests among young people in varied or in higher quality reading materials. One of the important reasons for this failure may lie in a lack of breadth of enjoyable materials now being offered.

REFERENCES

1. Cleary, Florence Damon. *Blueprints for Better Reading.* New York, N.Y.: H.W. Wilson, 1957.
2. DeBoer, John. "Teaching Critical Reading," *Elementary English Review,* 23 (October, 1946), 251–54.
3. Gray, William S. "Increasing the Basic Reading Competencies of Students," *Reading in the High School and College,* pp. 91–115. Forty-seventh Yearbook, National Society for the Study of Education, Part II.
4. Lee, Maurice A. "Nature and Causes of the Difficulties of High School Pupils in Reading and Interpreting Four Kinds of Material," *Journal of Negro Education,* 20 (Fall, 1951), 499–512.
5. Mackenzie, Gordon N. "The Role of Reading in Different Curriculum Designs," *Improving Reading in All Curriculum Areas,* pp. 46–50. Supplementary Educational Monographs, No. 76, November 1952.
6. Spache, George. "Classroom Techniques of Identifying and Diagnosing the Needs of Retarded Readers in High School and College," *Better Readers for Our Time,* pp. 128–132. Proceedings First Annual Conference International Reading Association, 1956.
7. Stewart, L. Jane, Heller, Frieda M., and Alberty, Elsie J. *Improving Reading in the Junior High School.* New York, N.Y.: Appleton-Century-Crofts, 1957.

Textbook Usage in the Intermediate-Upper Grades

Larry D. Kennedy

The elementary school pupil is expected to make the transition from a skill-centered curriculum at the primary level to an increasingly content-centered curriculum at the intermediate-upper grade level. It is at the intermediate-upper grade levels that the pupil encounters homework in increasing abundance. He is expected at these levels to demonstrate his proficiency in the subject matter he encounters through teacher-made tests. Further, he is expected to work toward mastery of the vocabulary and the concepts of social studies, mathematics, science, and English to a more complex degree than ever.

At the intermediate-upper grade levels, the pupil frequently encounters a number of teachers for the first time and, all too often, he *senses* a loss of the integrating experiences which characterized the primary level program. While the wisdom of departmentalizing subject matter at the intermediate-upper grade level, either in separate content classes taught by different teachers or within the confines of a single classroom with one teacher, may be challenged, the content orientation common to the secondary schools increasingly begins at the third or the fourth grade level. While elementary specialists may deny that content-centered rigidity is typical of the intermediate-upper level grades, it should not be assumed that *textbook* learning at these levels is any less overwhelming for the young child. The realization that the subject matter orientation of a school program begins, in reality, at this early level supports the need for direct instruction of pupils in usage of the content area textbook at the intermediate-upper grade levels.

The textbook plays a significant role in the school learning of the pupil. Rudman (1958) suggested that the classroom textbook provides *a course of study* for the pupil. This means that "...the textbook is responsible for three essential elements of any curriculum: 1] the content of the curriculum, 2] the skills to be learned, and 3] the sequence in which these skills are to be learned." The *reality* of school learning today, then, is such that the pupil's school success is equated to his mastery of the course of study—the textbook.

It is imperative that the pupil at the intermediate-upper grade levels receive specific instruction in textbook usage. Neither the teacher nor the pupil can afford to assume tacitly that social studies, mathematics, science, and English textbooks are similar to each other or to the basal reader to which they may have been accustomed.

Textbook Readiness: Guides to Textbook Structure

It is frequently the case that textbooks in science, English, mathematics, and social studies are distributed to the pupils on the first or the second day of school, identified by title, author, and subject area, and then promptly put to use. The pupil is told to "read pages 5 through 15" or to "look over Chapter 1" and so forth. Such assignments are not only in-

Reprinted from *The Reading Teacher*, 24(8), pp. 723–729. © 1971 by the International Reading Association.

adequate, they are decidedly premature. The teacher should devote a considerable amount of time to the development of "textbook readiness." Textbook readiness is concerned with providing the pupil with the knowledge and the skills required to use the textbook effectively and efficiently.

There are several elements or features of a textbook that teachers should consider. These include: 1] the table of contents; 2] the use of special devices that note significant content or skills; and 3] the questions at end of chapters.

Table of Contents

It is relatively easy for the teacher to forget that pupils are often unaware of the existence and the purpose of a table of contents. Actually, it would probably be nearer the truth to say that pupils are, indeed, aware of the presence of something called a table of contents, but that these pupils have never given more than passing consideration to its purposes. Yet, if one views a textbook as constituting a course of study in a particular content area, then it is essential that the pupil examine the table of contents in order to comprehend the scope and the sequence of the textbook.

The classroom teacher is generally free, of course, to select which units or sections in the table of contents will be taught. She should also discuss such information with her pupils. The value of directing specific attention to the table lies in helping to establish an "overview" of a semester's or a year's work. While it is true that each teacher uses the textbook differently, a discussion of the table of contents with the pupils can afford the teacher many opportunities to preview the course of study for her pupils and to invite them to join her in the preparation of a revised course of study for the class.

A discussion of the table of contents also introduces at least some unity into the work of specific content areas. A preview of the total program for the class provides the integration which pupils need when they are faced with what often seems to them to be unrelated content, skills, and activities. Essentially, when the teacher discusses the table of contents, she sets the goals or the purposes of the

content area. She defines the horizons of the area and, in a sense, enters into a contract with the pupils to guide them through the course of study.

Use of Signalling Devices

While one might argue the notion that "movies are better than ever," it is *certainly* true that textbooks are better than ever. This is not to say, of course, that textbooks are not misused. Indeed, a textbook can be only as effective as is the teacher who uses it. Writers and publishers in recent years, however, have taken special care to upgrade the textbooks for the pupil and for the teacher.

Current textbooks make use of a variety of "signalling devices" that tell the pupil that important information is being given. These "signalling devices" should be called to the attention of the pupil, and the teacher should follow through with specific examples in the textbook in order to prove to the pupil the value of such signals.

The pupils should be told to pay particular attention to italicized words. Words that are italicized are *not* to be read in the same way as non-italicized words. Such words are to be studied carefully. Similarly, the practice of using blue or red type to highlight important words or concepts is common today. The pupil should be directed to give specific attention to such words and concepts.

The use of bold-faced type for words or for entire sentences should be noted also. In social studies textbooks such type is used to set off the topic sentence of a paragraph or of a series of paragraphs. The pupils should be told that such sentences generally state what is coming up in the paragraph.

The use of additional signalling devices such as brackets around special directions or "color boxes" which contain key concepts of generalizations should also be pointed out to the pupil. It is not an overstatement to say that pupils frequently overlook or ignore such devices entirely.

Signalling devices, with the exception of foreign or unfamiliar words, are not generally encountered by the pupil in the books he reads for pleasure. The pupil has different purposes, however, in his reading of textbooks. Textbook reading requires the acquisition of knowledge and of skills, and a page in a subject area textbook cannot be read in the same way as a page in a basal reader or in a library book. The teacher cannot assume that the pupil can read a textbook page with the same efficiency and effectiveness with which he reads a page of fiction. It is the responsibility of the intermediate-upper grade level teacher to teach the particular "signalling devices" of the textbook. These devices are designed to serve as aids to the reader, and, as such, they should be taught directly.

Textbook Questions

Many teachers avoid the use of the questions provided at the conclusion of chapters or sections of textbooks. Admittedly, there are those questions which should be avoided, but, generally, only when used without regard for the individual and the collective content and skill needs of the pupils in the classroom. Certainly, teachers should not assign a host of questions to be answered in writing by each pupil. Such a practice is highly questionable. The teacher must ask herself: "How will the questions contribute to the mastery of knowledge and skills of my pupils?" Such a question should serve to insure against an unwise use of the questions and should help to *fit* individual questions to individual pupils.

Questions at the conclusion of a chapter or a section of a textbook can be used also to *introduce* the knowledge and skills in the chapter. Used in this fashion, the questions help to set the content or the skill purposes for reading. The pupils then read the chapter in order to answer the questions. The teacher should also feel free to add those questions which will help to meet her particular objectives for the chapter.

Questions to Guide Reading

It has been only in recent years that educators have given extensive attention to *why, how,* and *what if* types of questions. It is, of course, easy to ask *who, what, when,* and *where* questions and to evaluate the responses to such questions. In terms of the development of creative and critical thinking in relation to reading abilities and skills, teachers should move to

questions that challenge the pupils to think about what they have read and to react critically and creatively to their reading.

There is, of course, a place for knowing the *who, what, when,* and *where*. Indeed, more sophisticated thinking skills and abilities depend frequently upon the acquisition of such basic facts. It is when the teacher fails to go beyond the *who, what, when,* and *where* that pupils are *short-changed* in terms of total comprehension. In a social studies assignment, for example, the nature of the subject requires that the teachers ask *why* certain historical events occurred. Further, the teacher should ask *what if* of her pupils to determine whether they are able to grasp what might have happened if certain historical conditions had been altered in some way. The *new* mathematics programs focus their attention upon the *how* and the *why* of mathematics rather than upon rote memory of computational facts. Similarly, teachers of literature cannot hope to develop interaction with the story if they remain at the *who, what, when,* and *where* levels. Teachers should ask *why* characters behave they way they do, *how* the author uses writing to get his personal views across, and *what if* the story had taken place in a different setting.

The use of *how, why,* and *what if* types of questions leads the pupil away from memorization of names, dates, places, and so forth. With such questions to guide his reading, the pupil is able to get "below" the surface meaning of an assignment so that he might interact with the teacher at a more stimulating level.

Reading Readiness and the Textbook Assignment

Reading readiness is significant at the intermediate-upper grade levels in terms of "readiness" for the reading of the textbook assignment. Experienced teachers know that it is not enough to say "Read pages 38 through 45 for tomorrow." The textbook assignment must be thought through carefully by the teacher, and the lesson must be prepared in such a way as to insure optimal learning experiences with the subject matter.

When the teacher makes an assignment, she must be concerned with "getting the pupil ready" to read that assignment. In her preparation period, the teacher should consider the following questions:

1. Why am I assigning this material? What are my purposes? What do I want my pupils to know or to be able to do as a result of having read this assignment?
2. What new vocabulary words or new concepts will the pupils encounter? How can I help them "meet" these terms and concepts?
3. What sort of questions can I write to guide them and to give purpose to their reading?

The importance of focusing assignments upon specific purposes was noted by McKee (1966):

> Unfocalized assignments which fail to direct the pupil's attention to and arouse in him no curiosity about particular problems or questions to be considered tempt him to read with only the vaguest purposes, with little concern for what his reading matter is saying, and without applying appropriate reading skills he has been taught. (P. 224)

The classroom teacher must "focalize" her assignments in mathematics, English, science, and social studies if the reading of the pupils is to be effective. The pupils should be told the purpose or purposes of the reading assignment. If skill development in mathematics is the goal of the assignment, then the pupils should be told what skill it is they are to acquire and how they will be asked to demonstrate their proficiency. If the goal of a social studies assignment is the acquisition of basic concepts, the pupil should be so informed. It is the responsibility of the classroom teacher to channel the pupil's reading toward the desired goals so that he does not become lost in the content-maze of the assignment.

Vocabulary and Concept Development

In spite of several years of being told to look-up new or unfamiliar words, the pupil more often than not either attempts to figure out the word and its meaning from context clues—or he does not even attempt to get the meaning. The pupil who encounters new terms in his assigned reading of science, social studies, mathematics, and English is likely to skip-over such words in order to complete his assignment. While such a practice is, of course, not recommended, the reality of "home-work assignments" suggests that such is indeed the case. Failure to look up and to identify unknown words reflects inadequate reading-study habits and results in poor preparation for any subsequent discussion of the assigned material.

Rather than leave the learning of new terms to chance and to risk the concomitant lack of understanding of the assigned material, the teacher should, in her planning period, identify those new or difficult terms and present them to the pupils as a part of her "assignment-readiness." The presentation of these terms to the class also presents an opportunity for the teacher to review or to re-teach certain principles of phonics and of structural analysis. It is, in fact, this application of previously acquired word recognition skills to assigned content reading which demonstrates to the pupils the *continuing* value of word recognition skills.

New terms and concepts should be listed on the blackboard in the context in which they are used in the textbooks. It is important that the terms and concepts not be taught in isolation. The teacher is interested in reading comprehension within the context of the assigned material and not in the ability of the pupil to pronounce or to identify words in isolation. The practice of teaching vocabulary in isolation is similar to that of a master list of words which pupils are required to spell on Friday, but which are seldom or never used in the oral or the written speech of the child. The class discussion of words in context also gives the teacher the opportunity to point out how the meaning of words can be altered by the context of particular sentences.

Difficult concepts should be explained prior to the reading of the textbook. All too frequently, pupils are assigned concept-laden material to read only to find that they are unable to progress through the material because they do not understand initial concepts.

A textbook assignment is not intended to be a guessing game. It is the responsibility of the teacher to assist in the removal of reading obstacles. A careful explanation of the new concepts to be encountered leads to more effective reading since the pupil is introduced to the concepts prior to his reading of the material. Such initial discussion of concepts does not negate the significance of "discovery learning." Rather, it maximizes such learning. The pupil should not be set adrift to *discover* a concept. The teacher should use her assignment period as a time to sequence such discovery and *to maximize* its possibility.

Summary

The classroom teacher can, through thoughtful planning and careful teaching, give her pupils a headstart in their attempts to comprehend the content of the textbook. Such concern with the textbook does not alter the realization that a single textbook will not meet the individual needs of pupils. Rather, it accepts the harsh reality of school learning as it actually exists. While elementary teachers may well hope for that day when each classroom is a library and when the mastery of a textbook is not the determiner of school success, it is still important to do the best possible job of teaching with the tools and the aids at their immediate disposal.

REFERENCES

McKee, P. *Reading: a program of instruction for the elementary school.* Boston: Houghton Mifflin, 1966. P. 224.

Rudman, H.C. Patterns of textbook use—key to curriculum development. *The Elementary School Journal,* 1958, 58, 401–407.

Guiding Students Through Informational Text

Karen D. Wood

It is well documented that 90% of classroom instruction is based on the textbook (EPIE, 1977; Goodlad, 1976), yet evidence also indicates that many of the textbooks used in our schools are not well written (Armbruster and Anderson, 1981). Add to these facts the wide range of reading ability levels prevalent in any heterogeneous class, and it is not surprising that many students have great difficulty reading and comprehending their textbooks.

A viable solution to the problem of reading informational text is to give teachers a large repertoire of strategies for communicating textbook content. These should include the use of various types of reading guides.

Guides to Studying Text

The most common of the strategies or devices for helping students comprehend informational text is the reading or study guide, where students respond to questions or statements while reading the text. Research attesting to the effectiveness of interspersing questions in text dates back to studies in the 1920s by Distad (1927) and Washburne (1929), with more research as recent as 1986 (Wood). However, the study guide as it is known today did not receive attention until the advent of Herber's (1970) three level guide in which literal, inferential, and applied statements accompany text.

Since Herber's guide, numerous others have appeared in the professional literature. Among them are concept and pattern guides (Vacca, 1981), the guide-o-rama (Cunningham and Shablak, 1975), the learning-from-text guide (Singer and Donlan, 1980), glossing (Richgels and Hansen, 1984), and most recently the textbook activity guide (Davey, 1986).

The common denominator in all of these guides is that they were designed for secondary level students. Yet, elementary level students, particularly in grades 4 and above, need assistance in reading the many textbooks required in their content area courses.

Therefore, this article introduces three reading guides for helping upper elementary students comprehend informational text: the point of view reading guide, the reading road map, and the interactive reading guide. First, a rationale will be given anchoring these strategies in current research and theory. Then, examples of each type of guide will be presented along with guidelines for developing and using them in the classroom.

Based on Current Research and Theory

Foremost in the recent research and theory on comprehension is the notion that proficient readers use their existing knowledge to reconstruct meaning from text (Anderson and Pearson, 1984). One way to effect this reconstruction process, thereby expanding and modifying readers' views, theories, or ideas, is through strategic teacher questioning (Anderson, 1977). Elaborating, embellishing what is read through mental imagery and inferencing, is

Reprinted from *The Reading Teacher*, 41(9), pp. 912–920. © 1988 by the International Reading Association.

another way readers can use past experiences to reconstruct new information, enhance comprehension, and improve recall (Hansen and Pearson, 1982; Mayer, 1980; Reder, 1980).

The reading guides presented in this article use questions and other tasks to activate students' prior knowledge, to have them mentally and graphically translate the written content, and to encourage them to draw inferences while they are reading. In this way students are not merely adopting an alternative set of teacher or text oriented propositions, but rather they are interacting personally and socially (aided by their peers) with the printed material. Through this dynamic interaction, students engage in deep processing of text as they seek to reconstruct the author's message and make sense of what they read.

Point of View Reading Guide

The point of view reading guide uses questions in an interview format to allow students to experience events from alternative perspectives. Instead of just reading about a particular character, students actually become that individual. From Encyclopedia Brown to Ferdinand Magellan, students can read while simultaneously role playing. Thus, literary, historical, or scientific occurrences become real for the students, motivating them to want to read the assigned material.

The interview questions elicit both text based and reader based contributions from the reader. Because readers must essentially assume the schemata or more simply "get inside the head" of the character, their comprehension and subsequent recall are positively affected.

The guide show in Figure 1 leads readers through the War of 1812 by having them become significant people at that time: a merchant, a war hawk, a soldier under Perry's command, two future presidents, and a Cherokee Indian, to name a few.

Since this may be a unique activity for students, it will be necessary to thoroughly model the process first. Instruct the students to write their responses in the first person, elaborating whenever possible with information from their background of experi-

ences. Note the varying responses to the two questions that follow.

For example, student response to the interview question "In your opinion, were the Americans ready to fight? Explain why you feel this way," might be:

> "No, we weren't ready to fight. Some of us, the war hawks, wanted war. Others didn't. Some New Yorkers at the Battle of Niagara stood by as their friends got killed. We lacked unity. We didn't even have muskets and other equipment. Some of us had to use our own guns or borrow some."

The same basic question, "Was America ready to fight? Why or why not?" could be found at the end of the textbook chapter. However, it would likely signal a much different response from the students, similar to the one that follows:

> "No. Because at the Battle of Niagara, a group of New York soldiers, refusing to leave New York, stood and watched their outnumbered comrades, across the river, being killed."

Here, the student has used the question stem as a starting point and has copied the remainder of the information directly from the textbook. Such a text based response typifies those answers received in a classroom. Yet, notice how the former question from the point of view reading guide allows for elaboration, inferential thinking, and speculation. Note also how the interview format frees the students to use less stilted, non-textbook type language.

By merging the text based and reader based information, students engage in a mental recitation of the content as they put the new information in their own words. Psychologists have said this mental recitation is the most powerful of all study techniques (Pauk, 1974).

Although shown here as an adjunct to social studies material, the point of view reading guide can be used with other content fields. In literature, students can assume the roles of various characters as they react to events in a story. In science, they can describe the process of photosynthesis from the perspective of a plant or the act of locomotion from the perspective of an amoeba.

Chapter 11: The War of 1812

You are about to be interviewed as if you were a person living in the United States in the early 1800s. Describe your reactions to each of the events discussed next.

Planting the Seeds of War (p. 285)

1. As a merchant in a coastal town, tell why your business is doing poorly.

The War Debate (p. 285–7)

2. Explain why you decided to become a war hawk. Who was your leader?
3. Tell why many of your fellow townspeople lowered their flags at half mast. What else did they do?
4. What was the reaction of Great Britain to you and your people at that time?
5. In your opinion, is America ready to fight? Explain why you feel this way.

Perry's Victory (p. 287)

6. In what ways were your predictions either correct or incorrect about Americans' readiness to fight this war?
7. Tell about your experiences under Captain Perry's command.

Death of Tecumseh (p. 288)

8. Mr. Harrison, describe what really happened near the Thames River in Canada.
9. What was Richard Johnson's role in that battle?
10. Now, what are your future plans?

Death of the Creek Confederacy (p. 288)

11. Explain how your people, the Cherokees, actually helped the United States.
12. Tell about your leader.

British Invasion (p. 288–90)

13. As a British soldier, what happened when you got to Washington, D.C.?
14. You headed to Fort McHenry after D.C.; what was the outcome?
15. General Jackson, it's your turn. Tell about your army and how you defeated the British in New Orleans.

The Treaty of Ghent (p. 290)

16. We will end our interview with some final observations from the merchant questioned earlier. We will give you some names and people. Tell how they fare now that the war is over: the British, the Indians, the United States, Harrison, Jackson.

Teachers will need to model and provide examples before eliciting the student generated analogies which will "make the strange familiar" (Gordon, 1966). Thus, they will have incorporated the many benefits of metaphorical teaching in the instructional lesson.

Reading Road Map

The reading road map is an expansion and modification of the guide-o-rama introduced by Cunningham and Shablak (1975) and later adapted for elementary school use by Wood and Mateja (1983). As shown in Figure 2, the reading road map guides students on a journey through the text using missions (interspersed questions), road signs (reading rate indicators), and location signs (headings, page numbers, etc.). Since poor comprehenders tend to read all material at the same rate, often very slowly and laboriously or very quickly, the "road signs" help them learn to adjust their reading rate to coordinate with the significance of the concepts presented.

After a thorough explication of the purpose of the reading road map, students should skim both the map and the coordinating text selections to note

FIGURE 2
Reading road map

Chapter 13: Arthropods
Overall mission: You are about to take a tour of the world of the arthropods.

Location	Speed	Mission

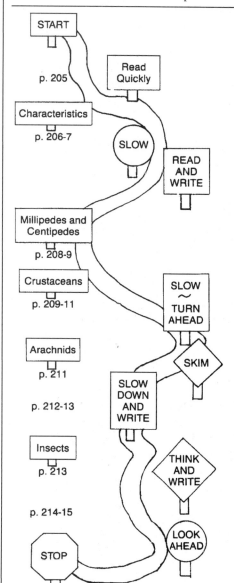

1. Name three major characteristics of arthropods.
2. a. What does *arthropod* mean? Find at least 2 other words with the root *pod* in them.
   b. Why is the exoskeleton so important?
   c. Briefly describe the molting process. Why does it take place?
   d. How are arthropods grouped?
3. a. Recall three traits of millipedes; of centipedes.
   b. How do millipedes protect themselves?
   c. Why are centipedes called "predators"? What other animals are predators?
4. a. How would you know a crustacean when you saw one? Where would you look for one?
   b. In your own words, tell how barnacles can be harmful.
5. a. How could you recognize an arachnid? (paragraphs 1 & 2)
   b. How and what does a spider eat? (paragraph 3)
   c. Retell the second paragraph on page 213 in your own words.
6. a. In what ways are insects different from the other arthropods?
   b. Fill in the following information:
      I. Insects
         A. Beetles
            1)
            2)
         B.
            1)
            2)
         C.
            1) social
            2)
7. What have you learned from looking at the pictures on pages 214–15?
8. Reflect back on the four types of arthropods. See how much you can remember about each type: millipedes, centipedes, crustaceans, insects.

their destination. Parallels can be drawn between the textbook journey the students are to take and an actual trip to another location. In reading, as with any mode of travel, it is much less confusing to look ahead, plan your course, and know where you are going before you get there.

Students can be assigned a partner or choose a friend with whom to travel. That is, they can pair up and discuss their guide with a partner, taking turns reading portions of the text and deciding upon the most logical answer. At selected points through the guide, the teacher may intervene to engage the students in a class discussion of their reactions so far. Upon completing the guide, the students are instructed to think back over their responses (their journey) and recall as much information (memories) as possible.

Interactive Reading Guide

Much empirical evidence supports using cooperative learning techniques in the classroom (Johnson and Johnson, 1985; Slavin, 1983). The interactive reading guide requires that students work cooperatively as they read and learn from the text (see Figure 3).

In a typical reading guide, students work alone while responding to a series of questions. However, with the interactive reading guide, the teacher directs the strategy in orchestral manner, sometimes requiring responses from individuals, pairs, or small groups. Additionally, instead of merely answering literal level or fill in the blank questions, students may be asked to predict, develop associations, read to a partner, reorganize information according to the text's structure, or recall in any order what was read.

After each segment activity or question is completed by the pairs or groups, the class, as a whole, discusses the responses given. Since the text material is divided into more manageable units and since extra time is spent on instruction, comprehension and long term retention can be enhanced.

In general, the class proceeds through the guide together, although the teacher may want to allow more advanced students to proceed ahead when judged necessary. To further facilitate the assignment, certain segments and activities may be given a time limit.

The partnership or small grouping arrangement required with this guide can be determined in advance. Students can be grouped who are socially and academically compatible, such that all will benefit from the knowledge and abilities of each other.

The teacher may select from several of the cooperative learning arrangements reported in the literature (Wood, 1987). One of these, Fader's Buddy System (1976), requires that students of varied ability levels become responsible for each other's learning. With the Buddy System, the disparity between ability levels is kept to a minimum so that students are neither bored nor threatened by other group members. However, the differences are great enough to ensure that group members can learn and benefit from the varied backgrounds and experiences of their peers.

The interactive reading guide may take several days to complete because it is designed as an inclass strategy and requires much student graphic and oral response. However, the class generated completed guide will provide a synopsis of textbook content beneficial for future study and review.

Guidelines for Classroom Use

A number of suggestions are given next to assist in the development and implementation of the reading guides described in this article.

Include a review of the content—Frequent review of information learned improves long term understanding and retention (Good and Grouws, 1979). As can be seen in each example, the culminating activity involves a mental and then written review of the major concepts, events, or people. Students are asked to associate and recall all they can, retrieving information while it is still readily available.

Be creative in designing the guides—The more creative the guide is in appearance and in content, the more likely students will want to engage in the reading assignments. A guide on the cardiovascular system for a health class, for example, may follow the shape of a heart with questions or activities marking

FIGURE 3
Interactive reading guide

Interaction codes:
- ◯ = Individual
- ◯◯ = Pairs
- ⊛ = Group
- ◯ = Whole class

Chapter 12: "Japan—An Island Country"

⊛ 1. In your group, write down everything you can think of relative to the topics listed below on Japan. Your group's associations will then be shared with the class.

Japan — location, land, seasons, food, products, industry, major cities

◯◯ 2. Read page 156 and jot down 5 things about the topography of Japan. Share this information with your partner.

◯ 3. Read to remember all you can about the "Seasons of Japan." The associations of the class will then be written on the board for discussion.

◯◯ 4. a. Take turns "whisper reading" the three sections under "Feeding the People of Japan." After each section, retell, with the aid of your partner, the information in your own words.
   b. What have you learned about the following?
      terraces, paddies, thresh, other crops, fisheries

⊛ 5. Put two pencils together and allow each person in the group to try eating with chopsticks. Discuss your experiences with the group.

◯◯ 6. With your partner, use your prior knowledge to predict if the following statements are true or false *before* reading the section on "Industrialized Japan." Return to these statements *after* reading to see if you've changed your view. In all cases, be sure to explain your answers. You do not have to agree with your partner.
   a. Japan does not produce its own raw materials but instead gets them from other countries.
   b. Japan is one of the top 10 shipbuilding countries.
   c. Japan makes more cars than the U.S.
   d. Silk used to be produced by silkworms but now it is a manmade fiber.
   e. Silkworms eat mulberry leaves.
   f. The thread from a single cocoon is 600 feet long.

◯ ⊛ 7. After reading, write down 3 new things you learned about the following topics. Compare these responses with those of your group.
      Other industries of Japan
      Old and new ways of living

◯ ⊛ 8. Read the section on "Cities of Japan." Each group member is to choose a city; show its location on the map in the textbook, and report on some facts about it.

◯ ◯ 9. Return to the major topics introduced in the first activity. Skim over your chapter reading guide responses with these topics in mind. Next, be ready to contribute, along with the class, anything you have learned about these topics.

significant locations. Likewise, guide questions and activities should stimulate creative thinking and engage as many of the senses as possible (see Figure 3, Number 5).

Group and pair students—The interactive reading guide described here is designed specifically to capitalize on the many advantages of cooperative learning. Yet all reading guides should have some element of student-to-student and student-to-teacher interaction. Not only has such collaboration been shown to improve achievement, but it also greatly enhances interpersonal relationships among students (Johnson and Johnson, 1985).

Skim guide and text before beginning—Skimming the guide and the text before beginning should become automatic to students after the initial explication and modeling sessions. This survey step helps to solidify their purpose for reading and allows them to "see where they are going before they get there."

Explicate and model—Ample research attests to the value of modeling and demonstrating skills and strategies before assigning independent practice (Berliner and Rosenshine, 1977; Duffy, 1981). It is essential that the purpose of the reading guides be thoroughly explained and students "walked and talked through" the assignment. In this way, they can begin to understand metacognitively why such guides can help them learn.

Circulate and monitor—The most effective teachers continually circulate and monitor class assignments (Evertson et al., 1984; Kounin, 1970). Such an involvement in the lesson allows the teacher to assist individuals or groups and to determine who may need further encouragement.

Follow with a discussion—Reading guides need teacher direction and are most valuable when students are not sent off to work alone or are not required to merely turn in their assignment when finished. Follow up discussions of guide responses are essential with each lesson to increase interest, learning, and later recall.

Use reading guides judiciously—Reading guides should not be designed for every chapter or selection. As with any strategy, their novelty would soon wear off and their utility diminish. Use of guides should be limited to portions of the text which may be difficult reading for students or which are particularly suitable for such modification.

Avoid assigning grades—Reading guides are adjunct aids developed to assist students with the reading of informational material. Therefore, they should not be graded in the competitive sense. Since the finished guides are often the result of group effort, group members should be given either a "complete" or an "incomplete," if graded at all.

Encourage strategic reading—Strategic readers read purposefully and with direction and they know what to do when something fails to make sense. In short, they know what strategies to use and when to use them (Paris, Lipson, and Wixson, 1983). Reading guides are a means of making students aware of the range of strategies necessary for successful comprehension. Yet it is essential to explain how these strategies generalize to other contexts within and outside the classroom environment and how they can still be employed independently when no reading guide is available.

Since teachers cannot provide one-on-one assistance to their students, reading guides have been called "tutors in print form" (Wood and Mateja, 1983). They help guide students through the reading of informational text by using questions or statements to reduce the amount of print students must deal with at a given time. When used as suggested, reading guides provide a vehicle to channel peer interaction, thereby using the most valuable teaching resource available in the classroom—the students themselves.

REFERENCES

Anderson, Richard C. "The Notion of Schemata and the Educational Enterprise." In *Schooling and the Acquisition of Knowledge*, edited by Richard C. Anderson, Rand J. Spiro, and William E. Montague. Hillsdale, NJ: Erlbaum, 1977.

Anderson, Richard C., and P. David Pearson. "A Schema Theoretic View of the Reading Processes in Reading Comprehension." In *Handbook of Reading Research*, edited by P. David Pearson. New York, NY: Longman, 1984.

Armbruster, Bonnie B., and Thomas H. Anderson. "Content Area Textbooks." Reading Education Report No. 23.

Urbana, IL: Center for the Study of Reading, University of Illinois, 1981.

Berliner, David C., and Barak V. Rosenshine. "The Acquisition of Knowledge in the Classroom." In *Schooling and the Acquisition of Knowledge*, edited by Richard C. Anderson, Rand J. Spiro, and William E. Montague. Hillsdale, NJ: Lawrence Erlbaum Associates, 1977.

Cunningham, Dick, and Scott L. Shablak. "Selective Reading Guide-O-Rama: The Content Teacher's Best Friend." *Journal of Reading*, vol. 18 (February 1975), pp. 380–82.

Davey, Beth. "Using Textbook Activity Guides to Help Students Learn from Textbooks." *Journal of Reading*, vol. 29 (March 1986), pp. 489–94.

Distad, H.W. "A Study of the Reading Performance of Pupils under Different Conditions on Different Types of Materials." *Journal of Educational Psychology*, vol. 18 (January 1927), pp. 247–58.

Duffy, Gerald C. "Teacher Effectiveness Research: Implications for the Reading Profession." In *Directions in Reading: Research and Instruction*, Thirtieth Yearbook of the National Reading Conference, edited by Michael L. Kamil. Washington, DC: National Reading Conference, 1981.

Educational Products Information Exchange. *Report on National Study of the Nature and the Quality of Instructional Materials Most Used by Teachers and Learners*. EPIE Report No. 17. Stonybrook, NY: EPIE Institute, 1977.

Evertson, Carolyn M., Edmund T. Emmer, Barbara S. Clements, Julie P. Sanford, and Murray E. Worsham. *Classroom Management for Elementary Teachers*. Englewood Cliffs, NJ: Prentice-Hall, 1984.

Fader, Daniel. *The New Hooked on Books*. New York, NY: Berkley Publishing, 1976.

Good, Thomas, and Douglas Grouws. "The Missouri Mathematics Effectiveness Project: An Experimental Study in Fourth Grade Classrooms." *Journal of Educational Psychology*, vol. 71 (June 1979), pp. 355–62.

Goodlad, John I. *Facing the Future: Issues in Education and Schooling*. New York, NY: McGraw-Hill, 1976.

Gordon, W.J.J. *The Metaphorical Way of Learning and Knowing*. Cambridge, MA: Porpoise Books, 1966.

Hansen, Jane, and P. David Pearson. "An Instructional Study: Improving the Inferential Comprehension of Fourth Grade Good and Poor Readers." Technical Report No. 235. Urbana, IL: Center for the Study of Reading, University of Illinois, 1982.

Herber, Harold J. *Teaching Reading in Content Areas*. Englewood Cliffs, NJ: Prentice-Hall, 1970.

Johnson, Roger T., and David W. Johnson. "Student-Student Interaction: Ignored but Powerful." *Journal of Teacher Education*, vol. 36 (July–August 1985), pp. 22–26.

Kounin, Jacob. *Discipline and Group Management in Classrooms*. New York, NY: Holt, Rinehart and Winston, 1970.

Mayer, Richard C. "Elaboration Techniques That Increase the Technical Text: An Experimental Test of the Learning Strategy Hypothesis." *Journal of Educational Psychology*, vol. 72 (December 1980), pp. 770–84.

Paris, Scott G., and Marjorie Y. Lipson, and Karen K. Wixson. "Becoming a Strategic Reader." *Contemporary Educational Psychology*, vol. 8 (July 1983), pp. 293–316.

Pauk, Walter. *How to Study in College*. Boston, MA: Houghton Mifflin, 1974.

Reder, Lynn M. "The Role of Elaboration in the Comprehension and Retention of Prose: A Critical Review." *Review of Educational Research*, vol. 27 (January 1984), pp. 312–17.

Singer, Harry, and Dan Donlan. *Reading and Learning from Text*. Boston, MA: Little, Brown, 1980.

Slavin, Robert E. *Cooperative Learning*. New York, NY: Longman, 1983.

Vacca, Richard T. *Content Area Reading*. Boston, MA: Little, Brown, 1981.

Washburne, John N. "The Use of Questions in Social Science Material." *Journal of Educational Psychology*, vol. 20 (May 1929), pp. 321–59.

Wood, Karen D. "Fostering Cooperative Learning in Middle and Secondary Level Classrooms." *Journal of Reading*, vol. 31 (October 1987), pp. 10–18.

Wood, Karen D. "The Effects of Interspersing Questions in Text: Evidence for 'Slicing the Task.'" *Reading Research and Instruction*, vol. 25 (Summer 1986), pp. 295–307.

Wood, Karen D., and John A. Mateja. "Adapting Secondary Level Strategies for Use in Elementary Classrooms." *The Reading Teacher*, vol. 36 (February 1983), pp. 492–96.

Classroom Organization for Instruction in Content Areas

Laura S. Pardo and Taffy E. Raphael

Chad, Megan, Anna, David, and Dennis, a heterogeneous group of children in Laura Pardo's urban third grade classroom, have been studying newspapers for approximately 5 weeks as part of a social studies unit on communication. To write their report about newspapers, they've gathered information from their textbook, taken a field trip to the city newspaper, interviewed an expert on newspapers, and read trade and reference books.

Laura organized instruction in three different ways to give the students optimal opportunities to learn new concepts and strategies, and to apply and practice these strategies in a variety of situations. The three forms of classroom instruction allowed students to (1) participate in teacher-led whole class lessons, (2) work in a cooperative small group, and (3) work independently.

By emphasizing the social nature of learning, Laura sought to create a classroom environment to meet the overall goal of content area instruction: to help students become skillful at learning and organizing content area information. Students should be able to meet this goal both when working independently and when working in a group.

In this article we examine three ways to organize classrooms to meet the goals of content area instruction. We begin by examining research on grouping practices that support students in their learning and organizing of content area information. We then follow Anna and her peers as they use selected strategies while participating in different forms of grouping during the class unit on communi-cation. We use the experiences of these students to illustrate how different grouping arrangements foster particular kinds of learning.

The Research Base: Grouping Practices

Using groups within classrooms has a long history, dating back almost 80 years to when ability was first used as a basis for forming small groups (Barr, 1989). Ability grouping has continued to dominate reading instruction in spite of research suggesting that the instruction received in the lower achieving groups differs substantially from, and is inferior to, that received by higher achieving children (Allington, 1983). Furthermore, research suggests that there is no justification for separating students into ability groups (Yates, 1966), and that instruction in hetero-geneous groups leads to higher achievement for all students (Dishon & O'Leary, 1984).

Issues of grouping are often ignored in content area instruction, where a single textbook is typical-ly used for students of all reading abilities, and in-struction centers on whole class lessons. Yet research indicates that students earn higher grades, develop more skill in critical thinking, and become better decision makers when they study in smaller cooper-ative learning groups (Johnson & Johnson, 1984; Slavin, 1985). Cooperative learning groups may produce academic benefits, including higher indi-vidual achievement, as well as social benefits. Also,

Reprinted from *The Reading Teacher*, 44(8), pp. 556–565. © 1991 by the International Reading Association.

learning within collaborative groups more closely parallels activities found in the workplace.

The research indicates that participating in heterogeneous groups can help students acquire and share content area knowledge, especially when the purposes of the groups fit the goals of the lesson or unit, the groups are heterogeneous, and the students have the necessary academic and social strategies to succeed in the group activities. Thus, determining the organization for a particular lesson depends on the purposes of the lesson, the content to be learned, and the strategies needed.

Selected Comprehension Strategies

Merely using a variety of grouping arrangements in classrooms will not automatically create independent and successful learners. Fundamental to students' success is learning a common vocabulary about strategies and learning the strategies themselves. Dennis, Megan, and their peers were able to take responsibility for planning, organizing, and writing their report on newspapers because of their familiarity with specific reading comprehension strategies. As seen in Table 1, these strategies included: K-W-L (Ogle, 1986), journals (Fulwiler, 1982), Author's Chair (Graves & Hansen, 1983), concept maps (Johnson, Pittelman, & Heimlich, 1986; Schwartz, 1988), QARs (Raphael, 1986), and Cognitive Strategy Instruction in Writing (Raphael & Englert, 1990). These strategies were the tools that provided students with the means to acquire and remember the content knowledge in the communication unit and other units.

Organizing for Content Area Instruction

Studying subject matter in Laura's classroom involved four broad phases. First, students needed to develop a general concept of the topic (in this case, communication). This would give them a shared understanding and vocabulary to use in discourse about the general topic and related subtopics. Second, students gathered information both about general con-

cepts and their specific subtopics, using a variety of information sources and comprehension strategies. Third, students organized and synthesized the information through charts and summaries. Fourth, students drafted and shared their final reports. Students' success in each of these phases was enhanced by their participation in reading and writing activities within appropriate grouping arrangements (see Table 2).

Teacher-Led Whole Class Discussions

There are several purposes for teacher-led whole class discussion, including: (1) introducing new strategies and concepts, (2) sharing related background knowledge, (3) building common experiences and reviewing previously presented ideas, (4) learning from difficult text, and (5) enrichment activities. The communication unit provided ample opportunities for students to participate as a whole class for each of these purposes. Lessons focused on the content to be learned and on processes or strategies that supported content learning (Roehler, Duffy, & Meloth, 1986).

Introducing new strategies and concepts occurred on 3 occasions: when the communication unit began and the concept itself was defined using a concept map, when the students used K-W-L to develop new concepts about newspapers, and when students learned to create an organizational chart as they reviewed information they had gathered during the unit. The K-W-L lesson, as students prepared to read the section of the text on newspapers, illustrates how process and content instruction were merged. During the W phase of the lesson, Laura asked students to think about their individual questions about newspapers.

Nina: Why does that black stuff get all over you?

Jenny: Newsprint.

Laura: Newsprint, Jenny said, but why does it get all over us?

Dennis: [interrupting] Ink!

Laura: Yes, why does that *ink* get on our hands?

TABLE 1
Selected comprehension strategies

K-W-L	This framework helps students build background knowledge and share common experiences. K stands for "What do I already know?" W stands for "What do I want to learn?" and L stands for "What have I learned?" It prompts students' thinking about: (1) their relevant background knowledge, (2) questions that reflect their purposes for reading, and (3) the information they learned from reading the text. Using K-W-L encourages students to attack informational text with a purpose, and recognize the information they have gleaned from it.
Focus journals	This type of journal encourages students to review their background knowledge, reflect on their previous learning, and predict their future learning. The journal focus is written on the board by the teacher each day before the students arrive. Students read the focus, reflect on their responses, and write in their journals. Frequently, the focus of the journal is on content area studies, though some days students choose their own topics. The focus journal helps students focus on their own learning and serves as a basis for discussion.
Concept maps	These visual organizers help students literally "map" their knowledge base. The maps can be used to help students understand a vocabulary term by having students identify the concept to be defined (e.g., communication); a superordinate category or phrase that helps them understand what it is (e.g., sending and receiving messages); traits (e.g., ideas from one person are shared with someone else; can be done out loud); and examples (e.g., newspapers, letters, telephone calls). Maps can also be used to organize information from different sources.
The author's chair	The author's chair provides students with a real audience as they share their journals, text, trade books, reports, and so forth. It is a special chair in the front of the room in which a child sits to read aloud to the rest of the class. During the time the child reads, he or she is speaking for the author. During content area study children may: (1) sit in the author's chair to read from their textbook to the rest of the class, (2) share their journal reflections and predictions with their peers, and (3) share their rough drafts for help in revisions and final drafts for general comments.
QAR	QAR teaches children about sources of information, helping students discover and use the many sources of information from which questions can be answered. It provides direction to those students who are overreliant on their background knowledge at the expense of information from texts, or those who are overreliant on the text as sole source of information and do not consider their own background knowledge and experience.
CSIW	CSIW is a framework for guiding students as they plan, organize, write, edit, and revise expository texts. A set of "thinksheets" serves as a basis for the teacher to model strategies. The thinksheets act as prompts for students to take notes and keep records about the information for their reports, to sustain their thinking about topics and as a basis for discussion. Thinksheets may be adapted to serve the specific needs students have as they gather and organize their information.

Chad's thinksheet (see Figure 1) illustrates how the children individually wrote questions about newspapers to guide their reading.

Because many students were not able to read the text comfortably, they read the section on newspapers with a partner. They completed the last column of their thinksheets individually, then participated in a teacher-led whole class discussion of the new concepts they had learned. The following segment illustrates how students made connections among earlier

TABLE 2
Patterns and purposes of classroom organization

Group size	Purposes	Strategies used	Examples
Whole class	Introduce new strategies and concepts Review previously presented ideas Build common experiences Share related background knowledge Learn from difficult text Enrichment activities	K-W-L QAR Author's chair	Concept map to begin unit K-W-L on newspapers Preparing for and taking field trip Modeling organizing information Reading and sharing textbook information (e.g., partner read; oral reading to group) Journal share
Small group	Apply and practice newly learned strategies and concepts with new texts Work collaboratively to create text (e.g., generate questions, gather information, organize and write drafts, revise) Encourage discourse about ideas in text	CSIW and adaptations Concept maps	Generating questions/setting purpose Gathering information from trade books Preparing interview questions Conducting interview of expert Organizing field trip information Drafting reports Peer conferences on reports Sharing among groups
Individual	Reflect on ideas, text, and interactions Set individual goals/purposes Apply and practice strategies, concepts Evaluate students' progress	Repeated readings Journals	Journal focus Generating questions Teacher/student conferences

discussions, the questions on their thinksheets, and what they had learned from reading:

Laura: Jenny, do you want to share with the class what you and I were just talking about, about what you learned?

Jenny: [reading from text] "Print means words in ink stamped on paper."

Laura: What does that tell you about one of your questions?

Jenny: It means that the newsprint comes off because it's *stamped.*

Laura: What question did you find the answer to?

Mike: The one about why does that black stuff come off on your fingers.

The connections that students made among the discussions, questions, and textbook were reflected in their reports. In a paragraph of their report, the students in the newspaper group discussed the importance of newspapers. This section was directly related to Dennis's and Chad's question, "What's so important about newspapers?" on their K-W-L thinksheets. They had also raised this question in class and on their field trip.

Sharing related background knowledge occurred in different ways. The students' journal entries served as a basis for a teacher-led whole group lesson in which students shared their knowledge about communication. This provided an introduction to students' initial reading of the textbook section in which communication was introduced. Students also shared background knowledge during the unit's culminating activity, in which each group presented its report to the whole class. What had been new concepts for each group gradually became their background knowledge, knowledge they were able to share with their peers and eventually the whole class.

FIGURE 1
K-W-L thinksheet

What do I Know?	What do I Want to know	What did I Learn?
I know that newspapers Are printed in black and white	What kind of papers do they use?	I learned that over 60 million people read news-paper a year.
Newspapers tell you what is going around your state or world	Who invented Newspapers?	Some Newspapers are printed evry day some are prin-ted on weekends
On Sundays they have comics	What's so important about Newspaper?	there are about 1,800 daily papers in the U.S. Many Large Communitys have more than one daily paper
	Why do you get Newsprint on your fingers?	
	What kind of ink do you use? Is it special	Newspaper is stamped instead of printed.

Building common experiences through teacher-led whole class discussions occurred throughout the communication unit. One way was through all students participating in field trips to such places as a newspaper office and television and radio stations. Each trip was framed by discussions about what they might see and learn, questions they might ask, and discussion about how information learned on each of the trips was related (e.g., people had a variety of jobs at the post office and at the newspaper).

Learning from difficult text can be frustrating for students with reading difficulties. It was important for these students to receive support and guidance during the teacher-led whole group discussions. Laura combined two purposes, helping students learn from difficult text and modeling strategies (e.g., notetaking and summarizing). For example, in one lesson, three students took turns reading aloud to the class from their social studies textbook. The students had rehearsed the one or two paragraphs they had been assigned, until they could read aloud fluently.

After each student finished reading his or her section to the class, Laura provided instruction. She thought aloud, stating that one way she remembers ideas later on is by writing down notes that will help jog her memory. She modeled stopping after each set of paragraphs to think about the main topics and the most important idea. She elicited ideas from students, provided her own thinking as a model, and modeled notetaking using a concept map.

Enrichment activities during the communication unit involved students listening to a modern form of communication: rapping. Two students from a local high school were invited to perform for the third graders. In an earlier unit, the enrichment activity involved students creating a videotape for their California penpals. The video was based on reports about their community.

Cooperative Small Groups

Cooperative small groups provide opportunities for students to: (1) practice newly learned strategies and apply newly learned concepts to further study in their chosen area, (2) work collaboratively to create texts, whether the texts be full reports, questions, or information synthesized from such sources as interviews of experts in a particular field, and (3) engage in discourse about the content and processes they are learning. Cooperative groups in the communication unit were formed to study subtopics such as newspapers, television and radio, and computers.

Application and practice of newly learned strategies. Students had worked with question generation and question answering as part of large group lessons with QARs, K-W-L, and concept mapping. They also had been asked to generate and respond to questions in their individual journals. The use of questions to guide learning was further emphasized in several small group activities.

To underscore that field trips were serious opportunities to learn more information, Laura had the students meet in their small groups to identify the questions that they planned to pursue during the field trip. Megan's question "Where do the colors come from?" helped focus students' attention on the printing press. Chad's question "How do you make a newspaper?" led them to notice the steps followed to create the daily paper. Their interest was reflected in a paragraph in their final report (note that all student writing samples are included without corrections for spelling, punctuation, etc.): "This is how newspapers are made. First the reporter finds a story then he/she writes the story. next an illustrator draws a picture for the story. Another person takes the drawing and draws it on a computer. Then the story is typed and edited. Last it is waxed and put on the page. Finally the newspaper is printed."

Working collaboratively to create text. In addition to the drafts of their reports, students created many other texts. These included interview questions and summaries of information gathered during the interview. One of the sources of information available to students in each group was an expert from the community (e.g., a supervisor from the local post office, a computer software engineer). Megan and the other students in the newspaper group identified what they already knew, what they wanted to learn, and the questions they wished to ask their expert. They then met with Sarah, whose family operates a city newspaper, and asked their questions. The answers were recorded on a second thinksheet (see Figure 2), which provided students with the opportunity to practice the strategy of summarizing, in addition to working collaboratively to generate the text.

FIGURE 2
"Expert interview" organization thinksheet

Organizing thinksheet

Question: *What kind of things you have a newspaper?*

Art   Traviling

Sports   Local

T.V.   adds

Bissness   comics

Question: *What's so impoment about newspapers?*

So you'll know what's going on all around you.

Question: *How is your newspaper made?*

It is written then ededitied, and printed and waxed then it is made.

Another opportunity to work collaboratively to generate text occurred in the writing of the drafts for their final reports. To create the first draft, each student volunteered to draft a paragraph on one of the areas they had collectively decided to include: names of newspapers, jobs in the newspaper office, sections contained in newspapers, how newspapers are made, and why they are important. Students then shared their paragraphs and discussed issues such as (1) the order of the paragraphs, (2) the accuracy of each other's information, and (3) the content of the introduction and conclusion.

Sections of their report reflected these discussions. Their sensitivity to different sources of information was seen in the introduction: "This report is about newspapers. We talked about them, we read books about them, and we visited the Lansing State Journal." Their individual questions, such as Chad's and Dennis's questions about the importance of newspapers, were reflected in their second paragraph: "This is what's so important about newspapers. You can see what's going on around the world. We read newspapers to see if theres danger and to see what the wether is. Adults read newspapers because they think it is very very important. And that's what so important."

The group's consensus about important categories of information (e.g., on the field trip and during the interview, asking how newspapers are made and focusing again on their importance) was seen in their inclusion of paragraphs containing such information. They agreed that an ending should reflect their goal that "we hope you learned from our report about newspapers."

Encourage discourse about ideas in or related to text. The many examples listed above illustrate the value of small groups. Small groups provided unique opportunities for students to engage in discourse about their topics and to use strategies for conveying their information. These opportunities helped students value each other as members of the community of scholars with knowledge of social studies topics. Students helped each other use strategies, such as question generation and summarizing, and learned

about content by means similar to those of mature learners in the workplace and nonschool sites.

Individual

As Table 2 suggests, the reasons for students to work individually include the opportunities to (1) reflect on their ideas, the texts they are reading, and their interactions with the teacher and peers, (2) set individual goals and purposes, (3) apply and practice strategies learned, and (4) provide information regarding individual progress.

Reflection on ideas, text, interactions. At the beginning of the communication unit, students were asked to reflect on what they already knew about communication by writing in the dialogue journals. Two focus questions guided their thinking and writing: What do you think of when you hear the word *communication*? What are some ways that you communicate? Different levels of knowledge were apparent, as seen in Chad's and Anna's journal entries.

Chad wrote a single paragraph in which he identified "taking, calling, and singh [sign] language" as ways people communicate. He then wrote: "I can communicate by calling or talking on the phone."

Anna used two text structures to convey her ideas. First she listed six ways people communicate: phone, talking, newspapers, letter writing, computer, and movies. Beneath that she wrote four paragraphs, each consisting of a single sentence identifying ways she communicates and expanding on ideas in her list: "I communicate by letter writing, phone & Talking that was I communicate. Like if I was calling my uncle I would be comunicating by phone. Or if I was writing a letter to my grandma. or if I was talking to my friend thats communiting."

Setting individual goals and purposes. A second reason for working individually is to set goals or purposes for one's reading. In the communication unit Laura used K-W-L as such an opportunity. The students individually completed the first column, identifying what they knew, and then participated in a whole class discussion in which they could learn from each other. Then Laura asked them each to consider what they would like to learn about newspapers. Figure 1 shows the five questions Chad identified to direct his reading.

Apply and practice learned strategies. Laura had taught students question generation as a strategy for identifying both what they already knew and what they wished to learn. The K-W-L lesson allowed Chad to set his own goals, and it also provided him and his peers with the opportunity to practice generating questions which might be answered through reading the textbook. Students also received practice in generating questions prior to using the trade and reference books.

Individual assessment. Assessment should occur within the context of instruction (Au, Scheu, Kawakami, & Herman, 1990). Thus, individual writing and reading activities provided natural opportunities to judge students' success in a variety of ways. For example, Chad wrote a journal entry about communication, a list of questions on the K-W-L thinksheet, and a related list of what he had learned.

All of these gave Laura information about his growing ability to identify important information, to generate relevant questions about the topic to be studied, to comprehend content area text, and to write to express ideas. Laura also could see the content Chad had learned from the text, and she could assess his knowledge of conventions of print and his penmanship.

Concluding Remarks

In this article we explored the use of various grouping arrangements in content area instruction. Anna and her peers experienced several rewards from the practices we described. First, over time they succeeded in working cooperatively with their peers on learning tasks, something that is often difficult even for adults. Second, they became risk takers. They were not afraid to try new forms of writing or different ways of conducting conversations to meet their goals, since they believed in their own abilities. Third, they made

noticeable improvements in their writing habits. They enjoyed writing and many chose to write in their free time. Not surprisingly, their writing skills improved. We saw these students progress from writing one or two word responses to sustained thinking and writing about content area topics.

Whether or not we should group children for instruction has been debated historically and continues to be debated today. The debate focuses on a wide range of issues, such as equity across groups, the validity of ability grouping, and the value of cooperative learning. This debate is nowhere more critical than in the content areas, where often a single textbook is mandated for use within a classroom and where whole class instruction provides a helpful contrast to the ability groups often used in the reading program.

Yet we should be cautious about maintaining only whole class instruction in the content areas, just as we are now cautious about only using ability grouping in the reading program. Perhaps we have been asking the wrong question about grouping practices. We suggest that the question is not "Should we have groups?" but instead "What groups should we have for what purposes?"

REFERENCES

Au, K.H., Scheu, J.A., Kawakami, A.J., & Herman, P.A. (1990). Assessment and accountability in a Whole Literacy curriculum. *The Reading Teacher, 43*, 574–578.

Allington, R. (1983). The reading instruction provided readers of different reading ability. *Elementary School Journal, 83*, 548–559.

Barr, R. (1989). The social organization of literacy instruction. *National Reading Conference Yearbook, 19–33.*

Dishon, D., & O'Leary, P.W. (1984). *A guidebook for cooperative learning: A technique for creating more effective schools.* Holmes Beach, FL: Learning Publications.

Fulwiler, T. (1982). The personal connection: Journal writing across the curriculum. In T. Fulwiler & A. Young (Eds.), *Language connections: Writing and reading across the curriculum* (pp. 15–32). Urbana, IL: National Council of Teachers of English.

Graves, D.H., & Hansen, J. (1983). The author's chair. *Language Arts, 60*, 176–183.

Johnson, D.D., Pittelman, S.D., & Heimlich, J.E. (1986). Semantic mapping. *The Reading Teacher, 39*, 778–783.

Johnson, D.W., & Johnson, R.T. (1984). Cooperative small-group learning. *Curriculum Report, 14*(1).

Ogle, D.M. (1986). K-W-L: A teaching model that develops active reading of expository text. *The Reading Teacher, 39,* 564–570.

Raphael, T.E. (1986). Teaching question answer relationships, revisited. *The Reading Teacher, 39,* 516–522.

Raphael, T.E., & Englert, C.S. (1990). Writing and reading: Partners in constructing meaning. *The Reading Teacher, 43,* 388–400.

Roehler, L.R., Duffy, G.G., & Meloth, M.B. (1986). What to be direct about in direct instruction in reading: Content-only versus process-into-content. In T.E. Raphael (Ed.), *The contexts of school-based literacy* (pp. 79–95). New York: Random House.

Schwartz, R.M. (1988). Learning to learn vocabulary in content area textbooks. *Journal of Reading, 32,* 108–118.

Slavin, R.E. (1985). Cooperative learning: Applying contact theory in desegregated schools. *Journal of Social Issues, 41*(3), 43–62.

Yates, A. (1966). *Grouping in education.* New York: Wiley.

Models for Using Nonfiction in the Primary Grades

Rosemary G. Palmer and Roger A. Stewart

Practitioners and scholars today are calling for the inclusion of nonfiction in primary-grade classrooms, where in the past fiction has dominated. With the increasing availability of age-appropriate nonfiction texts, this request can now become a reality. In the past, teachers and librarians steered primary-grade children into fiction, partly because most nonfiction in elementary schools was appropriate for intermediate-grade readers. As a result, when expository text was used in K–3 classrooms, teachers often read aloud and interpreted books too difficult for young children to read by themselves (Brown, 1998; Fielding & Roller, 1992; Palmer & Stewart, 2000, 2003). Now, with nonfiction available for emergent readers, students can read books on their independent and instructional reading levels. As a consequence, teachers and librarians face new and exciting challenges as they find, choose, and incorporate nonfiction into their instruction.

Teachers have not been left on their own to figure out how to use nonfiction. How-to texts are available to assist in selecting, evaluating, and teaching this genre (e.g., Bamford & Kristo, 2000; Hoyt, Mooney, & Parkes, 2003). Other books explain how to teach nonfiction writing (Stead, 2002), conduct research with expository text (Harvey, 1998), and use strategies and conduct investigations with informational text (Hoyt, 2002). In addition, a number of journal articles, some of which we cite in this article, provide information on using nonfiction in primary-grade classrooms. On the one hand,

this may suggest more work for teachers who already have full instructional agendas; but, on the other hand, it represents new resources for teachers to help students become lifelong readers for information and pleasure. We believe a synthesis of this information will help teachers as they include factual text in their instruction. This article provides a series of three models primary-grade teachers can use to structure their work with nonfiction.

We recognize that much of what is in this article can be found across a broad base of literature, including project-based learning, inquiry learning, comprehension instruction, and writing instruction. In addition, our three models are implicit in several published articles and books (e.g., Barclay & Traser, 1999; Perry & Drummond, 2002). Our purpose is to connect what others have done and provide a simple framework and common vocabulary for educators as they use more nonfiction and communicate with one another about it. This framework is compatible with standards and high-stakes testing because our models allow teachers to adapt instruction to the time they have for nonfiction.

Simply put, we live in an expository world. If we want young readers to effectively use this genre, they must be taught the necessary skills (Moss, Leone, & Dipillo, 1997). For example, if educators want younger students to conduct research with informational text, the students must learn how. They cannot jump to the level of independent research all at once. Our three models show primary-grade teachers how to scaffold instruction and answer the question

Reprinted from *The Reading Teacher*, 58(5), pp. 426–434. © 2005 by the International Reading Association.

"What do I do with nonfiction once I have chosen it?" Using the gradual release of responsibility (Pearson & Gallagher, 1983; Roehler & Duffy, 1984), our models represent a series of stages with the end product being independent use of informational books in the classroom. Gradual release of responsibility involves scaffolding from high levels of teacher support to more student involvement and responsibility. Instruction based on this model has been shown to enhance learning (e.g., Dole, Brown, & Trathen, 1996; Palincsar & Brown, 1984). We also believe our models represent evidence-based practice. We now turn to a preliminary overview of this evidence. Additional evidence is provided as we discuss the models.

Evidence-Based Practice

As we have explored nonfiction use in primary-grade classrooms and reviewed the research and resources on the topic, we understand the positive contribution expository text can make in early literacy development. Although nonfiction has not been emphasized in primary-grade classrooms (Duke, 2000b), we know that young students enjoy and sometimes prefer informational texts (Caswell & Duke, 1998; Duke & Kays, 1998; Duthie, 1994; Guillaume, 1998; Kamil & Lane, 1997; Kletzien & Szabo, 1998; Palmer & Stewart, 2003; Pappas, 1993; Reese & Harris, 1997). Research shows that younger students can effectively process expository text (Duke, 2000a, 2000b, 2003; Pappas, 1991, 1993). We also know that nonfiction motivates students as they search for answers to questions about their world (Guthrie, 1996; Guthrie & McCann, 1997; McMath, King, & Smith, 1998; Sweet & Guthrie, 1996; Yopp & Yopp, 2000).

Students are increasingly called upon to organize and display their learning. As a consequence, research and communication skills are being pushed into lower grades, creating the need for more expository text use. Nonfiction can help young readers engage in the critical thinking and research needed to build meaningful knowledge and understanding in content area subjects (McMath et al., 1998; Parkes, 2003).

We also have evidence that achievement improves when students read nonfiction. Some of this evidence comes from anecdotal accounts written by teachers who describe success with nonfiction and student research. We cite these studies throughout the remainder of the article. Other evidence comes from classroom-based studies. For example, struggling second-grade readers exhibited increased ability to focus on a task, follow directions, and work together (Schmidt, Gillen, Zollo, & Stone, 2002). They also demonstrated increased understanding of concepts in the unit. Richgels (2002) described a successful nonfiction program in a kindergarten classroom, and Korkeamaki, Tiainen, and Dreher (1998, 1999) stated that second graders learned strategies, applied them to reading and writing nonfiction, and enjoyed the instruction.

The Three Models

The three models teachers can use to structure their nonfiction work are (1) teacher-directed instruction, (2) scaffolded student investigation, and (3) independent student investigation. Demands on students and teachers increase as teachers scaffold students through each model, starting with Model 1 and moving sequentially through the two others. We illustrate the models with the topics of frogs and life cycles (see Table 1), although teachers can choose themes from other content areas—there are numerous nonfiction books now being published for social studies and other subjects. Strategies and teaching ideas provided under each model are not exhaustive but representative and illustrative of research-based instruction that can occur within that model. Before teachers implement the models, however, students need to become familiar with nonfiction.

Setting the Stage for Implementation

As teachers set the stage, they focus on familiarizing students with nonfiction and organizing for instruction. Teacher read-alouds are an important

TABLE 1
Examples of primary-grade nonfiction on frogs, baby animals, and life cycles

Frogs
Berger, M. (1994). *Those fabulous frogs.* New York: Newbridge.
Berger, M. (1995). *Leaping frogs.* New York: Newbridge.
Discovery links science—emergent: Set A. *A pond.* Littleton, MA: Newbridge.
Discovery links science—emergent: Set C. *Where's the frog?* Littleton, MA: Newbridge.
Discovery links science—emergent: Set D. *How do frogs grow?* Littleton, MA: Newbridge.
Heinrichs, A. (2003). *Frogs.* Minneapolis, MN: Compass Point Books.
Holmes, K.J. (1998). *Frogs.* Mankato, MN: Capstone.
Kalman, B., & Everts, T. (1994). *Frogs and toads.* New York: Crabtree.
Kalman, B., & Langille, J. (2000). *What is an amphibian?* New York: Crabtree.
Kalman, B., & Smithyman, K. (2002). *The life cycle of a frog.* New York: Crabtree.
Mitchell, M. (2003). *Life cycles: Frogs.* Minneapolis, MN: Lerner.
Murphy, P.J. (2002). *How a frog gets its legs.* New York: Rosen.
Saunders-Smith, G. (1998). *Frogs.* Mankato, MN: Capstone Press.
Shaefer, L.M. (2001). *What is an amphibian?* Mankato, MN: Capstone.
Tyler, M. (1997). *Frogs.* New York: Mondo.
Zemlicka, S. (2003). *From tadpole to frog.* Minneapolis, MN: Lerner.

Animals and their young
Animals and Their Young series. Minneapolis, MN: Compass Point Books.
Baby Animals series. Minneapolis, MN: Lerner.
Davis, S. (2000). *Baby animals.* Crystal Lake, IL: Rigby.

Life cycles and habitats
Life Cycle series. New York: Crabtree.
Life Cycles series. Littleton, MA: Newbridge.
Mitchell, M. (2003). *Animal life cycles.* Minneapolis, MN: Learner.
Ranger Rick: Animal Life series. Littleton, MA: Newbridge.
Start to Finish series. Minneapolis, MN: Lerner.

means to familiarize students with nonfiction. As teachers read aloud, students learn content, vocabulary, and "the sounds of print" (Duke, Bennett-Armistead, & Roberts, 2003; Duke & Kays, 1998; Moss, 2003; Moss et al., 1997; Pappas, 1991, 1993). Listening to and discussing nonfiction can activate background knowledge and motivate young readers to learn more about a topic. Teachers can use read-alouds to introduce the format and structure of nonfiction, discuss similarities and differences between reading nonfiction and fiction, and explore student interests and preferences. Through newsletters and school parent-night instruction, teachers can also encourage parents to read nonfiction with their students at home.

As setting the stage progresses, students and teachers prepare to move to Model 1, where systematic instruction with nonfiction occurs and students' knowledge of the genre and their capacity to work with it grows.

Model 1—Teacher-Directed Instruction
In the past, when teachers read aloud and interpreted difficult nonfiction, young readers learned information but failed to read expository text (Palmer & Stewart, 2003). Students must tackle expository text

themselves to become fluent and strategic readers of this genre. In order for students to do so, teachers need to directly instruct how to navigate and extract information (RAND, 2002). This requires a shift from teachers reading aloud difficult material to strategic reading instruction in appropriately leveled materials and from interpreting text to giving students skills to interpret text for themselves. But to do this, teachers need enough books—either classroom sets or multiple copies for small groups—and they need to model techniques and strategies for reading. For example, students should understand they can search for specific facts about a topic rather than read from cover to cover as in fiction. Organizational features such as headings, index, and glossary are comprehension tools; visuals (e.g., photos, diagrams, charts) supply additional information. Asking questions about text features, content, and vocabulary activates prior knowledge and helps students process text (National Institute of Child Health and Human Development [NICHD], 2000; Wood, Pressley, & Winne, 1990). Graphic and semantic organizer instruction improves comprehension and helps students visualize and remember information (Banikowski & Mehring, 1999; Marzano, 1998; Robinson, 1998).

There are many content reading strategies underpinned by research that can be taught. These are described in numerous books and articles (e.g., Duke & Bennett-Armistead, 2003; Harvey & Goudvis, 2000; Hoyt, 2002; Moss, 2003; Parkes, 2000; Tierney & Readence, 2000). We illustrate a few of these strategies as we describe what Model 1 looks like in classrooms. As young readers learn to use comprehension strategies through direct instruction and teacher modeling, they develop skills to independently access expository text in content area subjects.

A big book and class set of a nonfiction title are a great way to begin this process. Because "reading does not occur in a vacuum," readers need a purpose (RAND, 2002, p. 15). There are numerous ways to set purposes for reading. One of the most popular is K-W-L (Ogle, 1986), which we have observed primary-grade teachers use with nonfiction. List-Group-Label (LGL; Taba, 1967) is another strategy.

One second-grade teacher uses LGL to help her students set a purpose and access prior knowledge and experiences on a topic. Although research on LGL is not extensive, several studies encompassing a wide age range of students have shown promising results (see Tierney & Readence, 2000).

Applying LGL to the topic of frogs, the teacher asks, "What do you know about frogs?" Students write facts on sticky notes and put them on the chalkboard. As a class they organize the facts and place them under categories they identify. From these categories, the teacher helps the students generate questions (NICHD, 2000), which become their purposes for reading. For instance, to the question "Where do frogs live?" the teacher models how to locate answers in the table of contents and index of a Big Book. She turns to the pages listed, reads the information aloud while focusing on the question, and models how to extract facts while ignoring extraneous details. For example, in a section on habitats, the author explains that frogs live near water to keep their skin wet and then describes how frogs use their skin to breathe and drink by taking in oxygen and water. Although these details about the skin go beyond the question about where frogs live, they suggest a reason for the habitat. This extra information causes students to think critically and become active readers when the teacher asks, "Can frogs live in the desert? Why or why not?" This example also illustrates how to begin to model the critical reading process.

After completing the habitat question, the teacher selects other questions from the LGL activity and creates a simple study guide for students to record their answers. The teacher then helps students explore nonfiction books to answer such questions as "What are baby frogs like?" "What is the life cycle of the frog?" "What are other interesting facts about frogs?" This last question stimulates additional interest in the topic and provides a chance to share attention-grabbing information.

According to the National Reading Panel (NICHD, 2000), question answering can guide and monitor reading comprehension. Based on our research, we believe study guides are appropriate for primary-grade classrooms when they are used to model how to focus on, record, and organize information (Palmer & Stewart, 2003). This is unlike our nonfiction research in intermediate grades where we asserted that study guides and worksheets became fill-in-the-blank activities that contributed little to student learning (Palmer & Stewart, 1997). With younger students, a study guide serves as a tool for teachers to model key processes and for students to practice those processes as they learn to extract information from nonfiction.

After further fact gathering, students summarize their findings on their study guide and do hands-on activities with the text. Summarizing has a long history of research and has been shown to be a powerful comprehension strategy. In a meta-analytic study, Marzano (1998) found that teaching students to summarize significantly enhanced their learning. In addition to summarizing, students might make a diagram and label the parts of a frog or create headings in a book that has none. If the book lacks a table of contents, index, or glossary—or if they are incomplete—young readers can create or improve them. If students understand the structure of a text, they will better grasp its concepts (Duke & Pearson, 2002). The teacher can help students write a simple report from their study guide answers, then make a frog life-cycle wheel that graphically depicts the stages. (See Science and Technology for Children, 1992, or www.klru.org/butterflies for examples of life-cycle wheels.)

Part of teacher-directed instruction should focus on critical reading of nonfiction text (Lamme & Fu, 2001). Some nonfiction appears to be written quickly and contains confusing or conflicting information. Students need to understand that sometimes comprehension difficulties stem from problems in the text rather than in the reader. For example, in *Ponds and Rivers* (2000) young readers cannot tell which labels match the drawings in a life-cycle diagram. One nonfiction book names three stages of a frog's life while another describes four (Holmes, 1998; Zemlicka, 2003). A research-based strategy called Questioning the Author helps students develop the ability to read confidently and critically (Duke & Bennett-Armistead, 2003; McKeown, Beck, & Worthy, 1993; Sandora, Beck, & McKeown, 1999). Students learn

to ask, "What does the author mean?" if a text is unclear. We witnessed a third-grade teacher read several nonfiction books about planets to her class. When she encountered conflicting facts, she asked her students why this might occur. The class discussed how one book had a recent copyright date and, therefore, might contain more up-to-date information. The students also learned that discrepancies might occur because an author used incorrect information or did not include enough detail.

Once students have a foundation for reading expository text, teachers can help them choose appropriate books for independent reading. Today, young students can access nonfiction for independent reading on a variety of topics and reading levels because many publishers produce primary-grade nonfiction. Teachers can organize book tubs of leveled nonfiction on a single topic, such as frogs, or arrange them according to type of text: how-to, information, description, general topic, specific topic, or content area subject (Stead, 2002). Several teachers we know match students to texts in a variety of ways. For example, Kathy (pseudonym), a first-grade teacher, regularly assesses her students' reading levels, places nonfiction books in three or four tubs based on these levels, and attaches index cards to each tub with names of students at that level. When reading levels change, Kathy modifies the index cards accordingly, and as the class improves she adjusts the difficulty of the books in the tubs.

In Model 1, teachers model how to interact with and extract information from expository texts. They use nonfiction to teach content as well as comprehension and critical reading skills. The emphasis is on teacher-directed instruction. In Model 2, which we discuss next, the focus shifts to students taking more responsibility. This shift exemplifies the gradual release of responsibility that underpins our framework.

Model 2—Scaffolded Student Investigation

After working through the topic on frogs in Model 1, the teacher broadens the assignment to animal habitats and life cycles. The expanded topic allows for greater diversity of student interest and requires more books at appropriate reading levels to keep everyone reading and exploring. Because peer interaction promotes discussion and increases reading comprehension (NICHD, 2000), students now buddy up and select an animal based on the available nonfiction in the classroom. They read about their animal and discuss what they learn; then they answer questions on a study guide similar to the one used in Model 1. The buddies write a report from the study guide questions, create a life-cycle wheel and poster, and present information to the class. Research indicates that question answering, summarizing, and postwriting activities positively influence reading comprehension (NICHD, 2000; RAND, 2002). Next, students compare their animals to what the class learned about frogs. The class then makes an animal comparison chart and lists information under the categories of habitats, baby animals, life cycles, and interesting facts. Students compare animal life-cycle wheels and attach their wheels to the chart. Identifying similarities and differences and graphically depicting relationships improve comprehension and recall (Marzano, Pickering, & Pollock, 2001; RAND, 2002). We observed a second-grade teacher and her students complete a unit like the one described. The comparison chart was a focal point for discussion long after the unit ended.

As we have explained, Model 2 allows students to begin to independently use the reading and research skills they learned in Model 1 while the teacher monitors performance and behavior. We now turn to a description of Model 3 where students move toward independent use of nonfiction.

Model 3—Independent Student Investigation

After teachers scaffold students through the first two models, young learners should be ready to research topics of their choice. These investigations are student generated and, although adults may assist, are not sent home to complete. Students select a topic of interest, ask probing questions, gather and synthesize information, and create a product (Barclay &

Traser, 1999; Guthrie, 1996; Owens, Hester, & Teale, 2002; Perry & Drummond, 2002; Short, Harste, & Burke, 1996; Short et al., 1996). We have witnessed primary-grade teachers having great success with independent research projects. Students readily complete the task when they are adequately prepared, given freedom to pursue their interests through meaningful assignments, and provided an adequate and appropriate text base. A natural way to incorporate this model into the classroom is through thematic instruction, which is broad enough to capture all student interests.

After teachers have guided students through a class topic (frogs) and buddy topics (animals), they move to short-term projects that are self-selected and completed in three to four sessions. This allows teachers to further monitor students and double-check skills in reading, synthesizing, and reporting. Short-term projects are miniversions of independent student investigations. If these projects are successful, then students can dive into self-selected study that requires several weeks to finish. With short-term investigations, students might only explore one question, not unlike those described in Model 1 (i.e., What is the habitat of the frog?). They might create a brief report or visual for a short class presentation. These projects enable teachers to monitor students one more time before releasing responsibility to them for more in-depth investigations (Barclay & Traser, 1999).

We suggest two approaches for independent student investigations. A teacher can introduce a class unit, such as weather, and then have students choose subtopics that motivate them to become miniexperts. Either the teacher identifies subtopics or helps students find those that relate to the unit. The second approach gives students free choice of a topic. Both approaches, however, must be based on available nonfiction. In classroom observations, we have often noted too few books at appropriate reading levels for in-depth investigations. For example, we watched an enthusiastic teacher launch into a unit based on nonfiction only to find that she lacked sufficient numbers and levels of books. She spent more time scrambling to find books and coordinating the use of the ones she had than watching her unit unfold. Although adults can help students process difficult text, the core reading should be in appropriately leveled nonfiction.

For student-generated topics not related to a unit, the teacher might begin with an idea sheet or topic cards. An idea sheet helps students think about topics they might investigate. They fill in the blanks in unfinished sentences, such as "I have always wanted to learn about…" or "I have always wanted to visit…." Topic cards contain topics the teacher selects from state or district standards for students to organize according to interest. For example, with cards containing the words *birds*, *habitat*, *caterpillars*, *magnetism*, *healthy foods*, and *electricity*, a second grader may choose *caterpillars* as a first choice of study and *birds* as a second. Topic cards have an additional benefit of allowing teachers to control research based on available books.

After students pick topics, they do self-selected reading in appropriately leveled nonfiction to build background knowledge. They begin to ask probing questions, and the teacher helps generate meaningful and interesting questions to study. During designated blocks of time, students work alone or with peers or intermediate-grade students as they research, organize information, create a product, and orally present what they learned.

To organize information, students might create study guides patterned after those in Models 1 and 2. They might also "web" their questions and write answers on a separate sheet of paper. One second-grade teacher has students glue four library card pockets inside a manila folder. Then they write a research question on each pocket. As students find answers to their questions, they jot them on cards and place them in the appropriate pockets. Students compose reports based on these questions and answers. They also use the information to produce a product (e.g., nonfiction book, diorama, poster, pop-up book, or flipbook). Other authors suggest additional ways to help young students become independent researchers and writers (Barclay & Traser, 1999; Perry & Drummond, 2002; Schmidt et al., 2002).

The intrinsic motivation generated through exploring a self-selected topic is usually enough to keep most students involved. But students want to share what they learn, so an authentic audience, such as parents or other school classes, becomes important (Many, 2002). Students consider their audience as they plan their projects. After projects are completed, students practice their presentations and present their learning. Some schools have project fairs where students display their work and answer questions as parents, other students, and the public circulate through the displays. After they are finished, students reflect on their learning by completing self-evaluations about their use of time, completion of work, presentation, and suggestions for improvement. The teacher also evaluates each student's process and product.

During the implementation of Model 3, classroom management is important. Having a class full of students working on different projects can be intimidating even to veteran teachers. Some teachers monitor student progress with a wall chart listing steps to be completed. Students' names are placed on the chart, and, as they finish each step, the teacher lets them check it off. Other teachers put charts inside students' folders to check off during conferences, or they create contracts that accomplish the same management goals (e.g., Barclay & Traser, 1999). In short, teachers who are successful with Model 3 carefully and systematically monitor student progress.

Final Thoughts

Our models are a road map for primary-grade teachers to follow as they use informational books and as access to appropriate nonfiction expands. We have written elsewhere that a partnership between classroom teachers and librarians is essential for locating and using nonfiction (Palmer & Stewart, 1997). We underscore that assertion. But we also suggest that teacher partnerships are just as essential. Nonfiction can become an important tool in meeting standards and accountability requirements, but if teachers work alone, the process may be slowed.

Teachers are instructional engineers. Just as an engineer takes pride in seeing a structure or device come to fruition, teachers thrive on seeing students "get it" as a lesson unfolds. Nonfiction can become an important part of students "getting it" and teachers feeling pride in their work. To guarantee as much success as possible in this engineering process, we recommend that teacher teams begin by setting the stage and then moving sequentially through the models.

Throughout this article we have chosen our words carefully and restricted what we explored. For example, we used the term *investigation* instead of *inquiry* because we see investigation as a precursor to true student inquiry. In a similar manner, we did not consider the relationship between nonfiction research and the writing process or explain how to craft expository pieces using text structures, but other authors have (e.g., Barclay & Traser, 1999; Perry & Drummond, 2002; Vukelich, Evans, & Albertson, 2003). We did not delve into project-based learning, student inquiry, or community building in the classroom, but again other authors have (see previous citations). What our models provide is an organizing framework with common vocabulary from which teachers and librarians can collaboratively launch into more sophisticated instruction. But in order to take this next step, teachers need to read the references cited in this article and other relevant literature to obtain additional insights into nonfiction instruction. As collections grow, as teachers become comfortable with this new teaching resource, and as primary-grade students become independent researchers, nonfiction can be a vehicle for skill development and another source of reading enjoyment for young students.

REFERENCES

Bamford, R.A., & Kristo, J.V. (2000). *Checking out nonfiction K–8: Good choices for best learning.* Norwood, MA: Christopher-Gordon.

Banikowski, A., & Mehring, T. (1999). Strategies to enhance memory based on brain research. *Focus on Exceptional Children, 32,* 1–16.

Barclay, K., & Traser, L. (1999). Supporting young researchers as they write to learn. *Childhood Education, 75,* 215–224.

Brown, V.B.R. (1998). *First graders choosing books: "I wanna get that book, so I can read like Nathan."* Unpublished doctoral dissertation, University of North Carolina at Chapel Hill.

Caswell, L., & Duke, N. (1998). Non-narrative as catalyst for literacy development. *Language Arts, 75,* 108–117.

Dole, J., Brown, K., & Trathen, W. (1996). The effects of strategy instruction on the comprehension performance of at-risk students. *Reading Research Quarterly, 31,* 62–88. doi:10.1598/RRQ.31.1.4

Duke, N. (2000a). For the rich it's richer: Print environments and experiences offered to first-grade students in very low- and very high-SES school districts. *American Educational Research Journal, 37,* 456–457.

Duke, N. (2000b). 3.6 minutes per day: The scarcity of informational texts in first grade. *Reading Research Quarterly, 35,* 202–224. doi:10.1598/RRQ.35.2.1

Duke, N. (2003). Informational text? The research says, "Yes!" In L. Hoyt, M. Mooney, & B. Parkes (Eds.), *Exploring informational texts: From theory to practice* (pp. 2–7). Portsmouth, NH: Heinemann.

Duke, N.K., & Bennett-Armistead, V.S. (2003). *Reading and writing informational text in the primary grades: Research-based practices.* New York: Scholastic.

Duke, N., Bennett-Armistead, V.S., & Roberts, E.M. (2003). Bridging the gap between learning to read and reading to learn. In D.M. Barone & L.M. Morrow (Eds.), *Literacy and young children: Research-based practices* (pp. 226–242). New York: Guilford.

Duke, N., & Kays, J. (1998). "Can I say 'Once upon a time'?": Kindergarten children developing knowledge of information book language. *Early Childhood Research Quarterly, 13,* 295–318.

Duke, N.K., & Pearson, P.D. (2002). Effective practices for developing reading comprehension. In A.E. Farstrup & S.J. Samuels (Eds.), *What research has to say about reading instruction* (3rd ed., pp. 205–242). Newark, DE: International Reading Association.

Duthie, C. (1994). Nonfiction: A genre study for the primary classroom. *Language Arts, 71,* 588–595.

Fielding, L., & Roller, C. (1992). Making difficult books accessible and easy books acceptable. *The Reading Teacher, 45,* 678–685.

Guillaume, A. (1998). Learning with text in the primary grades. *The Reading Teacher, 51,* 476–486.

Guthrie, J.T. (1996). Educational contexts for engagement in literacy. *The Reading Teacher, 49,* 432–445.

Guthrie, J.T., & McCann, A.D. (1997). Characteristics of classrooms that promote motivations and strategies for learning. In J.T. Guthrie & W. Wigfield (Eds.), *Reading engagement: Motivating readers through integrated instruction* (pp. 128–148). Newark, DE: International Reading Association.

Harvey, S. (1998). *Nonfiction matters: Reading, writing, and research in grades 3–8*. York, ME: Stenhouse.

Harvey, S., & Goudvis, A. (2000). *Strategies that work: Teaching comprehension to enhance understanding*. York, ME: Stenhouse.

Holmes, K.J. (1998). *Frogs*. Mankato, MN: Capstone Press.

Hoyt, L. (2002). *Make it real: Strategies for success with informational texts*. Portsmouth, NH: Heinemann.

Hoyt, L., Mooney, M., & Parkes, B. (2003). *Exploring informational texts: From theory to practice*. Portsmouth, NH: Heinemann.

Kamil, M., & Lane, D. (1997, March). *A classroom study of the efficacy of using informational text for first grade reading instruction*. Paper presented at the American Educational Research Association meeting, San Diego, CA.

Kletzien, S., & Szabo, R. (1998, December). *Information text or narrative text? Children's preferences revisited*. Paper presented at the National Reading Conference, Austin, TX.

Korkeamaki, R., Tiainen, O., & Dreher, M. (1998). Helping Finnish second graders make sense of their reading and writing in their science project. *National Reading Conference Yearbook, 47*, 334–344.

Korkeamaki, R., Tiainen, O., & Dreher, M. (1999). Finnish second graders engaged in research: What interviews tell about their metacognition during inquiry. *National Reading Conference Yearbook, 48*, 120–133.

Lamme, L., & Fu, D. (2001). Sheltering children from the whole truth: A critical analysis of an informational picture book. *Children's Literature, 27*(2), 14–21.

Many, J. (2002). An exhibition and analysis of verbal tapestries: Understanding how scaffolding is woven into the fabric of instructional conversations. *Reading Research Quarterly, 37*, 376–407. doi:10.1598/RRQ.37.4.3

Marzano, R. (1998). *A theory-based meta-analysis of research on instruction*. Aurora, CO: Mid-continent Research for Education and Learning. (ERIC Document Reproduction Service No. ED427087)

Marzano, R., Pickering, D., & Pollock, J. (2001). *Classroom instruction that works: Research-based strategies for increasing student achievement*. Alexandria, VA: Association for Supervision and Curriculum Development.

McKeown, M.G., Beck, I.L., & Worthy, M.J. (1993). Grappling with text ideas: Questioning the author. *The Reading Teacher, 46*, 560–565.

McMath, J., King, M., & Smith, W. (1998). Young children, questions and nonfiction books. *Early Childhood Education Journal, 26*(1), 19–27.

Moss, B. (2003). *Exploring the literature of fact: Children's nonfiction trade books in the elementary classroom*. New York: Guilford.

Moss, B., Leone, S., & Dipillo, M. (1997). Exploring the literature of fact: Linking reading and writing through information trade books. *Language Arts, 74*, 418–429.

National Institute of Child Health and Human Development. (2000). *Report of the National Reading Panel. Teaching children to read: An evidence-based assessment of the scientific research literature on reading and its implications for reading instruction* (NIH Publication No. 00-4769). Washington, DC: U.S. Government Printing Office.

Ogle, D. (1986). K-W-L: A teaching model that develops active reading of expository text. *The Reading Teacher, 39*, 564–570.

Owens, R.F., Hester, J.L., & Teale, W.H. (2002). Where do you want to go today? Inquiry-based learning and technology integration. *The Reading Teacher, 55*, 616–626.

Palincsar, A., & Brown, A. (1984). Reciprocal teaching of comprehension-fostering and comprehension-monitoring activities. *Cognition and Instruction, 1*, 117–175.

Palmer, R.G., & Stewart, R.A. (1997). Nonfiction trade books in content area instruction: Realities and potential. *Journal of Adolescent & Adult Literacy, 40*, 630–641.

Palmer, R.G., & Stewart, R.A. (2000, November). *Nonfiction trade book use in primary grades*. Paper presented at the National Reading Conference, Scottsdale, AZ.

Palmer, R.G., & Stewart, R.A. (2003). Nonfiction trade book use in primary grades. *The Reading Teacher, 57*, 38–48.

Pappas, C. (1991). Fostering full access to literacy by including information books. *Language Arts, 68*, 449–462.

Pappas, C. (1993). Is narrative "primary"? Some insights from kindergartners' pretend readings of stories and information books. *Journal of Reading Behavior, 25*, 97–129.

Parkes, B. (2000). *Read it again: Revisiting shared reading*. York, ME: Stenhouse.

Parkes, B. (2003). The power of informational texts in developing readers and writers. In L. Hoyt, M. Mooney, & B. Parkes (Eds.), *Exploring informational texts: From theory to practice* (pp. 2–7). Portsmouth, NH: Heinemann.

Pearson, P.D., & Gallagher, M.C. (1983). The instruction of reading comprehension. *Contemporary Educational Psychology, 8*, 317–344.

Perry, N., & Drummond, L. (2002). Helping young students become self-regulated researchers and writers. *The Reading Teacher, 56*, 298–310.

Ponds and rivers. (2000). Denver, CO: Shortland Publications.

RAND Reading Study Group. (2002). *Reading for understanding: Toward an R&D program in reading comprehension*. Washington, DC: Office of Educational Research and Improvement/Department of Education.

Reese, D., & Harris, V. (1997). "Look at this nest!" The beauty and power of using informational books with young children. *Early Child Development and Care, 127–128*, 217–231.

Richgels, D. (2002). Informational texts in kindergarten. *The Reading Teacher, 55,* 586–595.

Robinson, D.H. (1998). Graphic organizers as aids to text reading. *Reading Research and Instruction, 37,* 65–105.

Roehler, L., & Duffy, G. (1984). Direct explanation of comprehension processes. In G. Duffy, L. Roehler, & J. Mason (Eds.), *Comprehension instruction: Perspectives and suggestions* (pp. 265–280). New York: Longman.

Sandora, C., Beck, I.L., & McKeown, M.G. (1999). A comparison of two discussion strategies on students' comprehension and interpretation of complex literature. *Reading Psychology, 20,* 177–212.

Schmidt, P., Gillen, S., Zollo, T., & Stone, R. (2002). Literacy learning and scientific inquiry: Children respond. *The Reading Teacher, 55,* 534–549.

Science and Technology for Children. (1992). *The life cycle of butterflies: Teacher's guide.* Burlington, NC: Carolina Biological Supply Co.

Short, K., Harste, J., & Burke, C. (1996). *Creating classrooms for authors and inquiries.* Portsmouth, NH: Heinemann.

Short, K.G., Schroeder, J., Laird, J., Kauffman, G., Ferguson, M.J., & Crawford, K.M. (1996). *Learning together through inquiry: From Columbus to integrated curriculum.* York, ME: Stenhouse.

Stead, T. (2002). *Is that a fact? Teaching nonfiction writing K–3.* Portland, ME: Stenhouse.

Sweet, A.P., & Guthrie, J.T. (1996). How children's motivations relate to literacy development and instruction. *The Reading Teacher, 49,* 660–662.

Taba, H. (1967). *Teacher's handbook for elementary social studies.* Reading, MA: Addison-Wesley.

Tierney, R., & Readence, J. (2000). *Reading strategies and practices: A compendium* (5th edition). Boston: Allyn & Bacon.

Vukelich, C., Evans, C., & Albertson, B. (2003). Organizing expository texts: A look at possibilities. In D.M. Barone & L.M. Morrow (Eds.), *Literacy and young children: Research-based practices* (pp. 261–288). New York: Guilford.

Wood, E., Pressley, M., & Winne, P.H. (1990). Elaborative interrogation effects on children's learning of factual content. *Journal of Educational Psychology, 82,* 741–748.

Yopp, R., & Yopp, H. (2000). Sharing informational text with young children. *The Reading Teacher, 53,* 410–423.

Zemlicka, S. (2003). *From tadpole to frog.* Minneapolis, MN: Lerner.

Developing a Love for Reading

Reading skill is useless without the
will to read; and surely the will to
read is impotent without the skill for
entry into the world which books
can open up to children.
—DORA V. SMITH (1959, p. 222)

Children early and easily discover the
pleasure of books; they need also to
discover the self-realization, the sense
of learning, the thinking, and the
changes in behavior that come from
mature reading.
—ROBERT A. MCCRACKEN &
MARLENE J. MCCRACKEN
(1978, p. 407)

The reading of literature is vastly
important to the cultural and
intellectual development of all
students....
—LINDA B. GAMBRELL
(2005, p. 590)

Issues and Innovations in Literacy Education: Readings From The Reading Teacher, edited by Richard D. Robinson. © 2006 by the International Reading Association.

The ultimate goal of all reading instruction should be to develop readers who see reading as an important aspect of their total lives. Although teachers often become overwhelmed with the details of daily activities, such as lesson planning, test scores, and skill learning, we must never forget that the result of our work must always be students who want to be lifelong readers. Although most students achieve some degree of success in learning to read, many, as adults, find reading to be a laborious chore that has little value in their personal lives.

David Russell (1951), an early pioneer in literacy education, stated more than 50 years ago,

> The test of a teacher's success in reading is not so much the children's scores on reading tests as the way pupils use printed materials. Do they turn to the book corner in the classroom when they have free time? Do they use the library regularly? Do they report on something read with genuine enthusiasm?
>
> The teacher who is helping build permanent interests in reading is accomplishing the highest aim of the reading program. The enthusiastic reader is the mature reader, for he is the person who will continue to give reading a large place throughout his life-time. (p. 14)

Although few would argue the importance of developing lifelong readers, the reality of today's literacy instruction presents many difficulties in attaining this worthy goal. Teachers often find themselves faced with increased pressure to achieve predetermined test score levels that in many cases set the objectives of the literacy curriculum instruction. Because outcomes such as "learning to love to read" and "becoming a lifelong reader" are subtle and, for the most part, not easily measured on standardized tests, they are often not emphasized by teachers.

Throughout its history, *The Reading Teacher* has been noted for its emphasis on the importance of developing lifelong readers as the primary goal of all literacy instruction. To this end, there has been a wealth of materials published for classroom teachers at all levels. Included in this section are a number of noteworthy examples for your consideration and reflection.

Section Readings

The first article, a brief piece by Leland B. Jacobs, sets the tone for what the primary goal should be for all reading instruction—that is, simply the encouragement of wide reading by students. The author addresses the issues surrounding the types of reading students select and what teachers should do to help in this selection process. For example, what should be the role of "popular" literature versus the more "traditional" books for today's students? This was an important question for educators almost 50 years ago and still is for teachers today.

Mabel F. Altstetter continues the discussion of the role of the typical literacy curriculum and how it seems to not train students to become lifelong readers. Based on this article, why do you think there exists this seemingly common problem related to developing a love of reading in our students? What suggestions are provided here for solving this literacy dilemma? Are these ideas generally workable in classrooms today?

Next, the article by Nicholas P. Criscuolo provides a list of practical suggestions for helping students learn to see reading as more than just a "school subject." Most of these ideas can readily be adapted to the modern classroom.

The literature circle has become a common reading activity in many classrooms today. Traditionally, this literacy model has been used predominantly with various types of fiction genres. However, in their article, Debbie Stien and Penny L. Beed suggest that literature circles would be just as appropriate with nonfiction writing. They provide a wide array of suggestions for how these ideas can be implemented in the classroom.

The final article by Sheryl O'Sullivan reflects recent thinking on the effective use of literature in the classroom literacy program. Suggestions are provided for teachers not only to encourage wide reading as a general principle, but also to stimulate character development in their students. In today's world where positive role models may be either few or of questionable value, this article provides an encouraging view of the role of literature in the classroom setting.

REFERENCES

Gambrell, L.B. (2005). Reading literature, reading text, reading the Internet: The times they are a'changing. *The Reading Teacher, 58*(6), 588–591.

McCracken, R.A., & McCracken, M.J. (1978). Modeling is the key to sustained silent reading. *The Reading Teacher, 31*(4), 406–408.

Russell, D.H. (1951). The mature reader. *Bulletin, IV*(2), 1, 13–14.

Smith, D.V. (1959). Developing a love of reading. *The Reading Teacher, 12*(4), 222–229.

For Further Reading on Developing a Love for Reading

The following articles from *The Reading Teacher* span nearly 50 years of discussion on various aspects of developing a love for reading in students.

Strickland, R.G. (1957). Making the most of children's interests in the teaching of reading. *The Reading Teacher, 10*(3), 137–138.
> Stresses the importance of determining individual student interests as a critical aspect in the development of an effective classroom literacy program of instruction.

Russell, D.H. (1958). Personal values in reading. *The Reading Teacher, 12*(1), 3–9.
> Describes mature reading as much more than "just saying the words successfully" and as including new and often personal meanings for each reader depending on his or her unique background experience.

Smith, D.V. (1958). Developing a love of reading. *The Reading Teacher, 12*(4), 222–229.
> Comments on the fundamental importance of developing a love and enthusiasm for reading in all students, no matter their reading ability.

Zirbes, L. (1961). Spurs to reading competence. *The Reading Teacher, 15*(1), 14–18.
> Presents a variety of useful classroom activities through which the teacher can enhance wide reading in a variety of genres as opposed to using many of the literacy assignments typically found in literacy instruction.

Yatvin, J. (1977). Recreational reading for the whole school. *The Reading Teacher, 31*(2), 185–188.
> Describes the development and implementation of a recreational literacy program for an entire school.

McCracken, R.A., & McCracken, M.J. (1978). Modeling is the key to sustained silent reading. *The Reading Teacher, 31*(4), 406–408.

Emphasizes the importance of the role of the classroom teacher as an active participant in the effective use of sustained silent reading (SSR).

Manley, M.A., & Simon, A.E. (1980). A reading celebration from K to 8. *The Reading Teacher, 33*(5), 552–554.

Summarizes a successful schoolwide effort to encourage wide reading in students with support from administrators, teachers, and parents.

Flood, J., & Lapp, D. (1994). Developing literary appreciation and literacy skills: A blueprint for success. *The Reading Teacher, 48*(1), 76–79.

Recommends specific organizational guidelines for classroom literacy instruction that emphasizes literature as a basis for meaningful discussion groups.

Menon, M.B., & Mirabito, J. (1999). "Ya' mean all we hafta do is read?" *The Reading Teacher, 53*(3), 190–196.

Describes a literacy program based on regular meetings of a fourth-grade and a sixth-grade class to discuss the various books they were reading, and on the ways that this interaction encouraged better attitudes in students about the importance of reading in their personal lives.

Gambrell, L.B. (2005). Reading literature, reading text, reading the Internet: The times they are a'changing. *The Reading Teacher, 58*(6), 588–591.

Reflects on the changing roles of reading in a modern society, noting the current influences of technology such as the Internet and computers.

Pleasure of the Popular

Leland B. Jacobs

Every year we can count on there being published over a thousand new books for children: picture-story books, fanciful tales, realistic stories, informational books, anthologies of prose and poetry. Of course, not all of these books are so appealing that they will go through printing after printing and thus live to a ripe old age. Nor are they all great by literary standards. Nor will all of them be truly child-like in their conceptions. In fact, some—if not many—will be pretty ordinary and a few will undoubtedly be even less than mediocre, just plain trash.

While, perhaps, a case could be made for reading trash, let us, instead, make some observations about "popular" books—books that may appeal for the present and then be replaced by other popular books. That these books do not reach the stature of "classics" does not negate their usefulness and their influence in the lives of young readers. If the child has derived pleasure from reading as a pastime, the book has served one important purpose. It has kept him reading.

In keeping the child reading, what else may the book not destined to be a classic do for the child? It surely touches him where he currently lives. Perhaps it helps him legitimately escape from what he believes to be a pretty humdrum existence. Perhaps it lets him stretch imaginatively in days and deeds to proportions that he would not or could not possibly try to reach in his own behavior. Perhaps it lets him become expert in some aspect of knowledge in which he chooses to develop greater expertness. Perhaps it lets him look at his desires and wishes in a new light. Perhaps it gives him new ideas to ponder, thoughts to mull over. Perhaps it puts romance into his otherwise rather stern world. In other words, a popular book is popular for sound reasons. In some dimension, as high adventure, as rollicking fun, as good companionship, as stimulating situations, as desired ideas and information, a popular book for the child reading it is clearly a worthwhile experience. In fact, to the child reader the book may even be "great" at that moment in his life.

Popular books of fiction are most frequently full of action and movement, peopled with strong characters, lively with current-day modes in language, and amply supplied with incidents that catch the tone of today's living. Popular informational books deal in uncluttered style, with what is timely not only in the world of nature and of human existence but also in terms of the questings of children to comprehend, to be knowledgeable, at the time in their lives when such knowing makes a real difference to them personally. Indeed, popular books are insistent books. They "read fast." They defy the reader not to turn to the next page. They get passed from one reader to the next with neat recommendations of merit. Thus the popular book serves childhood, serves it legitimately.

And one must never forget that the popular book is always in the position of perhaps being the source from which the child goes on to read great books. In Itaska State Park in Minnesota there is a tiny trickle of water without which there would be no Mississippi River.

Reprinted from *The Reading Teacher*, *12*(1), pp. 40–41. © 1958 by the International Reading Association.

How Full Is Full?

Mabel F. Altstetter

In the three and a half centuries since Francis Bacon said that reading maketh a full man, this pious statement has been mouthed millions of times until it belongs in the same category with mother, home and the flag. But what reading? What fullness? What man?

Americans as a nation are not readers. Until the advent of the "paper backs" the average was about one book for each adult annually. There can be no fullness of reading experience with such paucity. We defend ourselves by saying that we are a nation of doers, not readers and we do not even feel sorry for ourselves that books mean almost nothing in our lives. "Woe be to him who reads but one book" said George Herbert, and Samuel Johnson counseled a young man to read at least five hours a day to acquire information.

It is difficult to explain to the non-reader the deep satisfaction that can come with a rich experience in reading widely. It is possible to grow into such understanding by experiencing fullness on many levels as the individual grows. The kindergarten child who repeated over and over, "One misty, moisty morning" and said with shining eyes, "I like the feels of it," was surely tasting fullness. The fifth grader who liked

> Unto the utmost purple rim
> The happy princes followed him

was already knowing satisfaction from reading.

The shiver of delight that A.E. Housman speaks of, or the pleasure of recognition when hearing or reading an allusion, or the sense of identification that comes in one's own mind when reading, all are rewards that must be experienced to be understood.

Some people develop taste and a love of books without much help. Most people must have guidance and it is one of the greatest rewards of teaching to be the agent that puts children in touch with books. Not many of us will have a Bacon, a Carlyle, a Fadiman or a Van Doren among our pupils. The millions of children that throng the schools in our country today need help to know the fullness that reading can bring.

From the beginning of schools in our country there has been dependence on a single textbook in various fields. It is quite usual to find in a class of forty exactly that many copies of the same geography or history regardless of the fact that some children cannot read with understanding even a much simpler book. Biographies are lacking in many schools. The enrichment that a rounded reading of biographies can bring to history is immeasurable. Carlyle said that the history of the world is but the biography of great men. Historical fiction helps us to understand motives and characters that have shaped destiny. *Johnny Tremain* has done more to help young people understand the American Revolution than any text.

We have done a great deal in the United States in scientific research in how to reach the skills and mechanics of reading; we excel in methods of remediation. How is it then that children become adults who do not read?

In the first place, we have confused the acquisition of skills and their creative use. We have called

Reprinted from *The Reading Teacher*, 12(1), pp. 14–18. © 1958 by the International Reading Association.

the skills reading when they are no more that than a book of recipes is cooking. In the second place, children have in many places little or no materials for reading. It would seem crystal clear that if children are to read, they must have books. Between one-fourth and one-third of the children in school have access to no books other than their text books and a few supplementary readers. In many schools where there is a library the books are poorly selected. The presence of a library in a community does not mean that it serves a useful purpose of helping children enlarge their reading experience.

The high schools are required to have a certain number of books in order to meet the requirements of the regional accrediting agencies. For many children that is too late because a love of books and an interest in reading must parallel the acquisition of skills.

In the present day of publishing there is no reason for the lack of books in schools. Good books, both new and reprints of the old, pour from the presses. There are more books in the juvenile field than in any other. Why then are some children denied the right to read?

The blame must be placed squarely on the shoulders of the elementary teachers. That is a harsh thing to say but it is true. In general, teachers are not readers and have never known the delight and fullness that books can give. It is probably not too far from the truth to say that a teacher who does not know the enriching experience that books can give, will not provide "keys that open enchanted doors." A love for reading is contagious—it overflows from the life of the teacher to the children.

A certain school is required by the supervisor to have a library period. A recent visit to a fifth grade coincided with the library period. The teacher graded papers while the children gave desultory attention to a poor selection of books. The teacher glanced at the clock and with a Thank-goodness-that's-over tone said, "Put your books away and let's get to work." Small wonder that she later told the visitor, "These children don't care to read."

The teacher's colleges must take some of the blame. The course, and it is usually only one semester, in Children's Literature is given without relating it to the enriching of reading or deepening experience in general. A single anthology may constitute the only material read. In many places the course is a step-child taught by the faculty member who is free at that period. In one school not too long ago the coach was given the course to teach. That is an extreme case, of course. But it is true that students go out to teach with little or no knowledge of children's books and no conviction about the importance of having books where children can put their hands on them at any time.

No school is too poor to afford books for children. If teachers believe in their importance and are passionately eager for children to have them, ways will open. No superintendent or school board would expect an industrial arts teacher to function without tools or a home economics teacher to get along with only a cook book and a text book on sewing. A coach would not be expected to work without balls and other equipment. No janitor is expected to get along without brooms and mops. Yet books are the vital equipment of the elementary teacher if her children are to know fullness. The administration and the school board will floodlight the football field and buy expensive instruments and uniforms for the school band. They will provide thousands of dollars worth of work books and remedial reading machines. Why? Because they sincerely regard these things as important. We who believe that books are as necessary for children's minds as food for their bodies have done almost nothing to help parents and the administration to understand that if children are to read they must have books.

There has been much concern of late about the neglect of the gifted child. The gifted child does not sit with an adenoidal look and glazed eyes staring into space. A major characteristic of the bright child is his intellectual curiosity. What the presence of many books can do for the gifted is almost beyond belief. He will find answers to his questions and he will explore in fields where his teacher may not be able to lead him, if books are available.

The public library and the book-mobile are wonderful institutions but they are not enough.

Many schools do not have these helps. There is no substitute for having the books right where the children are—in the building and even better in the room. Recently a boy in the fourth grade brought a snake when he came to school. The teacher's repugnance was great. When the children eagerly asked, "What kind is it?" she replied, "Some time when you are down town go to the library and ask if there is a book on snakes." How much better if she had said, "On the library shelves there is a book about snakes by Herbert Zim and another by Raymond Ditmars. Read until you find out and we'll take time to have you tell us about it."

In any room library there must be a wide variety of subject matter areas and a wide range of reading difficulty. There is no such thing as a fourth grade book or a sixth grade book. Children must have what they can read and find interesting. There is no dearth of material; there is only a dearth of understanding of how important it is to have books.

From an economic point of view books are important. Wherever a real reading program with hundreds of books has been put into practice, reading scores have gone up amazingly and the need for remedial materials, machines and teachers has gone down. That can be an argument to use in getting books in the classroom.

The required book report has done much to turn children away from books. Who started the "Name the main characters; outline the plot" kind of book report? Certainly not a true lover of books but a sadistic person who wanted to make children suffer for the sin of reading. Few adults would read freely if they had hanging over their heads the prospect of having to outline for a teacher's red pencil to mark. If there must be some check-up, it should be given with a creative purpose of making children want to read more. Oral reports that share information and pleasure may have a good effect but can become boring if pressure is applied for all to report.

There can be no defense for the chart or other device that lists books read and thereby makes a comparison between the best and the poorest reader. The best reader *should* read the most books after all, and the poor should not have to compete.

Fullness on any level is the result of "satiable curiosity" as the Elephant Child well knew. It is good to keep in mind Kipling's

I keep six honest serving men
    (They taught me all I knew);
Their names are What and Why and When
And How and Where and Who.

Any child or adult who has learned the value of those words has reached an independence of teachers that will bring a life-time of satisfaction. Particularly in the fields of the social sciences *Why* and *How* instead of *What* will set in motion a chain of reading for answers and comparisons that give intellectual stimulation and awareness that will not accept a statement just because it is in print. It takes reading and evaluation to arrive at conclusions in answer to the question, "Was the purchase of Alaska a good investment?" The presence of only one text book in history and geography is woefully inadequate if a student is to use Kipling's serving men.

It should be made mandatory upon schools to make children aware of simple library tools and their use from the early grades on. It never ceases to amaze and sadden a college teacher to learn how little is known of the rich resources of information even an average library can supply.

Since the public library is the main resource for getting information we have an obligation to help children know something about it and its place in on-going quest for information and pleasure.

The building of a good reference library for the home is something that should concern all of us. A good dictionary, a good encyclopedia, an almanac of information such as the *World Almanac*, these are minimum essentials. A biographical dictionary, a geographical dictionary, a good atlas and globe are desirable.

It is important also that we help the student to seek advice about books to read. Teachers and librarians can help here. *Elementary English* and the *Horn Book* for children and *The Saturday Review* for both children and adults are dependable sources for guidance. *Good Reading*, a Mentor publication found at many newsstands, is an invaluable guide for adult reading in all areas and has sold by the hundreds of thousands.

Guidance in reading for both children and adults should be concerned with both breadth and depth of vicarious experience. Fiction is a good place to start because it has action which carries the reader's interest along. Fiction can deal with any subject, any time, any place. Historical fiction makes a time come alive and human motives and events assume enriched meaning. Social conditions, regional problems, minority groups are among aspects to be found in fiction. Aesthetic appreciation, fantasy, humor and mystery all can be found in fiction.

Biography, and what a wealth of it we have today, can inform and entertain. Travel, philosophy, science, drama, essays and letters, satire contribute much to fullness.

A reader learns, at first with guidance and then on his own, that reading is living and treasure for the taking. Thomas Carlyle said, "All that mankind has done, thought, gained or been: it is lying as in magic preservation in the pages of books."

Children are hungry for the satisfaction that reading can bring. They will vary in their reaction to the materials, of course. Not all children will respond eagerly to poetry in the same way but there is something for all of them to enjoy and it is folly to expect on an adult level appreciation for great poetry if the child has not grown through the various stages of enjoyment from Mother Goose and Milne, De La Mare and Sandburg to Euripides and Shakespeare.

A development in the last decade that rejoices the heart is the interest in god books that has come with the publication of the inexpensive "paper backs." They sell by the millions, their sale stimulated by their availability and cheapness. Teachers have had very little to do with their sale. Millions of people have never learned truly to read because they had no books and no guidance.

"Fullness" is an individual matter. The Van Dorens, the Churchills, the Bacons, the Emersons, the Thoreaus made their own fullness and delight. But each can have his own according to his capacity and his opportunity. We cannot do much about capacity; that is pretty well set when a child picks out his parents, but the opportunity—ah, there's the golden gift that teachers can provide. To help a child develop a love for worthwhile books is one of the finest things any human being can do for another. To stop with the teaching of the skills is downright cheating for that is only the beginning.

Effective Approaches for Motivating Children to Read

Nicholas P. Criscuolo

Classroom teachers need to get children to read freely for enjoyment. Because this need to motivate children comes up so often, it is very important to find practical activities to fill it. This article describes 12 practical, creative reading activities that have proved successful in getting children to read.

1. Invented Circumstances. Many opportunities exist within the framework of the reading program for children to write creatively about what they read. Often teachers ask children to alter the circumstances or locale of a story and write about what they think might have happened, or to write about what happened to the character after the story ended.

Fanciful stories are particularly appropriate for getting children to read and write. For example, write on the chalkboard the following sentences which are related to stories children have read:

> One day two kangaroos decided to take a bus downtown.
>
> On a hot afternoon the grizzly bear decided to stroll down Main Street.
>
> The Martian knocked on Mrs. Greene's door.

Ask children to write a story based on one of these story starters. Then have a Swap Shop period during which children swap their stories with each other.

Some teachers vary this activity by using an "add-to-the-story" technique which works best in reading groups or teams. One child adds a sentence to the first line and then passes the paper to the next pupil, who adds his/her own sentence to it, and so on. This permits everyone to participate. Some real "masterpieces" have been created this way! Completed stories can be posted on the bulletin board for everyone to read.

2. Rate It. Children enjoy some stories or books more than others. At the same time, they should be taught to be discriminating readers. Ask children to assign a numerical rating to the material read. For example, a 1 rating is "excellent" while a 4 is "poor." Discuss beforehand the criteria for assigning ratings. When the children have read a unit of stories in their basic texts and rated them, they can meet to reveal their ratings for individual stories and the reasons such ratings were given. Some lively discussions will ensue!

This activity can be varied by having the children write their ratings on colored file cards which represent the ratings, i.e., pink = excellent, blue = good, and so on.

3. Book Catalog. Basal readers often contain lists of trade books with themes similar to the themes of the stories in the basals. Too often these book suggestions are overlooked by teachers. In order to sustain reading interest, some teachers use these books as well as other trade books for enrichment and enjoyment.

A good way to promote trade books is to have youngsters draw pictures of the major event in a variety of books and write synopses of their contents. These are then compiled into an attractively cov-

Reprinted from *The Reading Teacher, 32*(5), pp. 543–546. © 1979 by the International Reading Association.

ered book catalog that is placed in the classroom's interest center or reading corner so that pupils can "shop around" for a good book to read.

4. Clipping Service. Ask students to bring current newspapers and news magazines to class. These periodicals provide an excellent source for large pictures and articles on leaders and events important in life today. Have the students clip these articles and pictures for a clipping file, which can be used as a stimulus for further reading about these topics and people.

Some teachers have the children keep their own folders with pictures of famous people pasted under appropriate fields. Encourage the children to locate written material to accompany the pictures and to share each other's folders.

5. You've Got My Vote! Just as we elect people to office, children can elect their favorite story characters. List the major characters from a popular book or basal text the children have read and tell them that there will be an election. Ask two children to team up—one to assume the role of the story character, the other to serve as campaign manager. They can pick a slogan, make posters, pins, and placards, etc.

When election day rolls around, the campaign manager for each story character introduces his/her candidate, while the candidate, assuming the role of the story character, tells the audience what he or she did in the story to receive their votes. The class then votes and a winner is declared.

As an extra treat, an election party can be held to celebrate the candidate's victory.

6. Feelings Unlimited. Have a Feelings Unlimited box in your room. Students write a short paragraph about how a character felt at a critical moment in a story recently read. The paragraph can be written on a file card with the child's name on the back. Writers can supply as many clues as they wish but must omit the character's name and the title of the book. Other students try to identify the book or story on the basis of these clues.

The Feelings Unlimited box has another important use: children can be encouraged to write their feelings about various story characters—pro or con—and place them in the box.

7. Photo Enthusiasts. For the most part, children like to be photographed. Bring in several rolls of film and take pictures of the children during various school activities. Ask the children to write commentaries to accompany the pictures and display them on the bulletin board for the class to read.

Inexpensive cameras can also be purchased and distributed to the children. Themes related to stories or books can be selected and children told to "click away." Commentaries can be written for each photo, compiled into a scrapbook, and placed in the reading center for the entire class to read.

8. Designing Inventions. Inventions fascinate children, and they often read about them and the people who have become famous for their inventions. To spark interest in this area, put the following possible inventions on the board: a homework machine, an automatic bed maker, an electric foot warmer.

Discuss these inventions with the children and then ask them to design their own inventions with a diagram and to write a short paragraph describing the uses of this invention.

Children can then swap and read about each other's inventions.

9. Bag Props. Have children go through a story or book and make a list of some concrete objects mentioned in it. Have them secure as many of the objects as possible or make them from bits of material, construction paper, cardboard, etc., and then put them in a bag which they can decorate.

Ask the children to share excerpts from the stories they have read. At the appropriate time, the youngster can fish into the bag for a suitable prop and display it to the group.

10. Secret Identities. When a group of children have finished a particular unit of stories or a book, ask each member to select a favorite story character and to write a short description of that character without divulging his or her name. Put these "secret identities" into a container or a large envelope or display them on the bulletin board. Keep an answer key, and as children think they know who the character is, they can check with you to see if their hunch is right. Children will have fun trying to guess as many identities as possible.

11. Armchair Travelers. Many of the stories and books children read are set in unfamiliar locales. Here's a good opportunity to learn about strange or faraway places. Travel agencies will usually supply posters, maps, and brochures about different countries. Children can prepare an illustrated talk on a place they've read about using these materials plus postcards, slides, and magazine pictures.

Some teachers have used a large map on which they highlight story locations. Pieces of yarn are extended from each story location on the map to a file card with a synopsis of the story.

12. Book Mates. Have children write and illustrate their own stories. Below each story the author must write his or her name. Each child puts her/his story in an envelope and addresses it to another youngster in the class. Designate someone to pick up the "mail" and deliver it.

It's a personal touch and youngsters will like to read their "mail." After a certain number of stories are written, they can be collected, grouped by authors, bound with the title "My Stories" and the author's name on it, and placed in the reading center for supplementary reading.

Since the teacher is the key to a successful reading program, he or she must see to it that the reading skills taught are enhanced through activities which increase pupils' enjoyment of reading. It's the smile, the chuckle, and the involvement in reading that indicate the success and worth of a classroom reading program.

Bridging the Gap Between Fiction and Nonfiction in the Literature Circle Setting

Debbie Stien and Penny L. Beed

Tom waved his hand eagerly at me, and the rest of his literature circle group soon did the same. On every face I saw an enthusiastic smile. I couldn't wait to hear what new discovery they had made during their literature circle conversation. "What's up?" I asked. "We're done, Mrs. Stien," exclaimed Tom (all student names are pseudonyms). "You're finished reading your book already? You just got started on Tuesday, and now you've all read and discussed it in three days?" I couldn't believe it. In five years of using literature circles, no group had ever read and discussed a book in three days. I had to find out if they really understood and appreciated the text, so I joined the group and we continued the literature circle conversation. Each member contributed to the conversation as the students made connections to their lives and other texts, discussed interesting words, and asked thought-provoking questions. From our brief conversation, it was obvious that these students had created some rich understandings. So why did they rush through the Magic Tree House fiction book *Civil War on Sunday* (Osborne, 2000)? "What's our new nonfiction book going to be, Mrs. Stien?" asked Tami. Suddenly I had the answer. "Is that why you finished your Magic Tree House book so quickly?" "Yes, we've been trying to predict what kinds of books you'll have for us to choose from that relate to the [U.S.] Civil War after reading *Civil War on Sunday*," explained Richard.

Now I was the one smiling—it was happening. My students were finding an appreciation for nonfiction. Moreover, I soon discovered that his newfound love of reading nonfiction texts wasn't unique to this literature circle group. It was apparent that all 22 students in my third-grade class were feeling the same strong motivation to read informational texts. My goal of getting students to read, value, and enjoy nonfiction texts was succeeding. Literature circles had provided an ideal environment in which students could share what was interesting to them in the books they read.

Long before this interaction occurred, I had learned to appreciate the value of literature circles to foster in my students a purpose and love for reading and a strong interest in *fictional* texts. This article tells of my exploration of literature circles as an instructional approach for engaging students with *nonfiction* texts.

Classroom Goals and Purpose

Two goals in my classroom are for every student to feel ownership and to take responsibility for his or her learning. I have found literature circles to be one of the best practices to help students meet these goals (Daniels, 1994, 2002; Fountas & Pinnell, 2001; Hill, Johnson, & Schlick Noe, 1995; Schlick Noe & Johnson, 1999).

Reprinted from *The Reading Teacher*, 57(6), pp. 510–518. © 2004 by the International Reading Association.

In my classroom, literature circles consist of heterogeneous groups of students who choose to read and discuss the same text. Group members agree on the amount of reading to be completed for each conversational meeting. Students then discuss what is important to them from their reading of the text. My role is that of a "floating facilitator." I am not a member of any group, but I join in briefly if I see an opportunity to ask a question or make a comment that would challenge or redirect my students' thinking and expand their conversation (Daniels, 1994, 2002).

Over the years, I have watched my students become more critical consumers of literature through conversations that exhibit their passion, empathy, beliefs, personal connections, and opinions of texts. Short (1997) confirmed that through literature circles, readers are given opportunities to become literate. The discussions that evolve in these groups support readers in becoming critical thinkers (Gambrell & Almasi, 1996). Students are empowered through literature circles and create their own destinations in the reading process.

In the last five years, when participating in literature circles in my classroom, students selected from a variety of fictional genres: fantasy, mystery, historical, realistic, and science fiction, and from themes that included "chocolate" and author studies. However, I began to worry that my students were not developing an appreciation for nonfiction. I was aware that most of the reading my students would encounter in their ensuing school years, and for the rest of their lives, would involve informational texts (Bamford & Kristo, 2000; Harvey, 1998). It was true that nonfiction texts were available to my third-grade students during sustained silent reading (SSR), and I did use nonfiction texts regularly in guided reading. However, I observed that interest in reading and discussing nonfiction texts and topics wasn't developing. Therefore, it became my goal to bridge the gap between fiction and nonfiction through literature circles.

I set out to support my students in using nonfiction texts in a literature circle setting. I wanted to observe their responses and to see if the dynamic student conversations that occurred when reading fiction texts in literature circles would continue with nonfiction texts. I also wanted to see if the roles children used to discuss fiction would transfer to nonfiction or whether they would create new roles that were as effective. Finally, I wanted to see if my students would become motivated to read nonfiction texts on their own. Therefore, to explore literature circles as an appropriate method for engaging students with nonfiction, I studied my students' responses to nonfiction texts in and beyond literature circles.

Participants and Methodology

All 22 students (10 boys, 12 girls) in my class agreed to be my coresearchers. These students represented a variety of learners: 5 students were identified as talented and gifted, (two to three grade levels above in reading); 3 students were on Individualized Educational Plans for reading and language arts (one to two grade levels below in reading); and 4 other students were reading half a year below grade level (based on fluency, accuracy, and comprehension).

I audiotaped the literature circle discussions to help me (and sometimes the students) monitor, analyze, and evaluate the quality of their conversations in both fiction and nonfiction literature circles. (Although some educators fear that the presence of a tape recorder will somehow change students' behaviors, I found that in literature circles, students quickly became caught up in their discussions and forgot about the tape recorder.) For my study, I found this to be an effective way to gather vital information without physically interrupting their conversations. In addition, I videotaped all of the lessons that I taught to introduce my students to the various aspects of literature circles. This included our talk about defining the terms *literature* and *circles*, the formation of a common definition of *literature circles*, modeling of what conversations should and shouldn't look like, and our discussions first about fiction and later about nonfiction roles in literature circles. I also took anecdotal records of the conversations I heard as I moved from group to group and of the comments students made at other times during the day about their nonfiction reading. I viewed and listened to the tapes and reviewed my notes throughout the study to inform my instruction and then again at the end of the study to look for evidence of growth and change in the students' responses and attitudes. I also kept records of nonfiction texts that the children chose to read during free time over the course of the year.

For the purpose of this research, I decided to create a four-question interview. My former student teacher conducted and audiotaped interviews with each of my students before we began literature circles and again at the end of the school year. Her participation allowed for consistency, and my students were at ease because of their familiarity with her. (The questions appear later in this article with the results.) Students also responded to additional questions (see Figure 1) at the end of the year to give even more feedback about nonfiction texts and literature circles.

Getting Started With Literature Circles

For my study, I started with fiction texts with the idea that, after the students became effective with literature circle discussions, we would adapt their discussions to nonfiction texts.

I included a lot of modeling and discussion to teach my students about literature circles, because it was a new concept for them all. First, I taught the students various ways they could have a conversation about literature. I modeled how to discuss literature daily during read-alouds and facilitated how to use discussion strategies during guided reading. I used six different roles adapted from Daniels's (1994, 2002) work with literature circles: Artful Artist, Word Wizard, Discussion Leader, Dramatic Reenactor, Story Elements Correspondent, and Personal Connector. The purpose of the roles was to assist students temporarily by giving them a unique way to think about the text they were reading; the roles allowed students to think about a story using various cognitive abilities and perspectives. They used role sheets to record their thoughts, and the expectation was that their use in class would be short term; it is important that students don't rely totally on role sheets and just read from them during their literature circle meeting.

FIGURE 1
Students' responses to interviews at the end of the school year

Question 1: What do you like about literature circles?

Fun sharing/talking	18		Everyone talks	9
Discuss what we want	16		Hear everyone's ideas	8
Like the books read	14		Tabbing	6
Learn about people/life	10		No hand raising	1

Question 2: How do you feel about role sheets versus tabbing?

Tabbing	18	Role sheets	1	Both	3

Question 3: Is literature circle discussion a good time to use nonfiction books?

Yes	22	No	0

Question 4: What were some different aspects of nonfiction literature circle conversations?

Learn about real people and topics	22
Deeper conversations	9
Less off-task behavior	6
Better reader with nonfiction books	4
Livelier conversations	3
Dates and years of events	2

To introduce literature circles, I taught the six roles during my whole-group reading time. It is important to model what a grand conversation sounds like (Roller & Beed, 1994; Samway et al., 1991). I spent a week modeling the roles and providing guided practice as the students tried out one role at a time in discussions of a fiction piece. Even during these "tryouts," the students seemed excited to share their roles and to converse about the story. This excitement about learning is supported by Vygotsky's (1978) theories of social interaction. In their discussion of Vygotsky's theories of learning, Au, Carroll, and Scheu (1997) stated,

> They [children] learn when they have the opportunity to engage with new ideas and make them their own.... Learning is seen in terms of the interactions of the individual with other people.... [L]iteracy begins as a social activity between people. The key to learning is the social support the child receives from adults and peers. (pp. 14–15)

Fiction Literature Circles

The first groups of literature circles focused on picture books by Patricia Polacco. I observed that engagement was optimal when group sizes were kept to four students, with no more than five. My biggest challenge was to get all students involved in interactive conversations, not just the sharing of their roles. We discussed this as a class. My modeling of interactive conversations with another third-grade teacher was effective in helping them understand the difference between just reporting information and building upon the comments of others. The ensuing conversations seemed more in depth; the students raised and discussed issues that surprised me. They discussed themes from the story that related to other books, movies, characters, or real people's lives. Vocabulary learning was important to them. Students helped one another create meaning by referring to the texts, to dictionaries, and even to thesauruses. They also appealed to their parents and me for more information about words to share in their groups. These "student teachers" were better able to help their peers because they completely understood the specialized vocabulary. The students looked forward to their twice-a-week literature circle conversations, and everyone came prepared. I observed that they were talking more about books.

Connecting Nonfiction to Fiction

After about two months of fiction literature circles, I felt that my students were ready to try nonfiction. I decided to connect nonfiction to fiction, hoping to ensure a new appreciation for informational texts. Biographies seemed like a natural bridge between the two genres, because they had some of the aspects of fiction, such as a character, but they were also nonfiction-based on facts. As a transition text between fiction and biographies, I selected *Hannah* (Whelan, 1991), a historical fiction story. The main characters are Hannah, who is a blind girl (about the age of my third graders), and the schoolteacher, who believes that Hannah should go to school. During this cycle, everyone read the same book, and literature circle groups continued their twice-a-week meetings.

After the groups finished reading and discussing *Hannah*, I used whole-group instruction to teach about biographies. Then we went to the library, located the biographies, and each student chose one to read for about 20 minutes. Next, they all shared two new facts about their character. We discussed characteristics of a biography and the type of information that is typically found in this genre.

I explained that we were going to read different biographies for literature circles, and the students seemed eager to get started. However, I asked the students first to think about our discussion roles. I invited them to decide which ones would still work with biographies and whether we should create some new roles. I wanted my students to understand that their conversations about biographies (and nonfiction in general) would probably differ from their fiction conversations.

Roles for Nonfiction: Biographies

As students brainstormed a list of characteristics of biographies, three new roles emerged. Richard suggested the role that came to be known as Fantastic Fact Finder. He explained that for this role, the students would find interesting or unique facts about the main character. These facts "wouldn't just be common facts that could be about most people." The rest of the students agreed, and we had our first new role.

The next conversation focused on dates that were important in the life of the person in the biography. Pam suggested that we create a role called Timeline Traveler. She thought that for this role, the students could make a timeline and record important dates in the person's life. Again, everyone thought that this was relevant to biographies, so we agreed on our second nonfiction role.

The last role added was that of Vital Statistics Collector. Debbie said that in this role, the students would report on personal information such as birth date, family members, schooling, important discoveries, and contributions. (See Figure 2 for these new biography role sheets.) Next, we decided which roles to keep from our fiction literature circles and which ones to discard. The students were unanimous in their choices of Personal Connector, Word Wizard, and Discussion Leader. Brian explained, "We can still use Personal Connector, because we can still make connections with the character, other books, and the world." "Word Wizard should stay because there will always be words that we want to talk about," shared Pam. Finally, Lori said, "Discussion Leader is needed so we will have questions to talk about."

Discussions About Biographies

To make the fiction to nonfiction connection after reading the book *Hannah*, the students had several choices of biographies of Anne Sullivan, Louis Braille, and Helen Keller. The students were eager to get started reading and discussing their biographies. After a reading period, I could hear side conversations throughout the day about the new information they had learned about their characters. Finally, it was time for the literature circle conversations. I scheduled 20 minutes, with an extra 10 minutes set aside in case students needed more time.

I took anecdotal records and continued to audiotape all literature circle discussions.

As I circulated and observed the five different groups, I could tell there was much to talk about. Students were focused and on task. They were really doing well applying the three new roles, and most students were putting themselves in the main character's "shoes," trying to understand what it must have been like to be handicapped.

A Typical Conversation

In this section, I include a conversation that was typical of most literature circle groups in my class. The transcript shows the way students helped one another to create understanding, how they used their imaginations to discuss what Helen Keller's life could have been like, and the way they used prior knowledge to make cross-textual connections. This group of two boys and two girls were average to above-average readers. Nancy, an above-average reader, had displayed a mature level of understanding and insight on literature discussions from the beginning. Tom, Tami, and Richard had made improvements in their abilities to have a conversation about what they had read as they gained more experience with literature circles. The group chose to read *Helen Keller* (Davidson, 1969). In one part of the discussion, Nancy asked, "How do you think Helen would be if she hadn't learned anything yet?" The other students had quick answers.

Tom: I think she would still be cranky, and mad, and throw stuff.

Richard: She would be so wild, and they would probably have to send her away to somewhere they could keep her locked up so she wouldn't destroy anything.

Nancy: But remember—they said they didn't want to do that.

Tom: Mrs. Keller said that she didn't want Helen to go away to school; she wanted Helen to stay at home.

Nancy: I think that she would be wild and that her mom and dad would get another teacher. But

FIGURE 2
New roles for "biography" literature circles

Timeline Traveler

Name _____ Date_____

Book title_____

Reading assignment: chapter/page _____ to chapter/page _____

You are the Timeline Traveler. It is your job to complete a timeline of the major events that happened to this person during his or her life. Some things to include are birth date, date of marriage, children, major accomplishments, date of death, and any other major life events that you feel are important to put on the timeline.

_____

Fantastic Fact Finder

Name _____ Date_____

Book title_____

Reading assignment: chapter/page _____ to chapter/page _____

You are the Fantastic Fact Finder. It is your job to share interesting facts about the person you are reading about. Share those facts that make this particular person interesting or extra special compared with most people.

Fantastic facts   *Page*

1. _____

   _____

2. _____

   _____

3. _____

   _____

Vital Statistics Collector

Name _____ Date_____

Book title_____

Reading assignment: chapter/page _____ to chapter/page _____

You are the Vital Statistics Collector. It is your job to share the personal information about this person.

1. Date of birth _____

2. Childhood home town, state, country _____

3. Family includes _____

   _____

4. Other important people_____

5. Hobbies or interests _____

6. Jobs or careers _____

7. Why is this person famous? _____

   _____

8. Date and cause of death_____

I don't think they'd find another teacher like the first one she had.

Tami: Whenever I read this, it reminds me about.... Did anyone see that movie about Helen Keller, with that little girl in it?

Tom: Yes!

Tami: This book always reminds me of that movie.

Tom: Yeah, with that little girl kicking and screaming. I can also make a connection to another book we read about a girl who was blind, but not deaf....

Nancy: *Hannah* [Whelan, 1991].

Tom: Yeah. Every time I read a chapter in this book, I remember about Hannah and try to make out things that are similar and stuff that's different.

Richard: There's much more that's different.

Nancy: Why is that?

Richard: Because it's so much easier to learn if you're only blind, than being blind and deaf.

During this excerpt, the students collaboratively were able to construct meaning for what they had read by using prior knowledge, information from the text, and by making logical interpretations of what they thought Helen's life might have been like. They also connected and compared the content with *Hannah* (Whelan, 1991), a text read earlier, and with the movie about Helen Keller. Three of the four students introduced subtopics and everyone contributed to and built on the comments of other group members.

All the groups in my class were similarly engaged; they commented that the time went too quickly. The students had no trouble using all 20 minutes, plus the extra 10 minutes that I had set aside. In fact, two groups were not ready to finish, so they were given time to finish their discussion during the following day's sustained silent reading period.

Throughout this cycle of literature circles, my students continued to compare information with

---

FIGURE 3
Fiction and nonfiction companion book titles

Fiction title	Nonfiction title
Civil War on Sunday (Osborne, 2000, Random House)	*A Picture Book of Robert E. Lee* (Adler, 1994, Holiday House) *Aunt Clara Brown: Official Pioneer* (Lowery, 1999, Carolrhoda) *Harriet Tubman* (Sullivan, 2001, Scholastic) *Meet Abraham Lincoln* (Cary, 1994, Random House) *Rosa Parks: From the Back of the Bus to the Front of a Movement* (Wilson, 2001, Scholastic)
Mummies in the Morning (Osborne, 1993, Random House)	*Mummies and Pyramids* (Osborne, 2001, Random House) *Secrets of the Mummies* (Griffey, 1998, Dorling Kindersley)
Revolutionary War on Wednesday (Osborne, 2000, Scholastic)	*George Washington: Soldier, Hero, President* (Fontas & Fontas, 2001, Dorling Kindersley) *The History News: Revolution* (Maynard, 1999, Scholastic) *If You Lived at the Time of the American Revolution* (Moore, 1997, Scholastic) *Sybil Ludington's Midnight Ride* (Amstel, 2000, Scholastic)
Knights at Dawn (Osborne, 1993, Random House)	*If You Lived in the Days of the Knights* (McGovern, 2001, Scholastic) *Knights and Castles* (Osborne, 2000, Scholastic)

FIGURE 4
Pre- and postliterature circle interview results

Question 1: Do you consider yourself to be a good reader?
Results: Prior to literature circles, 17 out of 22 students said they were good readers. After four months of literature circles, 21 of 22 students felt better about themselves as readers.

Question 2: Do you like to read?
Results: Before literature circles began, 16 students said that they enjoy reading. After literature circles, that figure improved to 20 of 22 students.

Question 3: Explain the difference between fiction and nonfiction; give an example of each.
Results: When I first introduced literature circles, 14 students could clearly explain the difference. Near the end of third grade, 21 students understood the difference.

Question 4: Do you choose to read nonfiction books on your own?
Results: Only 7 of the students replied that they read nonfiction in the first interview. In the second, this number increased dramatically to 18 students choosing nonfiction on their own.

group members and those outside their group. They would talk about these famous people from the time they first walked into the classroom until the end of the day. I had never seen so much interest or enthusiasm come from fiction reading. The students were meeting the goals I had set for nonfiction literature circles. Their conversations were exciting and lively, and my students were hungry to learn all they could about their text's main character.

Second Connection to Nonfiction

Even though biographies were first used in nonfiction literature circles, I also incorporated other forms of nonfiction texts. I had been observing the book choices of my students all year, and for some reason this class was especially interested in The Magic Tree House series by Mary Pope Osborne. I decided to build on their interest and began collecting multiple copies of four Magic Tree House titles and nonfiction companion books. (See Figure 3 for a partial list of companion titles.)

For this cycle of literature circles, I suggested to my students that they substitute "tabbing" for role sheets when preparing. They would tab a page with a sticky note and write an interesting comment or question on the note. When tabbing, they would have more freedom to apply all the roles if they wanted. The students were eager to begin, and they took their sticky notes and started reading. One student came back the next day with 23 tabs. I was certain that he would not have prepared half as thoroughly with a role sheet.

The conversations with tabbing included even more natural book conversations (Peterson & Eeds, 1990). There was an ease about who would share, and at times only a few tabs from each person would be shared because the conversations were much more in depth and time ran out. I decided to increase my time for literature circle conversations to 30–40 minutes, and there were always groups who needed their SSR time to finish the following day. Some students even wanted extra time to meet during recess.

Excitement and comprehension continued to flourish during nonfiction literature circle conversations. For example, in the following conversation, students explored understandings of cultural rituals in a different place and time. The text was *Secrets of the Mummies* (Griffey, 1998).

Brian: That's just gross! I can't believe that they would just toss them into a grave. They're children, just pure children.

Lisa: Yeah. I had no idea they would sacrifice such a good, almost perfect child for the hope of getting some rain.

Chris: I can't believe the girl's parents let the chief priests do this.

Dean: Remember, the book said that the girl and the family considered this an honor, but they were still a little scared.

Lisa: This is my *Kids Discover* magazine. It tells some of the same information about mummies, but there's lots of new stuff too. Look here on this page....

According to Rosenblatt (1978), accomplished readers respond to texts in both aesthetic (or personal) and efferent (text-based) ways. This excerpt indicates that these children are learning to expand their thinking across the spectrum of efferent to aesthetic response. The emotional response of every member of the group was high as they discussed the fate of a child in ancient Egypt. Their aesthetic responses of shock, anger, and confusion complemented their use of the facts found in the text to confirm and justify their points. Everyone was involved, and they all eagerly shared their interpretations and offered interesting comments. The conversation ended with a cross-textual connection. These results were even more satisfying to me because this group consisted of three struggling readers and one average reader.

Children's Responses to the Experience

When choosing fiction and nonfiction companion books, students told me that they selected those that appealed to their senses and motivated them to read. Most of the students reported that they "cruised" through the fiction books so that they could get to the nonfiction companion. For many of them, learning new, real-life information seemed to be very important. Their behaviors suggested that nonfiction reading gave them a new purpose for reading.

The differences in the children's responses to the pre- and postliterature circle interview questions reinforced my observations and the children's infor-

mal comments. Figure 4 illustrates the results from these interviews. From my observations of the children's free-choice book-reading behaviors, these results were valid. Biographies, as well as informational books on topics of interest, were popular.

Literature Circles Work With Nonfiction

In addition to the pre- and postliterature circle questions, the students were asked a series of four open-ended questions at the end of the year (see Figure 1). From this information I have learned that literature circles are an appropriate instructional practice to help students learn about and enjoy nonfiction. Third graders were interested in and capable of having lively, in-depth, interesting, and engaging conversations with nonfiction literature. Students assume ownership in selecting books about real life that appeal to them and in discussing what's important to them. Students can comfortably move from role sheets to tabbing to interactive conversations at the third-grade level.

There were other benefits as well. It was gratifying to listen to the students' conversations and watch how they carried over into other aspects of their classroom life. My students began to use their literature circle skills to discuss topics and problem solve across all curriculum areas. They improved considerably in their willingness to listen to one another and to value the ideas of others throughout the day. My students were truly in charge of their own learning, and they felt empowered (Samway et al., 1991). That's an incredible feeling, especially when you're 8 or 9 years old.

It has been an exciting journey watching my students become active participants in their literature circle conversations. They have developed a new love and appreciation for reading. It is even more gratifying to have my students help me learn more about an appropriate setting in which to use nonfiction literature in the best way possible. These third graders were truly coresearchers throughout this process. They became observant of their needs, sharing what worked well during their conversations, what areas needed improvement, and what they valued from the experience. Nonfiction is important in the lives of young readers, and it will continue to be throughout the rest of their lives.

REFERENCES

Au, K.H., Carroll, J.H., & Scheu, J.A. (1997). *Balanced literacy instruction: A teacher's resource book.* Norwood, MA: Christopher-Gordon.

Bamford, R.A., & Kristo, J.V. (2000). *Checking out nonfiction K–8: Good choices for best learning.* Norwood, MA: Christopher-Gordon.

Daniels, H. (1994). *Literature circles: Voice and choice in the student-centered classroom.* York, ME: Stenhouse.

Daniels, H. (2002). *Literature circles: Voice and choice in book clubs and reading groups.* York, ME: Stenhouse.

Davidson, M. (1969). *Helen Keller.* New York: Scholastic.

Fountas, I.C., & Pinnell, G.S. (2001). *Guiding readers and writers grades 3–6: Teaching comprehension, genre, and content literacy.* Portsmouth, NH: Heinemann.

Gambrell, L.B., & Almasi, J.F. (1996). *Lively discussions: Fostering engaged reading.* Newark, DE: International Reading Association.

Griffey, H. (1998). *Secrets of the mummies.* New York: Dorling Kindersley.

Harvey, S. (1998). *Nonfiction matters: Reading, writing, and research in grades 3–8.* York, ME: Stenhouse.

Hill, B.C., Johnson, N.J., & Schlick Noe, K.L. (1995). *Literature circles and responses.* Norwood, MA: Christopher-Gordon.

Osborne, M.P. (2000). *Civil War on Sunday.* New York: Random House.

Peterson, R., & Eeds, M. (1990). *Grand conversations: Literature groups in action.* Richmond Hill, ON: Scholastic.

Roller, C.M., & Beed, P.L. (1994). Sometimes the conversations were grand, and sometimes.... *Language Arts, 71,* 509–515.

Rosenblatt, L.M. (1978). *The reader, the text, and the poem: The transactional theory of the literary work.* Carbondale, IL: Southern Illinois University Press.

Samway, K., Davies, G., Whang, G., Cade, C., Gamil, M., Lubandina, M.A., & Phommachanh, K. (1991). Reading the skeleton, the heart, and the brain of a book: Students' perspectives on literature study circles. *The Reading Teacher, 45,* 196–205.

Schlick Noe, K.L., & Johnson, N.J. (1999). *Getting started with literature circles.* Norwood, MA: Christopher-Gordon.

Short, K. (1997). *Literature as a way of knowing.* York, ME: Stenhouse.

Vygotsky, L.S. (1978). *Mind in society: The development of higher psychological processes.* Cambridge, MA: Harvard University Press.

Whelan, G. (1991). *Hannah.* New York: Scholastic.

Books to Live By: Using Children's Literature for Character Education

Sheryl O'Sullivan

Good character consists of knowing the good, desiring the good, and doing the good.

(Lickona, 1991, p. 51)

The notion that schooling should be used to instill goodness in children is as old as schooling itself. Plato, for instance, said, "Education in virtue is the only education which deserves the name." However, the practice of character education has changed focus, changed names, and fallen in and out of favor in schools throughout history. Sometimes the focus has been more on religious indoctrination, as in the early Puritan schools, and sometimes more on values clarification, as in the 1970s work of Kohlberg. Regardless of what we call it or how we focus it, character education is an enduring idea. This article will discuss what character education means now, explore why schools should be involved in it, and, finally, examine ways to integrate character education with the curriculum through children's books.

Definition

The word *character* comes from a Greek word that means "to engrave." Literally, then, character traits are those markings engraved upon us that lead us to behave in specific ways. Ryan and Bohlin (1999) defined character succinctly as "the sum of our intellectual and moral habits" (p. 9). Schools, of course,

are hoping to instill good character markings rather than bad in their students, but whatever marks are engraved upon a pupil will lead to intellectual and moral habits that in turn lead to behavior.

Society is in general agreement about what constitutes a good character trait. In fact, numerous published lists of virtues are remarkably similar in content. C.S. Lewis (1947) drew from many diverse cultures and religions and identified the common virtues of kindness, honesty, justice, mercy, and courage. The Character Counts Coalition listed trustworthiness, respect, responsibility, caring, justice, and citizenship as core virtues (see www.charactercounts.org). From the ancient Greeks to the Boy Scouts, the enduring core values we live by are very similar and widely accepted. Character education is the encouragement of these virtues in our students.

The Role of Schools in Character Education

Ryan and Bohlin (1999) listed five important reasons why schools should engage in character education. The first two reasons are historical. Great thinkers from long ago and from divergent cultures have reminded us that the purpose of schooling is to help students not only to become smart but also to become good. The founders of the United States retained this belief. In fact, democracy was considered unworkable without an educated and morally responsible populace.

Reprinted from *The Reading Teacher*, 57(7), pp. 640–645. © 2004 by the International Reading Association.

The next two reasons have to do with current legal and societal mandates for character education. In the United States, character education has been recently endorsed by federal law and by many state laws. Guidelines established in 1995 by the U.S. Department of Education reminded schools that while they must remain neutral on religion they were obligated to actively impart civic values and a unifying moral code (Vessels & Boyd, 1996). In addition to these legal mandates, society repeatedly confirms its desire for schools to teach character. In a recent Gallup poll (as cited in Ryan & Bohlin, 1999), 97% of respondents favored the teaching of honesty; 91% favored teaching acceptance, patriotism, caring, and courage; and 90% wanted the Golden Rule to be taught.

Finally, there is the argument of inevitability for character education in schools. Wynne (1992) stated, "schools are and must be concerned about pupils' morality. Any institution with custody of children or adolescents for long periods of time, such as a school, inevitably affects the character of its charges" (p. 151). Many developmental theorists, such as Piaget, Kohlberg, and Vygotsky, stressed that children continue to develop their moral codes during their school-age years, and character development, for good or ill, will take place during these years. These developmental theorists and Wynne would accept that the literature students read will instill character traits in them unconsciously, even if these are never discussed or addressed directly in the classroom. However, schools would be wise to intentionally shape this development toward good by consciously using the existing curriculum for character education.

Integrating Character Education With the Curriculum

Authors repeatedly have affirmed the need to integrate character education throughout the school day if we hope to influence the behavior of students (Leming, 2000; Noddings, 2002; Ryan, 1996). One of the easiest ways to integrate character education with the curriculum is through the literature we ask

children to study. Kilpatrick, Wolfe, and Wolfe (1994) cited reasons for using literature study as a prime place for character education, including the fact that stories provide good role models for behavior as well as rules to live by. Guroian (1998) agreed that stories are much more effective than mere instruction in character for awakening what he calls the moral imagination. Guroian especially valued the use of metaphors in stories for helping children connect experiences and morals. He and Bettelheim (1989) specifically advocated the use of fairy tales for character education.

Choosing Books

O'Sullivan (2002) claimed that a wide variety of children's literature can be used for character education as long as teachers choose worthwhile books, move beyond literal to critical understanding of these books, and are intentional in focusing on the development of character during literature study. The following types of books should be included in character education.

- Well-written books containing moral dilemmas, such as *Princess Furball* (Charlotte Huck, 1989) for primary children or *Lyddie* (Katherine Paterson, 1991) for older students.

- Books with enough depth to allow moving beyond literal comprehension, such as the picture book *Knots on a Counting Rope* (Bill Martin Jr & John Archambault, 1987) or the chapter book *The Giver* (Lois Lowry, 2002).

- Books with admirable but believable characters about the same age as students, such as *Thundercake* (Patricia Polacco, 1990) for younger students and *The Moorchild* (Eloise McGraw, 1996) for older ones.

- Books across a wide range of cultures and with both boys and girls as lead characters, such as the picture book *The Rough-Face Girl* (Rafe Martin, 1992) or the chapter book *Esperanza Rising* (Pam Muñoz Ryan, 2000).

The deeper and richer the literature, and the stronger the characters, the easier it will be to include character education naturally in literature study. If a book is well chosen, the characters will probably display many different traits worth emulating and will apply these traits in situations young readers can understand. All it takes is a bit of practice to focus our attention on this area. So now let us examine some excellent children's books with the intention of using them for character education.

Picture Books

Miss Rumphius by Barbara Cooney (1982) follows the life of an atypical woman who travels widely, never marries, and follows her independent idea to improve the world. We meet Miss Rumphius as a young girl when her grandfather tells her she must do something to make the world more beautiful. We leave her as she is passing this challenge on to her young niece. Throughout her lifetime Miss Rumphius exhibits independence, resilience, courage, and care for the environment.

Strategy for use. This story lends itself easily to students writing either a journal entry or a book of their own. First, discuss the importance of setting goals and consider what a person should try to give back to the world. Miss Rumphius's three goals were to go to faraway places, come home to live by the sea, and do something to make the world more beautiful. Ask students what their three goals would be, then lead them to write stories about their own future lives.

The Rough-Face Girl by Rafe Martin (1992) is a Native American Cinderella variant in which two proud but beautiful sisters do not marry the desirable Invisible Being because of weaknesses in their characters. The Rough-Face Girl is not beautiful, but she has a pure heart and is judged worthy to marry the Invisible Being because she alone can see him.

Strategy for use. Cinderella stories make a very clear distinction between good and bad people in the story. There is no ambiguity, and this often makes it easier for young children to discriminate between noble and ignoble character traits. An easy graphic for doing this sort of comparison is the Venn diagram. A Venn diagram comparing the traits of the evil sisters and the Rough-Face Girl might look like Figure 1. This graphic should then be followed with ample

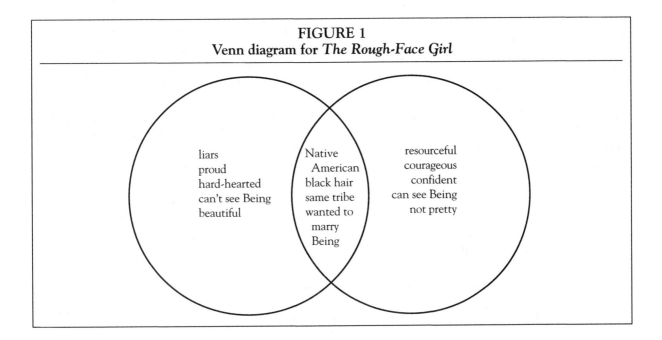

FIGURE 1
Venn diagram for *The Rough-Face Girl*

liars
proud
hard-hearted
can't see Being
beautiful

Native American
black hair
same tribe
wanted to
marry
Being

resourceful
courageous
confident
can see Being
not pretty

discussion focusing on why children chose to include the traits they did, what evidence from the story they have that these traits existed, and what distinguishes good from bad in the characters.

A Chair for My Mother by Vera B. Williams (1982) is about a matriarchal family consisting of a grandmother, a single mother, and a little girl who work together to rebuild their lives after their apartment burns. Their neighbors and extended family help them with many necessities, but it is up to the three of them to save the money to buy a soft chair. The story highlights the virtues of resilience, cooperation, courage, and love, though none of those words are ever mentioned.

Strategy for use. Ask students to find a favorite quote in the book and write it on an index card. The quotes should tell something about the virtues or values of the character. Put these index cards in a stack and draw one or two of them each day to begin your discussion of the book. The student who wrote the quote could be asked what he or she saw as the character traits exhibited in this quote and could lead the discussion that day. The following are examples of quotes from this book.

Girl:	And every time, I put half of my money into the jar.
Girl:	We went to stay with my mother's sister Aunt Ida and Uncle Sandy.
Grandma:	It's lucky we're young and can start all over.

Chapter Books

The Hundred Dresses by Eleanor Estes (1944) is an easy chapter book suitable for making the transition between picture books and longer works. In *The Hundred Dresses* a clique of popular girls teases another girl about her funny name and her life of poverty. One of the girls in the group, Maddie, does not like what is happening but makes no effort to stop the teasing. The girl, Wanda, also makes no effort to defend herself. When she moves away suddenly and it is discovered she really did have 100 dresses (beautiful drawings she had made) the clique

of girls, especially Maddie, has no way to assuage their guilt over their teasing.

Strategy for use. In the way the story currently ends, Maddie learns many valuable lessons but is never able to apply them to Wanda. This book is a perfect choice for doing a "choose your own adventure" rewrite with children. Stop after Wanda does not defend herself and ask students to write a new ending in which she does. Or stop after Maddie feels guilty but takes no action and write a new path for her in which she stops the teasing. Or help Maddie find Wanda after she moves away and write a path that allows Maddie to make peace with Wanda. This story has lots of alternative ways it could go, and the discussion surrounding the different choices will be rich in character education.

Bridge to Terabithia by Katherine Paterson (1977) is a book about two fifth graders who find in each other a kindred spirit. Both have complex and integrated personalities, and this sets them apart in their fifth-grade classroom, which is rampant with gender stereotyping. Both Jess and Leslie display many other admirable qualities. Jess is a scapegoat at home, yet he deals kindly for the most part with his sisters and parents. He has the gift of self-reflection, and when faced with a moral dilemma he recognizes it and tries to think of the right thing to do. For example, when he is faced with a bully who is picking on his little sister, Jess understands the need to stop the bullying but also recognizes that the bully is a person who deserves compassion. Leslie's circumstances also require her to be noble. She especially lavishes this nobility on Jess, showing him compassion, kindness, loyalty, and humility. While she often serves as the leader of the pair, she also humbly recognizes the many gifts Jess brings to the friendship.

Admirable as Jess and Leslie are, however, they are not perfect. Leslie is deceitful with her teacher and vengeful with the class bully. Jess is sometimes impatient with his little sister, and one time even hits her. Far from making these characters less admirable, the existence of negative character traits and their struggles with these are what make Jess and Leslie such good role models.

Strategy for use. Have students make clusters or webs using the positive and negative traits they find for the two main characters. On one large sheet of paper write *positive traits* in the center circle. On the other, write *negative traits* in the center. Students should print traits on the appropriate web and then put the page number from the book on which this trait was displayed. Use these clusters as the beginning of discussions about noble behavior, or lack of, and then apply these traits to students' own dilemmas. Figure 2 is an example of possible clusters for Jess.

A Wrinkle in Time by Madeleine L'Engle (1962) is another classic book with imperfect but noble characters. As in *Bridge to Terabithia*, the main characters also display many admirable traits, such as courage, compassion, discipline, and honesty. Meg and Charles Wallace, who are sister and brother, and their friend Calvin all set out on a fantasy journey to rescue Meg and Charles Wallace's father from the evil It. In this good versus evil story, Meg especially is called upon to mature quickly. The journey requires her to become more self-accepting, more confident, more courageous, and more giving than she had previously been in her school-day life.

Strategy for use. This book has a rather difficult writing style, and students may need help in discerning the deeper meaning behind some of the events. A good way to address this need in the classroom is to ask students to keep a double-entry journal in which they write actual quotes from the book on the left side and their interpretations of these quotes on the right. Using these journals as discussion starters will bring out the virtuous character traits that are woven everywhere throughout this book, but are sometimes partially obscured for children by the difficult language. Figure 3 is an example of a double-entry journal for this book.

More Books to Live By

These are only six books of a multitude of high-quality children's books that can be used for integrating character education with an already full school program. As the sample activities for these books show, infusing literature study with character education is more a matter of a slight change of emphasis rather than a new topic. Instead of examining characters as a literal concept in relation to plot and setting, teachers can examine character traits critically in relation to virtues. Several more books that

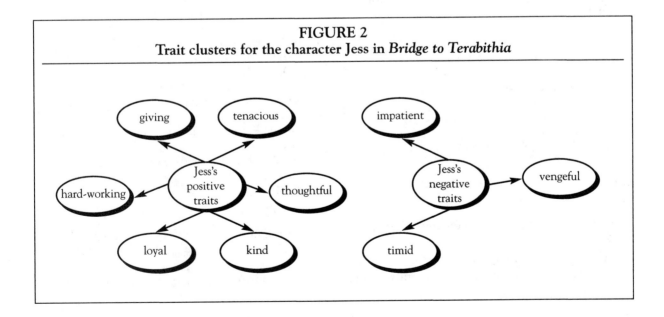

FIGURE 2
Trait clusters for the character Jess in *Bridge to Terabithia*

FIGURE 3
Double-entry journal for *A Wrinkle in Time*

What happened	What I thought
Mrs. Whatsit gave Meg a gift of her faults. (p. 100)	How can faults be a gift?
Charles Wallace was making jokes, and Meg said it was his way of whistling in the dark. (p. 117)	Does that mean he is trying not to show that he is afraid?
The evil It says, "I am peace utter rest. I am freedom from all responsibility." (p. 130)	He sounds really nice, but Meg shouldn't trust him!

More books for character education

Picture books
Emily by Michael Bedard
Fox Song by Joseph Bruchac
Flower Garden by Eve Bunting
Seven Silly Eaters by Mary Ann Hoberman
Toads and Diamonds by Charlotte Huck
Gittel's Hands by Erica Silverman
Mufaro's Beautiful Daughters by John Steptoe
William's Doll by Charlotte Zolotow
A Picture Book of Eleanor Roosevelt by David A. Adler & Robert Casilla

Chapter books
Chevrolet Saturdays by Candy Dawson Boyd
Bud, Not Buddy by Christopher Paul Curtis
Letters From Rifka by Karen Hesse
No Pretty Pictures by Anita Lobel
Same Stuff as Stars by Katherine Paterson
Holes by Louis Sachar
Tuck Everlasting by Natalie Babbitt
Ella Enchanted by Gail Carson Levin

---

school's work. It is inevitable that character education will happen during the elementary years. The only question is what sort of character will be developed in children during these years. By intentionally including discussions on character in literature study, we can help assure that children develop characters that know, love, and do good—perhaps our most important work as teachers.

REFERENCES

Bettelheim, B. (1989). *The uses of enchantment: The meaning and importance of fairy tales*. New York: Vintage.

Guroian, V. (1998). *Tending the heart of virtue: How classic stories awaken a child's moral imagination*. New York: Oxford University Press.

Kilpatrick, W., Wolfe, G., & Wolfe, S.M. (1994). *Books that build character: A guide to teaching your child moral values through stories*. New York: Simon & Schuster.

Leming, J. (2000). Tell me a story: An evaluation of a literature-based character education programme. *Journal of Moral Education, 29*, 413–426.

Lewis, C.S. (1947). *The abolition of man*. New York: Simon & Schuster.

Lickona, T. (1991). *Educating for character: How our schools can teach respect and responsibility*. New York: Bantam.

Noddings, N. (2002). *Educating moral people: A caring alternative to character education*. New York: Teachers College Press.

O'Sullivan, S. (2002). *Character education through children's literature*. Bloomington, IN: Phi Delta Kappa Educational Foundation.

Ryan, K. (1996). Character education in the United States: A status report. *Journal for a Just and Caring Education, 2*(1), 75–84.

Ryan, K., & Bohlin, K.E. (1999). *Building character in schools*. San Francisco: Jossey-Bass.

Vessels, G., & Boyd, S.M. (1996). Public and constitutional support for character education. *NASSP Bulletin, 80*(579), 55–62.

Wynne, E. (1992). Transmitting character in schools: Some common questions and answers. *Clearing House, 68*, 151–153.

could be used easily for character education appear in the Sidebar.

Character education is appropriate to teach in public schools. Historically, and by societal demand, character education is an expected part of the public

CHILDREN'S BOOKS CITED

Cooney, B. (1982). *Miss Rumphius*. New York: Viking.

Estes, E. (1944). *The hundred dresses*. New York: Scholastic.

Huck, C. (1989). *Princess furball*. New York: Greenwillow Press.

L'Engle, M. (1962). *A wrinkle in time*. New York: Dell.

Lowry, L. (2002). *The giver*. New York: Laurel Leaf.

Martin, B., Jr, & Archambault, J. (1987). *Knots on a counting rope*. New York: Henry Holt.

Martin, R. (1992). *The rough-face girl*. New York: G.P. Putnam's Sons.

McGraw, E. (1996). *The moorchild*. New York: Margaret K. McElderry.

Paterson, K. (1977). *Bridge to Terabithia*. New York: Dell.

Paterson, K. (1991). *Lyddie*. New York: Penguin.

Polacco, P. (1990). *Thundercake*. New York: Scholastic.

Ryan, P.M. (2000). *Esperanza rising*. New York: Scholastic.

Williams, V.B. (1982). *A chair for my mother*. New York: Scholastic.

Subject Index

Note. Page numbers followed by *f* and *t* indicate figures and tables, respectively.

MENTAL ABILITIES, 126
MENTAL RECITATION, 164
MENTAL SETTING, 93–94
MENTIONING, 102
METACOGNITION, 137
METAPHORS, 214
METHODS, 16, 22
METROPOLITAN TEST, 127
MISS RUMPHIUS (COONEY), 215
MISSISSIPPI, 28–29
MODELING: and content area discussion, 176; of literature circles, 205, 206; need for, 18; for reading guides, 169; of text selection, 115
MONITORING READING. *See* self-monitoring
MONITORING STUDENTS, 169, 187
THE MOORCHILD (MCGRAW), 214
MORAL IMAGINATION, 214
MORALS, 213–214
MOTIVATION: armchair traveler activity for, 202; bag props for, 201; book catalogs for, 200–201; book mates for, 202; campaign day for, 201; clipping service of, 201; effects of, 112, Feelings Unlimited box for, 201; inventions for, 201; IRA position statement on, 19–21; and phonics, 43; photos for, 201; secret identity activity for, 201–202; and student investigations, 187; teachers' tasks regarding, 114; writing for, 200
MUFARO'S BEAUTIFUL DAUGHTERS (STEPTOE), 218f
MULTIPLE STRATEGIES APPROACH, 117
MUMMIES AND PYRAMIDS (OSBORNE), 209f
MUMMIES IN THE MORNING (OSBORNE), 209f
MY VISIT TO THE AQUARIUM (ALIKI), 71, 72–73

N

NARRATIVE TEXTS: connecting expository text to, 206, 209f, 210–211; literature circles for, 206; popular books of, 195; teachers' tasks regarding, 114–115
NATIONAL ASSESSMENT OF EDUCATIONAL PROGRESS (NEAP), 25, 98, 137, 142
NATIONAL COUNCIL OF TEACHERS OF ENGLISH (NCTE), 106, 145
NATIONAL EDUCATIONAL MONITORING PROJECT (NEMP), 148
NATIONAL INSTITUTE OF CHILD HEALTH AND HUMAN DEVELOPMENT (NICHD), 25, 26, 27, 117, 184, 186
NATIONAL READING PANEL, 184

NATIONAL SCHOOL REFORM FACULTY, 30f
NELSON SILENT READING TEST, 127
NEWSLETTERS, 11
NEWSPAPERS, 11
NO CHILD LEFT BEHIND ACT (NCLB), 26–27
NO PRETTY PICTURES (LOBEL), 218f
NONFICTION. *See* expository texts
NORM REFERENCED TESTS. *See* standardized tests
NORMS, 126, 128
"NOT NOW!" SAID THE COW (OPPENHEIM), 69

O

OAK PARK ELEMENTARY SCHOOL, 59–60
OBJECTIVITY, 134, 136
OBSERVATIONS, 131–132
ON MY OWN QUESTIONS, 104
ONSET, 55–56
ORAL READING, 90, 127
ORAL REPORTS, 198
ORGANIZATION, CLASSROOM. *See* classroom organization
ORTHOGRAPHIC STAGE, 52
OUTLINES, 156

P

PARENTS: IRA position statement on, 23; IRA testing recommendations for, 144–145; newsletters for, 11
PASSIVE UNDERSTANDING, 84
PERSONAL CONNECTOR ROLE, 207
PERSONAL EXPERIENCES, 86, 157
PERSONAL RESPONSES, 114, 178
PHONEMIC AWARENESS, 53, 63–64
PHONETIC SUBSTITUTIONS, 40
PHONIC GENERALIZATIONS, 45–50
PHONICS: age of instruction in, 43–44, 56–57; approaches to, 64; debates regarding, 57, 59; decontextualization of, 59; definition of, 62; to develop word recognition, 38, 40; drills in, 41–42; functionality of, 43–44; goal of, 62; historical challenges of, 6–7; importance of, 51; and instructional cue crafting, 73; versus meaning making, 43; and motivation, 43; people's perceptions of, 51; principles of effective instruction in, 52–57; process of, 40; program content regarding, 42–43, 52–57; rationale for, 51–52; research conclusions regarding, 42; sample lesson of, 60–61; structural analysis's relationship to, 39; teachers' tasks regarding, 112–113

PHOTOS, 201
A PICTURE BOOK OF ELEANOR ROOSEVELT (ADLER & CASILLA), 218f
A PICTURE BOOK OF ROBERT E. LEE (ADLER), 209f
PICTURE BOOKS, 215–216, 218f
POINT OF VIEW READING GUIDES, 164–165
POLICY MAKERS. *See* legislators
POPULAR BOOKS, 195
THE POWER OF PROTOCOLS (MCDONALD, MOHR, DICHTER, & MCDONALD), 30f
PRACTICE ACTIVITIES, 22–23
PRAISE, 90
PREDICTABLE BOOKS, 53
PREDICTION: as prereading activity, 94, 100; in reciprocal teaching, 105–106
PREREADING ACTIVITIES, 94, 100
PRESENTATIONS, 187
PRIMARY GRADES, 181–188. *See also* elementary school students
PRINCESS FURBALL (HUCK), 214
PRINCIPALS, 5–6
PRIOR KNOWLEDGE. *See* background knowledge
PROFESSIONAL CERTIFICATION EXAMINATIONS, 139–140
PROFESSIONAL DEVELOPMENT: in coaching, 74; and collaboration, 28–29; in public relations campaign, 12
PROFESSIONAL LITERATURE, 13–14
PROFESSIONAL ORGANIZATIONS, 12
PROFESSIONAL STANDARDS AND ETHICS COMMITTEE, 11
PROGRESS REPORTS, 11
PROJECT FAIRS, 187
PROJECT ZERO, 29, 30f
PRONUNCIATION, 42, 47
THE PROPHET (GIBRAN), 13, 17
PROPS, 201
PSYCHOLOGY, 98
PUBLIC RELATIONS, 5, 11–12
PUBLISHING INDUSTRY, 14, 15, 195
PURPOSE, OF READING, 154, 161, 184

Q

QAR STRATEGY, 172; definition of, 173t; examples of, 174t; overview of, 103–105; question types in, 104
QUESTIONING THE AUTHOR STRATEGY, 185
QUESTIONS: about story maps, 99–100; after literature circle, 210f; classroom time spent asking, 99; and comprehension development, 82; direct instruction in answering, 102–105; to evaluate children's

literature awareness, 131; for expository reading in primary grades, 184–185; to guide textbook reading, 160; for higher level comprehension, 87–88; in point of view reading guides, 164–165; for prereading activity, 100; in reciprocal teaching, 105–106; for self-assessment, 147; in standardized test reforms, 137; in teachers' manuals, 99; in textbooks, 160; for vocabulary instruction, 101

R

RADIO, 7
RAMONA SERIES (CLEARY), 96
RAND, 184, 186
RAND READING STUDY GROUP, 111
RAPPING, 176
RATE, OF READING, 155
RATING BOOKS, 200
READERS, 111–112, 146
READINESS, 154, 158–162
READING: child's view of, 89; definition of, 21; fundamental skills of, 154–155; IRA position statement on, 21; overview of, 66–67; prerequisites for, 62; process of, 107, 116, 133–134, 135; time for, 16; writing's link to, 106–107, 117–118
READING ALOUD, 156, 182–183
READING CAMPS, 29
READING COMMITTEES, 5, 7
READING INSTRUCTION. See instruction
READING LESSONS: commonly taught, 14; parts of, 14–15; sample of, 60–61
READING, LOVE OF. See love of reading
READING RECOVERY PROGRAM, 54–55, 67
READING ROAD MAPS, 165–167
READING STRATEGIES, 94–95. See also specific strategies
READING SUCCESS NETWORK, 30f
THE READING TEACHER: goal of, 1; overview of, 1; summary points of articles in, 2, 34; and word recognition debate, 34
READING TESTS. See testing programs
REASONING, 81, 82
RECALLING, 157
RECIPROCAL TEACHING, 105–106
RECIPROCITY, 147–148
RECORD KEEPING, 131
RED RIDING HOOD (MARSHALL), 70
REFERENCE MATERIALS, 155, 198
REFLECTION, 178
REFLECTIVE CONFERENCES, 29–31

REFORMS: in assessment, 137–138; in individualization, 97; and NCLB legislation, 26–27; overview of, 27; regarding comprehension instruction, 97–98; teachers' role in, 27
REPEATED READINGS, 174t
REPUBLICAN PARTY NATIONAL STEERING COMMITTEE, 51
RESEARCH, PROFESSIONAL, 14
RESEARCH, STUDENT: regarding expository texts, 182; skills for, 185, 186–187; of study guides, 163–164
RESEARCHERS, 143–144
RESILIENCE, 147
RETELLING, 132, 147
RETROSPECTIVE VERBALIZATION, 81
REVIEW, OF INFORMATION, 167
REVISION, 107
REVOLUTIONARY WAR ON SUNDAY (OSBORNE), 209f
REWARDS, 90–92
RIGHT ANSWER SYNDROME, 87
RIGHT START TRAINING, 74
RIGHT THERE QUESTIONS, 104
RIME, 55–56
RISK-TAKING, 89, 90
ROLE MODELS, 214
ROLE SHEETS, 205
ROMANTICISTS, 17–18
ROSA PARKS (WILSON), 209f
THE ROUGH-FACED GIRL (MARTIN), 214, 215–216
RULE INSTRUCTION, 55

S

SAME STUFF AS STARS (PATERSON), 218f
SAMPLING PROCEDURE, 142, 145
SCAFFOLDING, 117, 185–186
SCHEMA, 112
SCHOLARS, 13–17
SCHOOL BOARDS, 11
SCHOOL CHARACTERISTICS, 17
SCIENCE: and content organization, 156; primary-grade nonfiction for, 182–188; reading road maps for, 165–167; reciprocal teaching in, 106
SECONDARY STUDENTS, 154
SECRET IDENTITY ACTIVITY, 201–202
SECRETS OF THE MUMMIES (GRIFFEY), 209f, 210–211
SEDL. See Southwest Educational Development Laboratory (SEDL)
SELECTIVE SAMPLING, 142, 145
SELECTIVE-CUE STAGE, OF WORD RECOGNITION, 73
SELF-CORRECTION, 90

SELF-MONITORING, 89–91, 117
SEMANTIC FEATURE ANALYSIS, 101
SEMANTIC MAPPING, 101
SEVEN SILLY EATERS (HOBERMAN), 218f
SHARE TIME, 96
SHARED BOOKS PROCEDURE, 95–96
SHORT-TERM MEMORY, 112
SIGHT VOCABULARY: definition of, 62; to develop word recognition, 38–39; introducing phonics after, 43. See also vocabulary
SIGHT WORD METHOD, 62
SIGNALLING DEVICES, 159–160
SILENT READING TESTS, 127
SKILL INSTRUCTION, 15
SKIMMING, 169
SMALL-GROUP INSTRUCTION: benefits of, 171–172, 178; for coaching, 74; for content area reading, 174t, 176–178; IRA position statement on, 23; literature circles for, 203–211
SOCIAL FUNCTIONING, 153
SOCIAL STUDIES: interactive reading guides for, 167, 168; point of view reading guides for, 164–165; questions to guide reading in, 160; reciprocal teaching in, 106
SOCRATIC METHOD, 16–17
SONGS AND SONNETS (DONNE), 17
SONGS OF INNOCENCE (BLAKE), 17
SOUNDS, 63–64
SOUTHWEST EDUCATIONAL DEVELOPMENT LABORATORY (SEDL), 30f
SPEAKING, 65f
SPELLING, 55–56
SPELLING-SOUND STAGE, OF WORD RECOGNITION, 73
SRA READING RECORD, 127
SSR (SUSTAINED SILENT READING) PROGRAM, 115
STANDARDIZED ORAL READING CHECK TESTS, 127
STANDARDIZED ORAL READING PARAGRAPHS, 127
STANDARDIZED TESTS: for comprehension assessment, 82–83; dangers of, 134, 141; effectiveness of, 130; and increased focus on comprehension, 97–98; increased use of, 133; interpretation of, 126; mandated, 142; misunderstandings about, 126–127; reforms of, 137–138; selection of, 127–128; uses of, 125–126, 140–141
STANDARDS, 126
STANDARDS FOR THE ASSESSMENT OF READING AND WRITING (IRA & NCTE), 145